Camille Saint-Saëns
On Music and Musicians

Camille Saint-Saëns
On Music and Musicians

Edited and translated by
Roger Nichols

OXFORD
UNIVERSITY PRESS
2008

OXFORD
UNIVERSITY PRESS

Oxford University Press, Inc., publishes works that further
Oxford University's objective of excellence
in research, scholarship, and education.

Oxford   New York
Auckland   Cape Town   Dar es Salaam   Hong Kong   Karachi
Kuala Lumpur   Madrid   Melbourne   Mexico City   Nairobi
New Delhi   Shanghai   Taipei   Toronto
With offices in
Argentina   Austria   Brazil   Chile   Czech Republic   France   Greece
Guatemala   Hungary   Italy   Japan   Poland   Portugal   Singapore
South Korea   Switzerland   Thailand   Turkey   Ukraine   Vietnam

Published by Oxford University Press, Inc.
198 Madison Avenue, New York, New York 10016

www.oup.com

Oxford is a registered trademark of Oxford University Press

Library of Congress Cataloging-in-Publication Data
Saint-Saëns, Camille, 1835–1921.
[Literary works English Selections.]
Camille Saint-Saëns on music and musicians / edited and translated
by Roger Nichols.
p.   cm.
ISBN 978-0-19-532016-9
1. Saint-Saëns, Camille, 1835–1921. 2. Music—19th century—History
and criticism. 3. Composers—France—Biography.
I. Nichols, Roger. II. Title.
ML60.S15213 2008
780—dc22   2007039011

1 3 5 7 9 8 6 4 2

Printed in the United States of America
on acid-free paper

EDITOR'S PREFACE

Many years after seeing Saint-Saëns at the first concert performance of *Le sacre du printemps* at the Casino de Paris in 1914, Stravinsky remembered him as "a sharp little man". If we take this judgment as being not entirely friendly, then Stravinsky was hardly alone in finding Saint-Saëns's sharpness something to be negotiated, a dangerous reef in the far from untroubled waters of Parisian musical life.

The "Saint-Saëns problem", insofar as there was one, stemmed from three interconnecting factors: in today's parlance, he was nobody's fool, he was an elitist, and he tended to shoot from the hip. Also it was not really possible to ignore him, or at least not until a little way into the twentieth century when, beset by Impressionism, Symbolism and various other isms, he began to indulge in his fossil impersonations—an act that did his posthumous standing no good at all. In retrospect we can see that in his very last years, between 1917 and his death in 1921, there was quite a lot to be fossilized about, especially in Paris. His reaction to Milhaud's *Protée*, that music in several keys at once could never be anything other than a hubbub and that happily there were still some lunatic asylums in France, was hardly surprising if we compare that music to his own luminous Clarinet Sonata of the same era, about as firmly in E flat as anything could be; and the fact that Milhaud framed this response and stuck it on his wall does not necessarily prove the case either way. It has to be said though that, nearly 90 years later, Saint-Saëns's piece is heard rather more often than Milhaud's.

On the surface, this sharpness is evident when we consider all the things he was against. "Theories are of no great value; works are everything"; "literary people are music's worst enemies"; "few people understand art";

"Ibsenism and its imitators are forms of mental aberration"; and, perhaps most tellingly, "when you want to mortify yourself, you enter a convent." This last statement gives a vital clue to one of the mainsprings of Saint-Saëns's own music, namely a Mozartian conviction that there were limits to noise and misery-inducing discord beyond which true music could not go. From this belief were born the deliberately "fossilized" sonatas of his last years, undoubtedly written as a challenge, not only to Milhaud, but to the various other fractious experimental oddities all around him that were taking succour, sometimes none too discriminatingly, from *Le sacre*. But we should not be misled by this picture of him as an old fogey. At least until he was 60, he was remarkably open to all kinds of music, as we can hear most enticingly in the Egyptian noises in the slow movement of his Fifth Piano Concerto of 1896; and in the early 1860s, when he taught Fauré at the Ecole Niedermeyer, it was he who introduced the students to the dangerous sounds of Schumann, Liszt and, yes, Wagner: or at least the Wagner of *Tannhäuser* and *Lohengrin*.

I won't preempt the reader's pleasure by paraphrasing what he himself says of Wagner with such wit and, in most cases, insight. But for him Wagner was a prime example of a composer who took theories to dangerous extremes, just as Milhaud was to do half a century later. Saint-Saëns was pre-eminently a man who believed in balance, in proportion, in the Delphic motto of "nothing too much". He was suspicious of the "Germanic preoccupation with going beyond reality" both in an inclination towards the mystic (not one of Saint-Saëns's own domains) and, in Wagner's case, in asking instrumental players for the impossible: from this came skimping, and from skimping a lack of clarity. It is in the interests of clarity that he wants the words in opera to be heard and so not too much going on in the orchestra, and certainly not too loudly; it is in the interests of clarity, rhetorical clarity, that he condemns enharmony as heretical, an unintended consequence of equal temperament that led to *Tristan* and beyond.

I will again leave him to explain what he understands by the word "melody". But I was surprised when putting together the notes for these translations at how many of them involved opera singers. Whatever he was against, he was without doubt "for" opera as a medium, in which of course he was very much a Frenchman of his time. "The voice," he says, is an instrument that "survives when the others pass by, are transformed, and die." He does not turn his back on the instrumental developments of his century—far from it, as we can see from his symphonic poems and their debt, acknowledged by him, to Liszt. But there can be no doubt that one of the major disappointments of his life was that only one of his 12 operas, *Samson et Dalila*, made it into the regular repertoire, and even that one owed its life to Liszt's performance of it in Weimar in 1877, rather than to the Paris Opéra, which finally got round to staging it only 15 years later. There is therefore, behind his engagement with opera and the operatic stars of the time, a tinge of regret at being, as he felt, ill used: in which context it may be noted that opera directors do not get off scot free.

The downside from the sharpness perceived by Stravinsky has been that Saint-Saëns has been too casually written off as a cold, calculating composer, overly concerned with form and correct syntax at the expense of "letting it all hang out", as that horrible phrase had it 20 years or so ago. The best response to this, in many cases, is the music itself, but only if you follow his written instructions (like his "grand-pupil" Ravel, he really did know best how his music should go) and play it with vigour and conviction: if you play it like Kalkbrenner, then of course it will tend to sound like Kalkbrenner.

To conclude this preface, I make two offerings towards a warmer, more generous portrait of the man and his music. He wrote that it was "not the absence of faults but the presence of virtues" that distinguishes the great composer. It could be argued that in this he was defending his own prolific record. Maybe he was, but his argument is nonetheless a strong one: could we be sure that Bach would have written *Wachet auf* or *Vergnügte Ruh'* if he had not also written many other cantatas of lesser worth? And a century or so after Saint-Saëns, Olivier Messiaen was talking of periods when he was "inspired" and others when he was "less inspired". Saint-Saëns fully accepted that "the spirit bloweth where it listeth" and that all composers can do is hone their technique so as to take advantage of any chances the spirit may provide (again, a point of view championed by Ravel). To this extent, he was a far freer and more open composer than he has been given credit for. He explains, in his article about his opera *Hélène*, how he was attracted not by her virtue so much as by her faults and asks, with some justice, "Who was ever interested in Menelaus?"

My final offering towards a more human portrait of the man is that he was capable of love. We see it in the touching correspondence with Fauré and also, in the present volume, in his memories of Berlioz and Bizet, and especially in his long article about Gounod, here translated into English for the first time. If we are to believe him (and why should we not?), this was a true meeting of hearts and minds. Altogether sadder is his article on Massenet whom, one feels, he might well have loved if that colleague had given him any encouragement.

There are then multiple layers beneath the crisp surface of Saint-Saëns's prose, enough to test any translator. But also there is an intimacy with the reader and an absolute refusal to be a Gladstone to our Queen Victoria and address us as though we were a public meeting. For me the chief joys of this selection lie in the positive virtues of the three factors I identified at the start as contributing to "the Saint-Saëns problem": his intelligence, his determination to maintain standards, and his addiction to plain, sharp speaking. Being a friend of his might have had its dangers, but the rewards were clearly immense.

ACKNOWLEDGEMENTS

I am grateful to Nicholas Anderson, Edward Blakeman, Roger Brock, Michael Bryant, Yves Gérard, Richard Langham Smith, Graham Melville-Mason, Barry Millington, and Jean-Michel Nectoux for their help, and to the excellent staff of the Music Department of the Bibliothèque nationale de France; also to my wife for tidying up my translations of Saint-Saëns's poems.

CONTENTS

Items marked with asterisks have not, to my knowledge, been translated into English before. The original provenance is given where this is known.

Part I

Music

1

INTRODUCTION

(Harmonie et mélodie,
Calmann-Lévy, 1899, 1–31)

Far be it from me to contradict those extremely sensible people who feel that an artist should cultivate his own art exclusively, and that his time is more usefully spent producing works rather than giving his views on the works of others. The problem is, the general public has begun to fret unconscionably about the opinions of artists, composers especially, and when the public has got something into its head, who can resist it? Before they have heard a note of Mr X or Mr Z, they want to know what his preferences and antipathies are; and if Mr X or Mr Z doesn't feel like speaking, then someone will speak for him.

So it is that I have read, in articles of pure invention, opinions supposedly held by me in which I attacked everything that those who have engaged in a serious study of music are accustomed to respect. That is how legends are born, and Heaven knows, legends have a habit of persisting! Some bright spirits have shown that this is how things should be: that legend will always be right and the truth always wrong. Not that I am stupid enough to want to change the opinions that anyone may form about me. I merely thought that there might be, here and there, one or two refractory spirits who preferred the real truth to the legendary one: it is for them that I have taken up my pen, and not for the pleasure of writing on staveless paper; manuscript paper is far more to my taste.

The fragments I have gathered together, taken here and there from articles I have published at various times, have nothing to commend them except their utter sincerity. I have also not jibbed at leaving, side by side, slightly different views of the same object, when they have been expressed at different periods. I enormously admire those who, in artistic matters, can make an instant judgment that they never change, even if I can't understand them. Music for me is like people—only really knowable over time. So many factors can influence one's judgment of this art that moves in time, like time runs quickly, and only through the more or less helpful caprices and moods of the performers reaches the more or less capricious audience, itself well or less well disposed!

The first time I heard Schumann's celebrated Piano Quintet, I was deaf to its fine qualities, to an extent that still amazes me when I think about it. Later on, I took a liking to it and for many years it filled me with an overwhelming, wild enthusiasm! . . . Since then, this fine fury has abated. While I still recognize this famous piece to be an exceptional work, and one that was epoch-making in the history of chamber music, I now find serious faults in it that make listening to it almost painful.

I had been aware of these faults for a long time, but refused to acknowledge them. You fall in love with works of art and, while that love persists, their faults are as though non-existent, or else they may even pass for virtues; then love falls away and the faults remain.

There are works you remain in love with all your life; there are others that triumphantly resist all the vicissitudes of taste. It is these, very rare, works that are the true masterpieces, and even the greatest masters don't create them every day.

After these confidential remarks, I don't imagine anyone will be surprised if I respond calmly to the accusation of having sometimes changed my opinions. In the matter of Wagner's music, I have been so bitterly reproached with burning what I once adored, that I am quite glad of the opportunity to explain myself on this point once and for all. We are allowed to change our minds about Beethoven or Mozart; but Wagner! . . . it is a crime, or rather a sacrilege. This is no longer a matter of art; we're talking about a cult.

Truth be told, it is not I that have changed, but the situation.

At a time when Wagner had got no further than *Lohengrin*, before we were able to foresee the transformations this powerful creative spirit was to undergo, and when we saw passages like the March from *Tannhäuser* and the Prelude to *Lohengrin* provoking howls of indignation, I never thought to be critical. I was on the side of art against the Philistines, and there was no other possible attitude.[1] Now the work is complete; the pas-

---

[1] Saint-Saëns is probably referring to the three concerts Wagner gave in Paris in January and February 1860, each consisting of the *Flying Dutchman* Overture, selections from *Tannhäuser*, including the March, the *Tristan* Prelude and selections from *Lohengrin*, beginning with the Prelude. Apart from the *Tristan* extract, the music was enthusiastically received by the audience; but not by the critics, to whom, as a mark of his contempt, Wagner had allotted no press tickets. He did send tickets to Berlioz, whose review appeared on 9 February. In a letter of 29 January Berlioz wrote: "Wagner has just given a concert that exasperated three quarters of the audience and enthused the rest. Personally, I found a lot of it painful, even though I admired the vehemence of his musical feelings in certain instances. But the diminished sevenths, the discords and the crude modulations made me feverish, and I have to say that I find this sort of music loathsome and revolting."

sage of time takes us further away from it each day, and distance allows us to judge his output in its entirety.

It happened that while his music was achieving the place in the musical world that was its due, it took over the press to an extraordinary degree and the bass drums of publicity beat an exuberant symphony in its honour. The Parisian public followed the press, and people who had covered their ears at the suave sounds of *Lohengrin* now shouted for joy and cried "encore!" at picturesque, exciting but fearful dissonances, that were for music what pickles are in the kitchen. Given that my viewpoint is not the same, it is surely natural that my impression should be quite different; it would indeed be amazing if it were not.

Ah well! All the same, I have not changed much. Some things that I didn't like and about which I reserved judgment, now I don't like for certain, that's all. It is true that I should now no longer write that Brünnhilde's awakening is "an enchantment". Not that the orchestral accompaniment to her awakening has ceased to strike me as enchanting; but what comes before it is so long and what follows so slow, and the prolonged trills of the two lovers so strange, that the few bars of the awakening proper seem to me insufficient compensation. On the other hand, my admiration for *Das Rheingold* has continued to grow, as it has for three quarters at least of *Tristan* and *Die Walküre*. But even while I admire the colossal power of *Götterdämmerung* and *Parsifal*, I cannot take to their complicated and, in my view, ill-balanced style. This criticism is, of course, only general: you would, I think, have to be totally unmusical not to admire Brünnhilde's funeral oration over Siegfried's body or the second scene of *Parsifal*.

Unfortunately, with Wagner it is never just a question of music; it is also a question of drama, and here he and I have to part company.

In the legendary days of Wagnerism, when for a brief moment the charming Gasperini was his prophet in France,[2] it was a matter of rescuing the lyric drama from the tyranny of routine and of the singers, in order to turn it into the great modern drama; and in accordance with the excellent idea that drama should reach out to the masses, there was talk of popular works whose subjects would be taken from legends that everybody knew, as opposed to works composed for an entirely fashionable elite who moved in a false, ideal world of the imagination that was inaccessible to the crowd.

Lohengrin fitted reasonably well into this programme. The libretto is sufficiently interesting; the declamation does not prevent singing and the singing does not slow down the action. For all its lofty qualities, the work

[2] Auguste de Gasperini (c. 1825–1868) was music critic of *La France musicale*, *Le Ménestrel* and *Le Figaro*. His book on Wagner was published in Paris by Heugel in 1866.

did not frighten the public. In fact, it is the greatest success, the *popular* success in Wagner's output. *Lohengrin* is in the repertoire of every opera house in Europe and America, except Paris, which it would have reached long ago but for political reasons.[3]

Then what happened? First of all, Wagner suppressed, one after the other, all the means of giving pleasure that opera had at its disposal in order to give free rein to the drama; then he suppressed drama and replaced it with a bizarre phraseology and a so-called philosophy whose meaning escapes me completely.

The drama of *Tristan und Isolde* is admirable in its initial conception, and the end of the first act provides one of the finest scenes to be found in the theatre. But, in the event, it became a succession of long conversations between two characters holding forth endlessly about the brilliance of the night and the darkness of the day. It is fine poetry, but it is not drama, it is an "armchair spectacle" with orchestra, an exquisite experience for those rare mortals who can read the score. I shall never be persuaded that it is good theatre to keep a character on stage for two whole acts, and what acts! It is a wilful abuse of the strength of both singers and spectators.

"The soul," says *The Imitation of Christ*, "has two wings, which are simplicity and purity." Wagner has constructed several dramas on this idea.

Lohengrin is an impassive character whose purity is his only good feature. Torn between love of Elsa and the loss of his power, he does not hesitate; he bids farewell to Elsa in the most affecting fashion, but he leaves.

Walther has never learnt anything, not poetry, not music: it is only through the simplicity of a happy nature that he "knocks out" the learned mastersingers. Here Wagner has, unintentionally, satirised himself. Naïvety is the least of his faults and any talented young composer would have no trouble writing far more appealing things than the great duet in *Parsifal*. But *Die Meistersinger* is an extraordinary work and the libretto is charming, despite its longueurs and some tasteless moments in Beckmesser's part where the *grotesquerie* is taken too far.

The whole of the *Ring* seems designed to lead up to the appearance of the hero Siegfried. And Siegfried is puberty and brute strength, nothing more. He's as thick as an ox, charges headlong into every situation and excites not the slightest sympathy. Parsifal is even worse; he is unwitting and pure, "reine Thor", words which, according to the most experienced Wagnerians, have no really precise meaning. And it is because he knows nothing and understands nothing that he finally manages to break the spells in which the holy men have allowed themselves to be entrapped.

[3] This complaint of 1885 was soon to be answered. The opera was first heard in Paris at the Eden-Théâtre on 30 April 1887. It was premiered at the Paris Opéra on 16 September 1891 and reached its 100th performance there on 28 April 1894.

Where is the philosophy in that?

Womankind in Wagnerian drama, initially loving and tender like Elsa or passionate like Isolde, becomes sublime with Brünnhilde who, in her love and sorrow, progresses from divinity to humanity—a bold idea, indeed a truly modern and philosophical one. But what becomes of this idea with the mystical, mysterious Kundry? "To understand the character of Kundry," says one commentator, "one had to have made a profound study of all ancient theologies." Heavens above! Some task, and one that takes us a very long way from popular drama.

I read somewhere that the appearance of the Parsifal text was an event not only of the aesthetic type but also ethical, marking a new era in the moral development of mankind. That is quite possible, and I am quite prepared to believe it once someone has provided me with some solid proof. Until that time I shall content myself with considering Wagner's works from an aesthetic point of view, which is quite sufficient for works of art.

If what I am saying were addressed exclusively to musicians, I could discuss in detail the musical questions thrown up by these colossal works. I could show how their style, which in principle is fairly humdrum and out of keeping with the loftiness of Wagner's conceptions, was first of all refined, but then became increasingly complicated, multiplying notes needlessly, abusing the resources of music to the point of wastage, and ultimately requiring of voices and instruments things beyond what is possible. His disdain for rigid structures, which was not yet a feature of his early works, comes across initially as liberating and emancipating, but then, in the late works, gradually turns into a licence that destroys all form and balance. He is constantly swept away by the typically Germanic preoccupation with going beyond reality. In this sense his instrumentation draws much of its character from passages that are impracticable and can only be played more or less accurately. The "Summoning of Fire" in Die Walküre is the acme of this procedure. The result is extremely beautiful, but surely it is dangerous to encourage players in this kind of attitude? "More or less" can easily become a habit. In some theatres where Wagner is given often, the orchestra plays out of tune and the singers sing out of tune, and no one notices: the ears of both players and audience have been untuned.

Given all these points, you can appreciate whether it's easy to reach a decisive judgment on works that are so complex and so different and which, from Rienzi to Parsifal, embrace so many varying styles. The Wagnerians have a simple way of dealing with this problem: they admire everything. One will tell you quite seriously that, when you go to a performance of one of the master's works, you must lay aside all critical sense; another will say that such and such a passage involving singers is beautiful, quite apart from the effect of the voice parts. Other composers are continually being accused of lacking conviction even when their theories are not wholly understood; but Wagner can write the most widely divergent things, and his conviction will never be brought into question.

He can either rely on formulas to the point of monotony, as he does in *Tannhäuser* and *Lohengrin,* or break free of them as in the works that followed: "That's fine! He intended it that way."

He can sit on the same chord for 60 bars in a moderate tempo, or modulate with every note: "That's fine! He intended it that way!"

He can launch into extremes of polyphony, or write duets and choruses in unison: "That's fine! He intended it that way."

He can set up realistic scenes like the arrival of the swan in *Lohengrin* and the spinning chorus in *The Flying Dutchman,* or turn his back on reality of any kind and have characters remaining immobile like wax figures for whole scenes, whole acts: "That's fine! He intended it that way!"

And I shall join the Wagnerians in repeating "That's fine! He intended it that way," since I stand for the freedom of art and genius before all things.

But I also reserve the right to retain my own freedom, to admire what I like and not to admire the rest; to find long what is long, discordant what is discordant, and absurd what is absurd. That is precisely what the Wagnerians refuse to allow. They grab you by the throat, and you have to admire everything all the time, come what may. People who are unable to play the simplest thing on the piano, and who don't know a word of German, spend whole evenings deciphering the most difficult scores in the world and singing this music in which every note can only be understood in relation to the word it sets, at the end of which they are faint with admiration. Wagner was the inventor of everything; there was no music before him and there can be none after. Don't talk to them about the vulgar insult Wagner threw at France after the defeat in the Franco-Prussian War; it would only provoke fury—against you! Note that it is not a question of a passing remark, such as can easily escape one accidentally in a letter or a newspaper article; it was an intentional piece of writing, reprinted in the author's lifetime and included in the definitive edition of his complete works.[4]

Behind this lack of respect for all decency and this insatiable need to go on listening to the same things—please note—in these Wagnerian circles and societies that seem to have spread gradually over the whole world, whatever the standard of performance, there lies something other than

---

[4] Wagner's "comedy in the classical manner" *Eine Kapitulation* (*Une Capitulation* in French), written in 1870, was described by Bernard Shaw in *The Perfect Wagnerite* as "that scandalous burlesque in which the poet and composer of *Siegfried,* with the levity of a schoolboy, mocked the French republicans who were doing in 1871 what he himself was exiled for doing in 1849". It caused widespread and lasting resentment in France.

the love of art: it is sectarianism. Of course, any man capable of inspiring such fanaticism is an extraordinary being; but I am fearful of sectarians and prefer to keep a safe distance from them.

"You dismiss Wagner," they say to me, "after studying his music and profiting from it." Not only do I not dismiss him, I am proud to have studied his music and profited from it, as was my right and duty. I did the same with J. S. Bach, with Haydn, Beethoven, Mozart and all the masters of every school. That does not mean that I have to say of each of them that he alone is God and that I am his prophet.

Ultimately it is not Bach, or Beethoven, or Wagner that I love, it is art. I am an eclectic. It may be a serious fault, but I am unable to cure myself of it; one cannot change one's nature. Furthermore, I am passionately in love with freedom, and I cannot allow people to tell me what I should admire. Enthusiasm to order is something that makes my blood run cold and prevents me from enjoying the finest masterpieces.

When all is said and done, if I allow myself to criticise Wagner's works, it is from an entirely relative point of view. In order to judge them sensibly, one has to put them in context and compare them with the plays of Goethe and Schiller. German theatre does not appeal to the French temperament and, seen from a German perspective, it is not within my competence. My own perspective is French, which is not to say one that is Parisian or man-about-town. Let's not exaggerate, please.

From this perspective Wagner's dramas seem to be full of faults—or, if you prefer, full of qualities that could never accord with the French character. Even so, people will manage, by means of an intense campaign of articles, lectures and carefully presented performances, to persuade the French public that it understands German art, just as they have persuaded it that it understands Italian art. They have certainly succeeded in whipping up enthusiasm for Italian tragedy! The fact is that they will succeed—and indeed have already succeeded only too well—in making the public unresponsive to the art of France, which is tantamount to destroying French art at its very source, because there is no art without a public. Art is a language: a preacher in the desert has ceased to communicate.

So what lies behind this propaganda for a foreign art, promulgated so energetically by people whose good intentions are equalled by their lack of sense? A profound error, and an illusion.

The error is belief in the continual progress of art.

Victor Hugo has said the last word on this question of artistic progress in his marvellous book *William Shakespeare*, and I shall not be so presumptuous as to try and add to what he says.[5] I recommend anyone wanting

---

[5] Hugo's *William Shakespeare* was published as part of the tercentenary celebrations in 1864.

to enlighten themselves on this topic to read the instructive pages in the chapter headed "Art and Science".

There the great poet shows irrefutably how continual progress is a law of science but can never be a law of art, and how the greatest perfection in the means employed does nothing to make works of art more beautiful. There can be no question of Hugo pleading his own cause here, given that he worked so hard to perfect the tools of literature!

Elsewhere, after painting a brilliant, wide-ranging series of portraits of the great geniuses who have brought honour to the human race, he adds:

It is possible to equal these geniuses. But how?
By being other.

Yes, by being other, and that answer is the condemnation of the Wagnerians' theories. Even if Wagner's works were perfect, that would be no reason to imitate them.

Wagner introduced a fruitful idea into the world, namely that lyric drama was the drama of the future and that it was necessary, so that it could march resolutely onward towards its goal, to free it from the impedimenta of traditional opera—the demands of singers and the idiocies born of routine. He interpreted that idea in his own fashion, which was perfectly suited to him; and for precisely that reason, extremely bad for everyone else.

Did he himself not change styles with every work? Is his system in *The Flying Dutchman* the same as in *Tristan?* Is his system in *Tristan* the same as in *The Ring?* Did he not sometimes even forget about systems altogether, as when he wrote a large Italian ensemble in *Lohengrin,* and unison choruses in *Parsifal* that go unremarkably from tonic to dominant, accompanied by repeated triplet chords in the style of M Gounod? And did he not prove in doing so that, being the great artist that he was, he relied primarily on that instinct to which, for want of explanation, we give the name "inspiration"?

Genius does not show a path, it beats a path for itself which it alone can follow. To want to follow it is to condemn yourself to impotence and ridicule. Take up its lead, but interpret it in your own fashion. So much for the error.

The illusion is to think that critics can influence art. Critics analyse and dissect. The past and present both belong to them; the future, never.

Critics are powerless to create new forms; that is the business of artists, and for that all they need is freedom. To advise and instruct them is the surest way to confuse them or make them sterile.

Now Wagnerian critics are singularly intolerant; they don't allow this, they forbid that. There is an embargo on exploiting the resources of the human voice, or of treating the ear to a cleverly constituted vocal ensemble. The system of obligatory melody has been succeeded by that of obligatory declamation. If you don't fall into line, then you are prostituting art, sacrificing to false gods, I know not what else. I really do wonder where such asceticism is leading.

Obviously no labour is too great in the cause of giving the public a taste for elevated enjoyment and refined pleasures. But to offer it "cruel beauties", as the smart saying is, to serve up a banquet of refined suffering and elevated unpleasantness, is surely excessive, and smacks of mortification. When you want to mortify yourself, you don't go to the theatre; you enter a convent.

That is the situation at least "in our lovely land of France". Young composers, if you want to amount to anything, remain French! Be yourselves, of your own time and country! What people show you as being the future is already the past. The future is with you. Unfortunately, as I said earlier, there is no art without a public and the public are not with you. They have been subjected over the last half-century to such praise of Italian and German art that they do not believe in French art. Let someone announce the arrival of a foreign opera and they run to hear it as though going to see a fire, even at the risk of returning home crestfallen, as was the case after the premiere of a certain Italian opera. But when works such as *Faust* or *Carmen* reach the stage, then they will wait to go and see them until the rest of the world has signalled its acclaim. Paris used to make reputations, now it merely confirms them; it receives light instead of giving it; this sun resigns itself to the modest role of moon.

But even that is not all. At a time when the whole world proclaims us to be the masters of theatre, people start questioning this superiority and saying we could learn things from the theatre in Germany. Who say this? Frenchmen.

These Frenchmen are happy to protest their patriotism, when they get the chance, and no one would wish to cast doubt on this. They are no doubt excellent Frenchmen, just as those subjects of King Priam were excellent Trojans when they all agreed to bring the Greeks' doomladen horse into Troy and cheerfully set about the destruction of their fatherland.

One last word.

I admire Wagner's works profoundly, for all their bizarre nature. They are superior and powerful, that is enough for me.

But I have never belonged, do not and will not belong to the Wagnerian religion.

March 1885

2

ART FOR ART'S SAKE

("L'art pour l'art",
Ecole Buissonnière,
Pierre Lafitte, 1913, 135–140)

M emories in France may be short, but no one is likely to forget the memorable meeting of academics at which a brilliant writer, in introducing a delightful poet, humorously reminded the company that he had been a captain in the hussars and used his rank as part of an epigram.[1] At this same meeting the eternal question was raised about art for art's sake.

Here firstly is M de Mun,[2] talking to M Henri de Régnier:[3]

—You were saying that art has nothing to do with being moral, and never runs the risk of being immoral so long as it remains strictly objective and impersonal, that's to say when it does not take sides. Allow me to stop you here. Not to take sides is precisely what I think a writer is forbidden to do. Art, in my view, is the adornment of ideas; if it is not that, if it limits itself to being *merely the concern for form, for the cult of beauty for its own sake,* whatever may be the actions and thoughts it is masking, *it seems to me to be no more than the useless exercise of a sterile facility.*

The useless exercise of a sterile facility! That's easily said and with that, with the stroke of a pen, a host of masterpieces stand condemned. But it is important that we understand one another. M de Mun is speaking here of the art of writing, and in that case he may indeed be right, even if it is possible to raise some objections, as we shall see later. But he does not nar-

---

[1] This reference remains obscure.

[2] Comte Adrien de Mun (1841–1914) was a leading anti-republican. On the strength of his speeches and pamphlets, he was elected to the Académie française in 1897.

[3] The novelist and Symbolist poet (1864–1936). In the early years of the twentieth century, he was a close friend of Ravel who used quotations from his work as epigraphs for *Jeux d'eau* and for *Valses nobles et sentimentales.*

row his terms of reference down initially; he speaks, to begin with, of *art*, and this word can be interpreted in a number of ways. There is Art, with a capital A; there are the Fine Arts, from which it would be wrong to exclude music—we shall see why; there is literary art and poetic art; and there are a whole number of other arts, some more or less closely connected with art proper, others sharing no more than the name.

So what is Art?

Art is a mystery. It is something that responds to a particular sense, one unique to the human species, which is usually called the aesthetic sense—an inexact term because *aesthetic sense* signifies a sense of the beautiful, and what is "aesthetic" is not necessarily beautiful. A sense of style would be nearer the mark.

This sense is possessed by some savage peoples. Some of these primitive tribes have weapons and utensils that show a remarkable feeling for style, which they lose when they come into contact with civilization.

By art, if you like, we mean only the Fine Arts, including the art of decoration.

Music, as I have already said, should be included in these.

I shall astonish nearly all my readers when I say that few people understand music. For most of them it is what Victor Hugo described as "the vapour of art", something that is for the ear what perfumes are for the nose, a source of sensations that are vague and necessarily formless like all sensations. But the art of music is something quite other. It possesses line, shape, instrumental colour, all within an ideal sphere that some of us inhabit from earliest childhood, like the author of these lines, some reach through education, but many others never know at all. In addition it possesses the faculty of movement, denied to the other Fine Arts. Music is the most mysterious of them; but the others are mysteries too, as we can easily see.

The first artistic manifestation takes place through attempts at reproducing objects, a practice that goes back to prehistoric times. And what is the first thought that comes into a man's head in such a situation? It is to mark out, with a stroke, the contour of an object whose image he wants to preserve. This contour and this stroke do not exist in nature. And in that lies the whole principle of art: basing yourself on nature to turn it into something else that responds to a special and inexplicable need of the human spirit.

There is nothing more fantastical and pointless than the advice so often given to artists, to be true! Art cannot be true, although it should not be false. It should be *artistically* true and produce an artistic translation of nature that satisfies the *sense of style* I mentioned above. When it has satisfied this sense, it has attained its goal; no more can be asked of it. This is not *the useless exercise of a sterile facility*; it is an attempt at satisfying a legitimate need, one of the most aspirational and respectable needs of human nature: the *need for art*.

Consequently, why should we demand of Art that it should be useful, or moral? It is both of those things in awakening noble, pure feelings in the hearts of mankind. That was Théophile Gautier's opinion, but not Victor Hugo's. The sun is beautiful, he used to say, and it is useful. True, but the sun is not a work of art.

In any case, how many times did Hugo contradict his own theories by writing poems that consist entirely of brilliant descriptions and splendid imagery!

But we are discussing art and not literature. Literature enters art through poetry and moves away from it through prose. Even if some great prose writers have managed to make their work artistic through the beauty and harmoniousness of their paragraphs and the picturesqueness of their vocabulary, prose by its very nature is not art. Also, if we except crude indecency, what would be immoral in prose ceases to be so in poetry, because here art regains its rights as soon as poetry appears: the form eclipses the content. That is why a great poet, Sully-Prudhomme,[4] preferred prose to poetry when he wanted to write philosophy, because, if he turned to poetry, he was afraid of not being taken seriously.

That is also why parents take their young daughters to operas whose plots, if heard without music, would terrify them. What Christian has ever been shocked by *La Juive?* What Catholic has been appalled by *Les Huguenots?*[5]

And it is also because prose moves away from art that it does not sit well with music, despite the current fad for this uncomfortable union.

As for poetry, there has been a trend to make it artistic to the extent of reducing it to mere form and writing verses bereft of any kind of meaning; but this fancy was short-lived.

Let us return, please, to M de Mun's aphorism.

"Not to take sides," he said, "is what a writer is forbidden to do." The eminent orator is absolutely right where prose works are concerned; but it would be possible to differ from him in the case of poetry.

In a marvellous ode called *La Lyre et la Harpe,*[6] Victor Hugo brings together Paganism and Christianity; each of them speaks in turn, and the

---

[4] René-François-Armand Prudhomme (1839–1907) was a poet and essayist who won the first Nobel Prize for Literature in 1901. His poems were set by Fauré ("Ici-bas!", "Au bord de l'eau", "Les berceaux") and Duparc ("Soupir", "Le galop"), among others.

[5] At the end of Halévy's *La Juive*, Rachel is hurled into a boiling cauldron; Meyerbeer's *Les Huguenots* contains a stabbing in church and (offstage, it is true) three executions and a massacre.

[6] This poem, from *Odes et ballades* of 1828, was set by Saint-Saëns for soloists, choir and orchestra in 1879.

poet, in the final verse, seems to agree with both of them, which does not prevent the ode from being a masterpiece. In prose, that would not have been possible. In the poem, the poetry carries all before it.

How is it that geniuses like Victor Hugo, distinguished minds, whom I know to be the profoundest of thinkers and critics, refuse to see that Art is a special entity, responding to a particular sense and having nothing to do with anything that is not itself? We have to admit that art accommodates itself wonderfully to morality and passion, but even so it remains sufficient unto itself: and it is then that it is at its greatest.

The first prelude of Bach's *48* does not express anything, and it is one of the marvels of music.

The *Venus de Milo* does not express anything, and it is one of the marvels of sculpture.

For completeness's sake it is as well to add that, in order to avoid immorality, art must be addressed to people who have a feeling for it. Where an artist sees only beautiful forms, the unenlightened will see only nudity. I have seen one good fellow scandalised by Ingres's *La Source*.[7]

To summarise: just as morality has no call to be artistic, so Art has no call to be moral. Both have their functions and are useful in their own way. The aim of morality is morality: the aim of Art is Art, and nothing else.

3

HARMONY AND MELODY

("Harmonie et mélodie",
Harmonie et mélodie,
Calmann-Lévy, 1899, 1–36)

I

What is music?

Music is one of the branches of the world's art, like literature, painting, sculpture and architecture.

Music is the youngest of the arts. This is not the place to embark on its history; let us merely say that, even if the elements of music are as old as

---

[7] Painted in 1856 and now in the Musée d'Orsay in Paris, this picture is a full frontal of a girl carrying on her left shoulder a pitcher from which water is pouring.

humanity, the art of music in the true sense of the term, the art of music as we understand it, dates from the 16th century. It is not surprising that it should still be ill understood, ill defined and even ill taught; for a proper theory of music has still to be produced, despite the number of theories that have been put forward, from the theories of theorists to the theories of critics.

One of the most widespread is the following: music consists of two elements, melody and harmony: harmony, a secondary element, is derived from melody; melody is born spontaneously, it is a product of genius; harmony is a product of calculation and learning.

This theory is based on no fact; it is even contrary to the facts in every respect; but it has had the good fortune to be taken up by a number of writers who were not musicians, seducing them with its apparent logic, and, as it has been around a long time, it has acquired the pernicious strength of a prejudice. It is in the name of this prejudice that fine pieces are attacked and great composers persecuted. Fine pieces always triumph in the end, but great composers sometimes die while they're waiting, as in the case of Berlioz or Bizet.

We do not intend to trace the origins of this war, which had already reached fever pitch in the time of the Gluckists and Piccinnists. This was a war between rival schools and, even if posterity has come down on the side of the former, we have to admit that Piccinni's admirers did have a point. Since then the fight has become less principled! But in any case, even leaving aside the fact that Gluck was a genius, for his supporters to win was entirely logical; he brought the traditions of French opera back together again, giving dramatic action and sung declamation the primary roles. Not that the melodic school accepted defeat: secretly it began to prepare the revenge that Rossini was to take so stunningly, helped by the most brilliant company of singers that ever lived.

This revenge was not accomplished without difficulty, despite Rossini's colossal powers and the talent of his interpreters. French good sense rebelled against the imposition of Italian "gurglings"; influential critics took it upon themselves to prove that good sense was wrong, that the roulade was the true means of expression for tragic opera, and that Italian music was the only music in the world. Perhaps they would never have succeeded, had they not found the way already paved by a writer of great authority—a man whom nobody would dare to attack unless fortified by the truth: namely, that it's possible to be a great writer and not understand a thing about music.

In 1814 Stendhal published a collection of letters, with the devious title *Lives of Haydn, Mozart and Metastasio*, which were devoted entirely to the glorification of Italian music. This book became the bedside companion of the majority of critics. The astonishing frivolity of its basic message is concealed beneath an appearance of learning that was bound to impress the ignorant.

I beg permission to dwell for a moment on this book, whose disastrous influence is still felt today, both in the world at large and in the press, even though the book itself has long been forgotten.

Music, according to the author, consists entirely of tunes; everything else is accompaniment, something totally inferior: the less important this accompaniment is, the better. Haydn is brought in as a witness and is made to say: "If you have a good tune, your composition, *whatever it is*, will be good and is bound to give pleasure."

It's true that a little further on we find the exact opposite: "Haydn followed an extremely original principle . . . Every motif was useful to him. 'The whole art of composition,' he used to say, 'lies in how you treat a theme and develop it.'"

The mediocrity of the writer's approach is striking, viz.:

> The science of sounds is so vague that one can never be certain of anything to do with them, except the pleasure they afford at any given moment.
> One needs only application and patience to produce nice-sounding chords; but to discover a fine tune demands genius.
> Do you want to know whether a tune is fine? Take away its accompaniment.
> If, in music, the physical pleasure it gives us is sacrificed to some other feature, then what we are hearing is no longer music.
> Melody is the principal means of producing this physical pleasure; harmony comes afterwards.

I am sure there is no need to underline how degrading for art this idea is of physical pleasure, which keeps on coming back. As for the author's views on music in general, he manages to refute his theories himself by being unwise enough to turn to practical matters and by delivering judgments that time has not confirmed.

For instance he compares Pergolesi and Cimarosa to Raphael, Piccinni to Titian, Sacchini to Correggio; while Mozart is compared to Dominiquin[1] and Gluck to Caravaggio. Judgment on Beethoven is delivered thus: "When Beethoven and Mozart himself piled up notes and ideas; when they went in search of quantities and bizarre extremities of modulation, then their symphonies, all learned and replete with science, had no effect;

---

[1] Domenico Zampieri (1581–1641), known as Dominiquin, was best known for his frescoes. His paintings are generally recognised as being accurate rather than inspired.

whereas when they followed in the footsteps of Haydn, they touched every heart."

When this sentence was written, Beethoven was 44. He had already written the Pastoral Symphony, the Seventh and the Fifth, three works that changed the face of the musical world. The author, though, has no problem dismissing anything that runs against his theories. For instance he mentions J. S. Bach only in passing, telling us that he learnt about modulation . . . *in Rome!* Which is rather like saying that Raphael learnt to draw in Berlin. But maybe he meant another Bach and muddled him up with the prodigious artist whose glory would have put absolutely in the shade those minor stars he so continuously admires—Galuppi, Benda, Guglielmi, Traetta and the rest, whose light has never reached us.[2]

Elsewhere he turns Palestrina into the creator of modern melody: an utterly false assertion, still repeated to this day.

He exhibits the deepest disdain for the immortal Rameau, the greatest genius France has ever produced; he declares indeed that the French have never had any music and never will have—a calumny that lives on. He moans continually about the decadence of art: Cimarosa, Haydn and Mozart are dead and nothing will replace them!

"Maybe I am being unfair," he says near the end, "to MM Mayer, Paër, Farinelli, Mosca[3] and Rossini, who have high reputations in Italy." So, a contempt for Beethoven and a misunderstanding of Rossini—that is where the idea of *melody for melody's sake* led someone of indubitably superior intelligence. Basically he has mistaken the pleasant and generally irresistible sensation produced by a beautiful voice on the least cultivated ear, for a love of music. Even choirs leave him more or less unmoved; a solo voice that can be tasted at leisure like a sorbet, that is true pleasure:

"What is the task of the voice? . . . to be beautiful and to show itself off. That is all. To achieve this, accompaniments must be fairly quiet, the violins should play pizzicato and, in general, the voice should sing in slow tempi." This idolatry of the voice culminates, in the final analysis, in the obliteration of music. And is it not amusing to see Rossini despised by the same man whose judgment was to defend him later on?

I should make it clear at once that I am not attacking any composer or any school, only a particular line of criticism. Rossini has joined the immortals, and in any case the war between the French, Italian and German schools is over, like that between the Classical and Romantic composers.

---

[2] Baldassare Galuppi (1706–1785) was the most important Venetian composer of his time; Georg Benda (1722–1795) was a church and opera composer; Pietro Guglielmi (1728–1804) composed some fifty comic operas in Italy and London; Tommaso Traetta (1727–1779) was an opera composer who in some senses anticipated Gluck's reforms of the medium.

[3] Opera composers born in 1763, 1771, 1769, and 1775.

II

No, music is not an instrument of *physical pleasure*. Music is one of the most delicate products of the human spirit. In the recesses of his intelligence, mankind possesses a particularly intimate sense, the *aesthetic sense*, by means of which he perceives art: music is one of the means of setting this sense in vibration. Behind the sense of hearing, with its marvellous capacity to analyse sounds, to distinguish the differences in their intensities, timbres and qualities, there lies, inside the complexities of the brain, a mysterious sense that responds to something quite different.

You know the *Pastoral Symphony*. You've heard that peasants' round dance, which gradually gains pace to the point of giddiness, of madness. At the climactic point everything suddenly stops and, without a transition of any kind, the double basses play *pianissimo* a note outside the prevailing key.[4] This note, almost inaudible, is like the sudden spreading of a black veil; it is the shadow of implacable fate appearing in the midst of the festivities, an indescribable anguish that no one can escape. From the point of view of the ear and its "physical pleasure", or even of cold reason, this note is absurd because it destroys the tonality and logical development of the movement. And yet it is sublime.

It appeals therefore neither to the ear that wishes to be caressed, nor to that short-sighted reason that battens on to phrases which are as regular as a geometrical figure. There must then be something in the art of sound that passes through the ear like a porch and through reason like an entrance hall, and that goes on further. All music that lacks this something is to be despised.

To modify one of Stendhal's aphorisms, we should say: "If, in music, the ideal with which it should before all else provide us is sacrificed to physical pleasure, then what we are hearing is no longer art." Seen from this angle, music takes on a different character: the perspective is quite other and certain questions become meaningless. It is no longer a matter of finding what gives more or less pleasure to the ear, but what expands the heart, what elevates the soul, what awakens the imagination by opening up for it the horizons of an unknown and superior world. This means that the question of whether one aspect of the art takes precedence over another becomes wholly irrelevant. This clearly defined melody is in fact useless, that succession of chords without any melody is profoundly beautiful; on the other hand, it happens that a melody of extreme simplicity may soar instantly to the greatest heights, while pretentiously manufactured works crawl painfully along the ground. There is no recipe for making masterpieces, and those who advocate this or that system are simply quacks.

[4] Movement IV, bar 1.

But let's come back to physical pleasure.

This pleasure is real; it cannot be the aim of music, but it is the attraction by which it seduces its audience. Melody alone, with the aid of rhythm, is capable of charming a certain kind of public. Who are these listeners? They are firstly all those people who, by reason of their inferior capacities, cannot rise to an appreciation of harmony; that is beyond dispute. They include the peoples of ancient times and also Orientals and African negroes. The music of Africa is childish and without interest. The Orientals have made detailed researches into melody and rhythm, but know nothing of harmony; as for the Greeks and Romans, all the efforts that have been made to prove that they knew harmony have merely served to demonstrate the opposite.

When Stendhal said: "Melody is the principal means of producing physical pleasure; harmony comes afterwards," he was talking not in aesthetic terms but in historical ones. Harmony *arrived* with the development of Western civilization, with the development of the human spirit.

Those people who deny progress and believe that the ancient world was superior to the modern one may deny the importance of harmony in music and concentrate exclusively on melody. Others, if they wish to be logical, will recognize that before the birth of harmony music was in some sense rudimentary and that it lacked the use of its principal organs. The development of harmony marks a new stage in the evolution of humanity. There has been much discussion as to whether harmony grew out of melody, or melody out of harmony. Such discussion is pointless. Both things exist in nature. It was merely the case that, while the most savage peoples were able to take melody and develop it more or less, harmony could grow only within the cradle of the refinements of modern civilization and of the amazing achievements of the Italian Renaissance.

It is perfectly reasonable to say: "One needs only application and patience to produce nice-sounding chords, but to discover a fine tune demands genius." And we could say with equal reason: "One needs only facility to produce a nice-sounding melody; but to discover fine chords demands genius." Fine melodies and fine harmonies are both products of inspiration; but it is obvious that discovering fine harmonies needs a far more powerful and organised brain than imagining fine melodies.

Currency has been given to the idea that harmony was the product of *scientific* reflection, and that inspiration had nothing to do with it. How has it come about then that the geniuses who discover fine melodies are also the only ones to discover fine harmonies and that no mediocre academic has, for example, been moved to write the "Oro supplex et acclinis" from Mozart's *Requiem,* which is no more than a succession of chords? The truth is that real composers discover both fine harmonies and fine melodies spontaneously, and that "science" is irrelevant to the question.

Whatever opposing factions may claim, putting together all the elements of a complex work will always be the achievement of a superior mind. The love of fine harmonies is also the mark of a listening public that has reached a high point of culture.

People who only like melodies are unconsciously confessing that they are unwilling to take the trouble to appreciate and coordinate the different elements of a complete work so as to understand it as a whole; as for assuming they would be unable to even if they wished and accusing them for that reason alone of being in the rearguard of the progress of civilization, we shall not be responsible for adopting such a challenging position. Whatever the case, such people, together with Orientals and savages, make up the public whose inertia blocks the course of art across the world; they don't realise that the most profound and exquisite musical pleasures are unknown to them; they are like children who think they have attained happiness by eating jam.

(Author's Note: Since writing these lines, my ideas about Oriental music have changed slightly.)

III

There is the melody of the theorists, the melody of composers and the melody of melody-mongers.

For the theorist every succession of notes is a melody. This narrow point of view has to be that of anyone wanting to discover melody in the works of 16th-century composers, the most prominent of whom is Palestrina. The melody-loving critics who claim to find true melody in Palestrina simply prove that they don't know this master's music.

Not only is the music of this school bereft of melody, but its rhythm is vague, albeit complicated and carefully thought out, and its tonality often imprecise. This music is therefore conceived within a system diametrically opposed to the one continually espoused by the critics I have just mentioned. It is extremely difficult in our own era to perform such works well, since they contain no indications of speed or nuances and their performing traditions are lost. But when, by dint of care and intelligence, a reasonable performance is achieved, then they produce a great impact; which seems to prove that a striking and predominant melody, sharply defined rhythms and a firm tonality are not the indispensable things they have been made out to be, and that music is not the most perishable of the arts, as people will insist on saying.

Whatever the truth may be, it is clear that melody, after being eclipsed in the 16th century by the new and magnificent development of harmony, then reclaimed its rights, and that music in our time cannot do without it. Here we reach the nub of the matter: there is melody and melody, just as there are pianists and pianists.

Take a lovely passage from Beethoven: the theme of the Andante of the 5th Symphony. For a musician it is a noble, beautiful and affecting melody: for a melody-monger it is not a *melody*. This theme is not foursquare; it doesn't come to a conclusion, it stops on a kind of question mark, and it is another theme that seems to descend from the heavens in reply which closes the paragraph. It is supremely beautiful, but could never please a melody-monger.

These people recognize a melody by the vocal character of the theme. Beethoven's is instrumental in character.

Instruments may never lay claim to the charm of voices, but on the other hand they possess quite special resources and their development has allowed instrumental music to take an extraordinary leap to heights that vocal music had never dreamt of. Of course it is possible to use instruments like voices; but, as a general rule, the style for voices and instruments can never be the same and it would be a mistake to confine instrumental music exclusively to themes that were vocal in character: if it often does employ them, that's because it is much easier to use them than to avoid them.

No one could accuse Mozart of melodic poverty, but he pursued the chimaera of unmelodic instrumental music for many years. The overture to *Così fan tutte* is an unsuccessful attempt along these lines, and the absence of melody is painfully apparent. The overture to *Don Giovanni* is a kind of compromise. In the overture to *The Magic Flute* the problem is completely resolved: no shred of a singing phrase anywhere, an extraordinary complexity and, as a result, a clarity and charm and an irresistible impact. It is a *tour de force* that only Mozart could bring off.

You often find ideas in the instrumental works of the great masters that could be termed *collective*, being made up of several melodic shapes heard simultaneously. The theme of the Allegro of the *Egmont Overture* is one of this kind. Such ideas are the product of a superior art, but will never please those who love only melody in the true sense of the term, because it is impossible for one voice to sing them and for some listeners to retain them in their underexercised memory. That is why people continually demand simplicity and clarity in music with an affectation that makes one think of M Sardou and his famous *sainte Mousseline*.[5]

[5] This slightly obscure reference seems to be to lines in Théodore de Banville's poem *Dans la fournaise*, dedicated to the journal Gil Blas "pour l'anniversaire de sa naissance" in December 1880:

> L'éclectique Messaline
> En courant son guilledou,

Music can avoid being complicated: but it can only be relatively simple since it is, by its very nature, a complex art. A melody is not a work, any more than a line is a poem. Music cannot really be simple and clear for everyone without renouncing most of its resources; in which case it removes any interest from its harmony, rhythm and instrumentation so as not to distract the listener's fragile attention from the melodic line. It even takes care not to make this line too unconventional. The cost is that it descends into the realm of the vulgar; it is categorised as melodic, scenic, easy to understand, and the daughter of inspiration. But suppose it is reluctant to clip its wings? Then it is learned music, and the composer is a pedant who does not know how to conceal his learning—he is a pretentious nincompoop, an algebraist, a chemist, a what you will.

It is in these terms that the public are educated and that people discourse on the art of Beethoven. They used to talk the same way in Rameau's time—nothing changes.

Here are some passages of a curious piece of criticism from some fifty years ago, which shows rather amusingly how far these sorts of ideas can take you:

> Music is in the arts what love is in life [a good start, but wait for the end]. Music has one unfortunate failing for those who practise it and reflect, but luckily musicians do not spend much time reflecting [how kind!]. Their most brilliant productions wither more or less instantly, and they are unarguable deprived of that immortality that is the privilege of the other arts. . . . The strange thing is that it is only simple music that lasts [there we are]. It is what the experts call "little music" and often treat with disdain: romances, for instance. But while the best and most satisfying of these romances live in mankind's memory and cross the centuries [good for romances!], it turns out that, with the exception of the odd decrepit and lonely admirer, the greatest works, that have cast a spell over audiences and been proclaimed the masterpieces of the century, like finales, symphonies and masses, do not last as long as twenty-five years; after this brief immortality, they are forgotten, despised even,

---

Chante sainte Mousseline
Sur un thème de Sardou.

(The eclectic Messalina,
while doing the
rounds of the nightspots,
sings 'sainte Mousseline' to lines by Sardou.)

Victorien Sardou (1831–1908) was a playwright, now best known for *La Tosca* (1887), on which Puccini based his opera.

in favour of other idols which will be despised in their turn. Fashion, which has very little influence over the other arts and is powerless against their finest products, is almost all-powerful over music.

There are several possible reasons for this. Basically, music is song; and song is ideas. Harmony does, no doubt, add engaging effects and it supports and seconds the melody. But many composers, drunk on their studies of harmony, are led to undervalue melody, which is not there for the taking. These foxes without tails . . .

Those are reasons indeed.

If these composers, these foxes, had tails, music would not go out of fashion so quickly. Reactionary criticism has always had these grace-ful turns of phrase and insult has always been quick to take the place of reason. Take this phrase about Berlioz: "He is a member of the Insti-tut, I grant you, but which member?" In our day insult is paired with calumny.

From the moment when you are suspected of belonging to a particu-lar school, you are accused of harbouring the strangest opinions and holding to the most bizarre notions. The author of these lines, who reveres the masters, has been portrayed as dragging everything that is respectable through the mud and has been condemned, as a penance, to listen to a Beethoven symphony, on the assumption that he would find this the most appalling of punishments!

Back to our reading . . .

These foxes without tails too often pretend to have a profound dislike for anything that is merely melodious or elegant or, in a word, singing. Nothing is worthy of attention unless a mass of voices or instruments is crossing and combining, so that you lose yourself in a labyrinth and need to be a genius to find your way out. In my view it would be better to have the wit not to enter in the first place. These are prodigious efforts, this sublime music par excellence which does not last more than thirty years [a moment ago it was twenty-five—so there's some progress], and when it is no longer fashionable, you cannot imagine how it ever was; while the prettiest romances, the hunting and popular songs, the country airs, are still heard with pleasure.

At least that's frank, and the author has earned his spurs as an *enfant terrible*. The conclusion to be drawn from this great school of simplicity is that we should prefer songs like "Au clair de la lune" and "J'ai du bon tabac" to *Guillaume Tell*, *Les Huguenots*, *La Juive*, *Don Giovanni*, the nine Beethoven symphonies, the *Missa Papae Marcelli*, the *St Matthew Passion* and *Israel in Egypt*.

IV

Music is still so young that it does not realise its strength or suspect its power.

So what is music? Who will take on the task of defining it? It is an architecture of sounds; it is a plastic art that models, in a kind of clay, the vibrations in the air; it has colour of a sort, like painting; but it goes past like the wind, a second carries it away and it is no longer there. Wrong! Engraved on bronze, it is firmly fixed: the printing press takes it and spreads it throughout the world. It becomes literature, it becomes a *book*, universal and indestructible. People of every country read it and understand it, whatever their language and race, and future generations will receive it intact.

Works of literature have for many years uniquely enjoyed the privilege of immortality, and Horace was right to say that he had erected a monument more lasting than bronze.[6] Bronze breaks, painting fades: the book remains. And now a new art comes along, also more lasting than marble or bronze. Literature senses a rival; and note how it receives and treats this newcomer! By instinct, writers hate music; even those who claim to like it invent some grave fault in it, such as being a frivolous art, or of becoming out of date within a few years; or else they only accept music by composers who are either dead or foreign; at the very least they do their best to curb the development of this new art in their vicinity, in their native country.

"You should not make your debut in a new opera," wrote Alfred de Musset, "because it is in the works of the masters that true music is to be found." Which did not prevent him from calling music elsewhere "the most perishable of all the arts". Note how Diderot speaks of Rameau, "who put on paper such a quantity of unintelligible imaginings and apocalyptic truths about the theory of music, which neither he nor anyone else can ever really have experienced; and from whose hand we have a number of operas made up of harmonies, bits of tune, disjointed ideas . . . , and who, after burying the Florentine opera, will in turn be buried by the Italian virtuosi." *The Barber of Seville* consisted of "vague confusion, formless scribbles, bizarre combinations, German racket, badly developed phrases, crazy modulations, eccentricity" (according to Augustin Thierry).[7]

Music goes out of fashion like everything else in this world, neither more nor less. Tragedy has gone out of fashion, romantic drama has gone

[6] "Exegi monumentum aere perennius" (I have built a monument more lasting than bronze), *Odes* III, 30.

[7] French historian (1795–1856).

out of fashion, but have not died of it. The general public understands nothing of 15th-century painting or of the arts of the Middle Ages; we see people knocking down masterpieces of Gothic architecture in order to turn them into ruins, because the Gothic is only beautiful as a ruin, by moonlight. It is doubtful whether fashionable people get pleasure from looking at Dürer's engravings. How many of them get to the end of *The Divine Comedy* or *Orlando furioso*, let alone the *Iliad* or the *Odyssey?* What could be more unfashionable than dead languages?

For art, being out of fashion is the beginning. Where fashion ends, posterity begins. Music can, if it wishes, be an art of sensation; it excites the masses, drives crowds to delirium. Once this noise is over, it becomes a statue: immobile and silent, it remains itself.

It is wrong to think that music forcibly drags along in its train an army of singers and instrumentalists. You can read a Beethoven symphony by your fireside as you can read a tragedy by Racine; neither of them needs to be played for them to exist.

Those same people who deny the durability of works of music cannot believe what they are saying, because they praise the ancient masters at the expense of the new. The truth is that they fight against the invasion of music with every means and every weapon that come to hand. Since they cannot compel it to be silent, they want to reduce it, to make it a lowly art, something contemptible and charming—as Roqueplan[8] described it: an art of enjoyment. Hence this out-and-out war against all serious music, this hypocritical enthusiasm for singing and melody, a false doctrine whose emptiness we have been attempting to demonstrate.

There are people who think they like flowers because they cut them to make bouquets: for them the plant, with its marvellously organised ensemble of roots, stems and leaves, does not exist; its whole *raison d'être* is the flower, and a plant that doesn't flower is of no interest. There are others who study the plant as an entity, who follow its development, admire the wonderful balance of its parts, its elegant, delicate or powerful outlines, and for whom the flower is to be cherished only on its stem, in the fullness of its life. Are we to say that such people are flower-haters? Then why say that composers hate melody, just because they won't sacrifice everything else to it? No one hates melody; what are detestable are the idiocies and vulgarities that are promoted under the banner of melody.

Composers are requested to conceal their technique. But what is meant in this case by technique is quite simply talent, and, when you have it, you

---

[8] Nestor Roqueplan (1804–1870) was editor of *Le Figaro* and then, with Edmond Duponchel, administrator of the Opéra and Opéra-Comique from 1847 to 1854. Of the second part of *Les Troyens*, he commented that "the text is such that anybody could have written it; the music is such that nobody would want to have written it."

should use it, not stick it in your pocket; while it may be polite not to parade it, it would be fairly stupid to act as though you didn't have it, just to please those who haven't got any.

Musical criticism is written, not by musicians, but by literary people, and so music is delivered up to its worst enemies, and if all the advice proffered to it were followed, its death would ensue. No one says to composers: "be great, be strong, be sublime!" Instead, "be easy to understand, be accessible to the masses!" At this very moment, composers thinking of writing new works for the Paris Opéra are advised: "To be a dramatic composer, you do not need to prove your talents for algebra or chemistry. If, *primarily,* your works are visually aware and melodic, then *everything else will be forgiven them, if necessary.*"

It is a veritable summons to musical debauchery.

One of the most unusual characteristics of this war, waged by literature on music for so long, is its extreme harshness. It is impossible to write serious works of music without exposing oneself to being dragged in the mud and treated like the lowest of the low. *You don't have the right,* apparently, to compose in a certain manner. It's quite common to see writers professing the most liberal opinions, then turning into extreme authoritarians when they start to rail against music; and after demanding the freedom of movement, the freedom of association, the freedom of the press and the freedom of printed matter, they demand the slavery of the freest of all the arts.

Music laughs at all this rage; she laughs at the calumnies heaped upon her. What does she care that she is accused of being ephemeral? She lives, she will live, she will prevail.

She will prevail because she is the art of advanced peoples, the expression of a civilization whose development is reaching a supreme intensity, unknown to other ages and other peoples.

The writers who stand in the way of musical progress, sometimes out of conviction, sometimes for whatever unimportant reason, are innocently putting themselves under the wheels of the chariot that is leading humanity into the future. The chariot may slow down as it crushes them; but stop, never!

One can only feel sympathy for these unfortunates, led on by a bizarre fatalism to sacrifice their strength and talent in an impossible task, lacking either reason or glory, for which nobody in the world will thank them. Because they don't understand what they're saying, they repeat the same trivialities from one generation to the next with a courage that deserves a better outcome. It is truly puzzling to see these intelligent people committing themselves to such an ungrateful task; one day or the next they must surely tire of it. Already more than one of them has gone over to the enemy: in the end they all will. That day the battle will be won. We shall not speak of "the Fine Arts and Music", but of "Music and the Fine Arts". And if Music has a place apart, it will be the place of honour.

July 1879

4

THE BIRMINGHAM FESTIVALS

("Festivals de Birmingham",
Harmonie et mélodie,
Calmann-Lévy, 1899, 141–154)

Thanks to their grandness of scale, the importance they have in the sight of the English and their ancient origin, the Birmingham Music Festivals deserve to be noticed. There, as on the banks of the Rhine, a festival consists of a series of concerts lasting several days. Nothing similar exists in France, where any concert is boastfully called a festival if it is larger than usual.

Our musical celebrations in the west of France are the only ones that could be compared with those of England or Germany, but they are by no means of the same importance.

Strange as it may seem, English musical attitudes are still largely misunderstood on the continent, and I'm amazed at some of the bizarre ideas about our neighbours' tastes that are current in Paris. Just because we have occasionally heard female salon singers from the land of Shakespeare singing like magpies, we have drawn the conclusion that the English are, by nature, resistant to music. We have a picture of them applauding any old thing, and not caring whether a piece is good or well performed as long as it has two essential ingredients: favourable publicity and the name of a famous composer. More than one artist has, to his cost, found that this is far from the truth. But when you don't enjoy the success abroad that you're used to, you don't normally advertise such failures when you get home. So the French public often believes that Madame X and Mademoiselle Z have had triumphs in London, when in fact they experienced precisely the opposite. As I write, I'm holding Pandora's box. If I were to open it! . . . Fear not; it shall remain closed.

In order to set up concerts in London, whether as a performer or a composer, you must have a reputation. It is of course very hard to reach the public in any country in the world, but in London it is an even more difficult business than elsewhere. Concert organisers face considerable costs, and engage only those artists capable of "turning a profit". It's true that they don't oblige artists to play or conduct for free, as they do with us. In France, we have persuaded composers and performers that they were of a superior nature and could live on fame, as the gods used to survive on ambrosia. With regard to composers, let us not speak; but for performers it's another matter. They did not long put up with this superhuman regime: some were stranded in the teaching profession, others went off to earn their living outside France.

English audiences have one great quality: patience. They are reserved without being mistrustful and, if they are not exactly prodigal with their applause, they are not grudging either. They are extremely conservative and never tire of the most frequently heard pieces, once they have been accepted into the canon. But, on the other hand, they willingly lend their ears even to extremes of novelty and are as quick to understand their secrets as any audience in the world. If they don't understand a piece at first hearing, they content themselves with not applauding and do not make a parade of passionate hostility towards it. In short, they are not excitable. They don't go in for the wild gestures and stormy expressions of continental audiences, who are so dearly prized by those artists that thrive on emotions and danger. But then one can't have everything in this world.

The Birmingham Festival is a philanthropic institution. Its purpose is to support the city's general hospital, which was founded in 1765. At that time Birmingham had only 35,000 people, instead of the 400,000 it has today.

The city found it was unable to meet the growing costs of the hospital and so, in 1768, it had the idea of putting on a festival in St Paul's Chapel, which raised 800 pounds. The concert included the Handel oratorios *L'Allegro, Il Penseroso, Alexander's Feast* and *Messiah.*

The second festival did not take place until ten years later and the third was given in 1784. Since then, a series of concerts has been organised regularly at three-year intervals. In 1834 the Town Hall was built and the festival, which had moved from Saint Paul's Chapel to Saint Philip's Church, made its definitive home in this splendid building. The 1837 festival is known for the first appearance there of Mendelssohn, who conducted the performance of his recently completed oratorio *Saint Paul;* it had already been given that same year in Düsseldorf, Liverpool and London.

At the 1840 Festival, Mendelssohn conducted the *Hymn of Praise,* known in Germany as *Lobgesang* and in France as *Symphonie-Cantate.* This work had been premiered in Leipzig the previous June at celebrations of the 400th anniversary of the invention of printing. 1846 is the red letter day in the history of the Birmingham Festival; that is the date of the premiere of *Elijah,* Mendelssohn's masterpiece, specially written for the occasion and conducted by the composer. This work placed Mendelssohn on a pedestal beside the greatest masters and, despite the efforts of Fétis, the illustrious director of the Brussels Conservatoire, to pull him down from it, he has remained firmly *in situ.*

The performing forces available to the Birmingham Festival are huge: they are very close to those for the large concerts at the Universal Exhibition in Paris at the Trocadéro Palace, with the difference that the voices and instruments, instead of being lost in too large a space with its inevitable echoes, are heard in a hall holding nearly two thousand people and not five thousand.

Furthermore, this hall is a rectangle in shape, or an elongated square, and not an ellipse, like the Trocadéro or the Albert Hall in London. Architects seem to be very fond of ellipses and adduce in support of their preference a number of highly plausible scientific reasons. But they confuse the production of one single sound with a musical performance, and start from a premise that seems wholly erroneous. There is no doubt that if you produce a sound at the mathematical centre of the ellipse in a hall of this shape, the sound will be heard equally and perfectly throughout the building. But as it is impossible for 500 performers to gather on a mathematical point, they will be increasingly badly placed, the further they are from the point in question. It follows that, for an ensemble of players to produce the collective effect on a listener that the composer wanted, they must be put in a setting so organised that there is no such central point.

Also, as M Cavaillé-Coll has so rightly explained, curved surfaces deform sounds in the same way as curved mirrors deform reflections; and so it is impossible to hear the music clearly. One is then forced, in order to stifle echoes and unwanted resonances, to have recourse to absorbent surfaces which damp down any superfluous vibrations. In the Birmingham Town Hall, all the sound produced is utilised; the most delicate instrumental solo and the finest nuances of the voice reach the ear of the listener without effort, and the unleashing of powerful massed sonorities does not lead to confusion. It is one of the best large halls in existence.

The Festival orchestra is made up of 28 first violins, 26 seconds, 20 violas, 17 cellos and 17 double basses, making 108 strings in all. There are four flutes, four oboes, four clarinets, four bassoons and one contrabassoon. Two trumpets, two cornets, four horns, three trombones, an ophicleide, two harps, four timpani and percussion instruments, bringing the total number of players to 146. What's more, the hall possesses an enormous organ, made by Mr Hill, an English builder, which has 77 stops: the pedal alone has 15, including three of 32 feet.

It will be noted that the woodwind instruments come in groups of four, and not two as in ordinary orchestras. It was the same for the official concerts at the Paris Exhibition, with the exception of the oboes. Some composers imagine that oboes are as powerful as trumpets and trombones. This opinion prevailed in the music committee of the Universal Exhibition, and two unfortunate oboists were condemned to battle against a vast orchestra in an immense hall, while the flutes, clarinets, bassoons and even, I believe, the horns had the advantage of numbers. It is difficult to conceive of anything more absurd.

The chorus, around a third of whom are amateurs, consists of 95 sopranos, 90 altos, 95 tenors and 80 basses. Of the 90 altos, 45 belong to the ugly sex, since nature has not provided a large enough supply of low female voices. Thanks to this heroic but necessary arrangement, the alto section, so important in oratorios, is given a breadth and solidity that allow it to stay on equal terms with the redoubtable tenor section alongside it. While the French refuse to take similar steps, we shall always have to note with regret the feebleness of the alto line in their traditional choirs.

I wish those who deny the English any musical feeling could hear the choral singers of Birmingham. Good intonation, exactness of time and rhythm, a pleasant sound, this marvellous chorus has them all. If these singers aren't musicians, they do precisely what they would do if they were the best musicians in the world. You can ask them at the last moment for different nuances or speeds from the ones they're used to, and they will do immediately and to perfection what you ask of them. They take awkward tunings and fearful pianissimos on high notes in their stride. That such singers are not well prepared for music making is something I cannot concede; and, even if I could, that would be reason to grant them a greater merit than to others who, though better prepared, still do not achieve such good results. So let us recognize frankly the abilities of others: not to do so will harm no one except ourselves.

There is no doubt that singing can be as good in Paris as it is in England. The choirs conducted by M Lamoureux,[1] in his performances of Handel and Bach oratorios, reached a state of perfection that could not be surpassed. But such performances are, with us, no more than incidental, instead of being, as elsewhere, the result of permanent organizations. The fact is that it is not possible to find in France a large enough number of amateurs who love music enough to devote themselves completely to regular and extended rehearsals. M Bourgault-Ducoudray[2] put on performances of *Alexander's Feast*, *Acis and Galatea* and a Bach cantata, but

---

[1] The conductor Charles Lamoureux (1834–1899) used the orchestra that bore his name to promote Wagner, but also the younger generation of French composers and, as indicated here, a certain amount of Baroque music.

[2] Louis Bourgault-Ducoudray (1840–1910) won the Prix de Rome in 1862 and was professor of music history at the Conservatoire from 1878 to 1908.

then had to give up his superhuman efforts, which had affected his health. Before him, M Vervoitte[3] had conducted a society for sacred music that made a brilliant appearance, but then suddenly vanished. For the musical honour of France it is much to be desired that these efforts should be repeated and that MM Vervoitte, Bourgault and Lamoureux find successors. But perhaps it would be as well, if one wanted to get French amateurs interested, not to devote such efforts too exclusively to the music of Handel.

In England, Handel is the basis of oratorio, the daily bread of every musical feast. Since the beginnings of the Birmingham Festival, no single one has been without a performance of *Messiah*, and not to the detriment of other Handel works. After the well-known triumphant arrival of *Elijah*, that too is a regular ingredient. These two works seem destined to appear for ever on the festival programmes—a situation that is not without monotony, and one shudders to think what would happen if a third work were to come along and gain the same measure of public favour.

This conservatism comes though from other reasons than purely musical administration: in the matter of oratorios, English dilettantism is combined in a complex manner with devotion, and devotion of a quite special kind. England has been at times both Catholic and Protestant; at heart, it could never be Protestant like the Germans nor Catholic like the Latin races. England is biblical, and the Old Testament occupies a place in its religion almost equal to the one it has in Judaism. Hence the striking success of works like *Israel in Egypt, Elijah* and *Solomon,* whose stories will never have for audiences on the continent the interest they have for the English. Even if the ultimate triumph is reserved for *Messiah,* which is performed everywhere all the time, the Gospel, in their eyes, is still the Bible. This is a nuance that one feels very strongly in England, but it is very difficult to explain it to anyone else.

August 1879

---

[3] Charles Vervoitte (1819–1884) was organist at the church of St-Roch from 1859 to 1873 and then at Notre-Dame until his death.

5

MUSICAL ECCENTRICITIES

("Divagations musicales",
Au courant de la vie,
Dorbon-Aîné, 1914, 45–51)

Throughout history, opinions about art, and especially about the art of music, have been subject to strange aberrations, to wild eccentricities. An art gives rise to a powerful suggestion, and through it the moon instantly appears as green cheese. The public in its innocence falls in with these crack-brained ideas. When you go back and read what someone like Stendhal said about Cimarosa, or what Balzac said about Rossini, you're amazed at the opinions they foisted off on their contemporaries; who listened to them open-mouthed, truly believing that if they failed to find everything in this Italian music that people wanted them to, it was because they were incapable of understanding it.

Fifty years ago one did not dare express a doubt as to the quality of famous operas which nowadays are regarded as deficient in melody, harmony, instrumentation, everything . . . Beethoven, in those days, the divine Beethoven was "algebra in music". Don't imagine I invented that: those are things one can't invent.

So, without descending pointlessly to personalities, we should not be surprised at certain opinions since in this matter, as in others, there is nothing new under the sun. But surely it is permissible to warn certain readers, assuming there are some of goodwill, and put them on their guard against the assertions of certain persons who, while doubtless acting in good faith, are also over-persuasive? You will have understood by now that we are talking about those people—a goodly number, as we know— who go forth under the banner of the great Richard and, beneath his shadow, fight a fight that has long been purposeless.

It is not enough for them that their God triumph: victims have to be slaughtered on the altars.

First, Mendelssohn. His output is uneven. But *Elijah, A Midsummer Night's Dream*, the Organ Sonatas, the Preludes and Fugues for piano, the *Scottish* and *Italian Symphonies* . . . You try and match these!

We are asked to believe that when he first appeared he was accepted without a struggle, because his "mediocrity" immediately put him on the public's level. Don't believe a word of it!

I attended the first Paris performances of the *Dream* and of the Symphonies, and I still remember the lances I broke over them. At early performances of the *Dream*, I saw elderly habitués of the Conservatoire Concerts digging their nails into their foreheads and asking in desperation why the Société des Concerts should be forcing its subscribers to undergo such horrors . . . it took time for this audience to discover the "Berceuse" [Nocturne], then the "Scherzo", then the "March", then the "Agitato" and then, finally, the Overture. It was a long process!

Another victim is Meyerbeer. The knives are out particularly for *Les Huguenots*, because of its resounding and long accepted success. On this front a powerful ally has been found in an article by Schumann, in which he says that *Les Huguenots* is not "music".

Unfortunately, when Schumann, with his wonderful talent, tried to write for the theatre, the result was *Genoveva. Genoveva* is certainly music, and charming music, but it does not work in the theatre, as everyone agrees. And so the authority of Schumann's judgment on *Les Huguenots* is undermined. On the other side we have the opinion of Berlioz—not the most indulgent of men, as we know—who in his famous *Traité d'instrumentation* quoted extracts from the great duet, "that immortal scene". Such praise, I feel, is not to be ignored.

Once the victims have been sacrificed, then the task is to affirm that the God is right in every respect (otherwise he would not be God): this means claiming for him, in addition to the numerous brilliant qualities he possesses, those that he lacks.

Emphasis will be laid, for instance, on his prolific melodic invention, and on his clarity. Certainly he can be clear when he wants to be, just as certain women can be virtuous when the mood takes them; but those are not the ones we normally call "virtuous". Virtue is not Helen, but Penelope; clarity is not Wagner, but Mozart.

Some apologists have even gone so far as to claim that the Wagnerian repertoire contains no technical difficulties for the orchestra and that there are not even any "awkward moments", while the truth is that there are some passages that are not merely difficult or awkward, but actually unplayable.

I have in front of me a very well argued and interesting article on "the future of lyric drama". The author attacks the noble genre, with its kings, heroes, gods and sumptuous costumes, as well as everything that belongs to legend or mystery or to the almost ubiquitous need to place the action in distant countries and eras. As I read it, I began to fear that I was head-ing for a denial of Wagner's life's work, because it had always seemed to me that it was full of gods and heroes and legends and mystery, and that when Wagner wanted to deal with real life, he turned to the costumes and customs of ancient times.

I was wrong. Siegfried's forge and Hans Sachs's shoes are enough to turn the *Ring* and *Die Meistersinger* into works of realism. But don't imagine that Wagner was capable of realism of a vulgar kind! Like Beethoven, he rejects the direct imitation of Nature, he does not imitate the sound of iron, he substitutes the man for the thing, the blacksmith for his tool, expressive art for pure imitation; and the writer continues for some time in this vein.

It's all very charming; but it's not true. A part for an anvil, a real anvil, is part of the orchestration, written into the score. The effects Wagner gets from it are highly picturesque, and if he has not substituted "expressive art for pure imitation, the blacksmith for his tool", I must humbly confess to not being offended. What's more, in *Rheingold* he introduced a whole orchestra of anvils, large, medium and small, who kick up a din for quite some time. They make a crescendo while the orchestra gradually dies away and play on their own for several bars; after which they make a decrescendo while the orchestra gradually returns to normal: their appearance and disappearance are part of the general ensemble. It is an extremely original and striking idea. I heard this effect for the first time in Munich, in the performances organised by order of King Ludwig II[1] against the composer's wishes, and which he did not attend. The passage for the anvils unaccompanied gave the listener a sensation of vertigo which presumably Wagner disliked when he heard it at Bayreuth, because he cut it in rehearsal. I miss them, as I miss the castanets in *Tannhäuser*, which used to click away in ternary rhythm when the Bacchanal motif comes back, and which have likewise been removed.

Gods, heroes, distant lands and times, all of these are extremely useful in opera and it would be pointless to say otherwise. But they are not indispensable, as M Charpentier has successfully demonstrated in *Louise*.[2] But M Charpentier, true man of theatre that he is, has got round the difficulty by all kinds of ingenious means; he has even transported us to fairyland, with his vision of an illuminated Paris seen from the heights of Montmartre.

To return to our subject, can we not see things as they really are? And what aberration makes people reason falsely, when they are capable of doing so accurately, as is the case with those I've mentioned? One of them

[1] Saint-Saëns mistakenly refers to him as Louis III. There were three performances, on 22, 24, and 26 September 1869.

[2] Gustave Charpentier's opera was premiered at the Opéra-Comique on 2 February 1900.

has said quite rightly: "Essentially, art does not change. It is men who change their opinions over its means and limits. Once they have finally come to the conclusion that these limits are entirely arbitrary and that everything has a right to life in the city of the beautiful, then they will more easily grasp the fecundity of art, which is inexhaustible."

Let us conclude with those excellent words and express the wish, if not the hope, that they may be read and appreciated as they deserve, and that they may serve to regulate opinions in the future.

6

HÉLÈNE

(Au courant de la vie,
Dorbon-Aîné, 1914, 71–76)

A long time, a very long time ago I had this vision: of Helen fleeing in the night, arriving desperate and exhausted at the beach, a long way from her palace, and being joined by Paris—then the love scene, resistance finally swept away, the ultimate flight for the two lovers after a despairing struggle . . .

I have never been able to see Helen simply as a woman in love: she is the slave of Destiny, the victim of Aphrodite sacrificed by the goddess to her glory, the price of the Golden Apple; she is a powerful figure whose sin evokes no sniggering, but rather a kind of holy terror. See her on the ramparts of Troy, of that city upon which her presence visits ruin and disaster: when she passes by, the old men of Troy stand up and salute her. Later we find her with her husband, a queen doing the honours of her palace, and no one thinks of reproaching her for her past, her abandonment of Menelaus, the years she spent in Troy, the innumerable Greeks who died for her! The daughter of Zeus finds in her path nothing but honour and respect.

I dreamt then of setting to music the flight of the two lovers; but we know how this has been parodied, and with what sharpness and success.[1] To get an audience to respond seriously to these epic characters who had

---

[1] In Offenbach's *La belle Hélène*, premiered on 17 December 1864.

become laughing stocks was, for a long time, an impossible notion. I put the project off for later and, as time went by, I forgot about it.

Then came a request from M. Gunsbourg—which I resisted at first, only for him to make it even more strongly. This was enough to reawaken my memories, and to bring before me once again Helen and Paris more alive than ever.

Initially I had the idea (a lazy one, I confess) of finding a collaborator; but then a collaborator would perhaps want to add his ideas to mine and spoil the simplicity of my conception. I made up my mind to work alone.

Alone? Not entirely. Following the French classical composers, I took as my helpers Homer, Theocritus, Aeschylus, Virgil and even Ovid. Scholars will have no difficulty in discovering their contributions to *Hélène*. Without Virgil, would I have dared to give the description of Priam's palace, its gilded roofs, its walls covered with polished, shining bronze and decorated with impressive statues, probably multicoloured, in an ensemble that almost makes Gustave Moreau's strange structures seem realistic! Would I have dared write the line:

> Dans le sang de ses fils Priam est égorgé?
> (Priam is slaughtered in his sons' warm blood?)

With my notes taken and my scenario sketched out, I had now only to get down to work. At the time[2] I was the guest in Cairo of His Highness Prince Mohammed Ali Pasha, the brother of the Khedive. I enjoyed complete freedom, and a peace that no visitors dared disturb, frightened away as they were by huge, superbly uniformed, formidably armed young men, who were the guards of the palace gate.

I could not say how, before any of the text was written, I came by the first musical phrase, to which I subsequently set the line:

> Des astres de la nuit tes yeux ont la clarté!
> (Your eyes shine brightly like the stars at night!)

I had got as far as that when the manager of the Khedive's theatre had the notion of putting on a grand concert in aid of Breton seamen and of filling it entirely with music by me.

So there I was, suddenly busy with meetings and rehearsals, and forced to practise the piano in order to fulfil my part in the ceremony. All of that was incompatible with work on a project in its critical early stages. Very regretfully, I put *Hélène* aside, and when I later tried to pick up the

[2] The spring of 1903.

threads, it was no longer possible: I was disoriented, out of tune! I had to put an end to my delightful stay in Cairo and go and search for what is generally called inspiration in the middle of the desert, in the Thebaid or Ismaïlia, a haven of light and silence: Ismaïlia, the Prince of Arenberg's favourite spot, is a divine place.

Here can be found blessed solitude, tempered by a highly civilised group of people of both sexes who are employees of the Suez Canal Company. Surrounded by their families, they form a little elite colony, including two talented poets! And as these charming people are extremely busy, they people the solitude without disturbing it.

In 12 days I had written my libretto and soon I embarked at Port Said for the journey back to Paris, where I was expected for rehearsals of a revival of *Henri VIII* at the Opéra.[3] When this revival was over, I found I was tired. My "composing machine" was no longer functioning, and it needed a week's rest in Biarritz and another week in Cannes to restore it. Then I remembered that the spa town of Aix-en-Savoie backed on to a mountain covered with flowers, with wonderful panoramic views on all sides, and easy to reach thanks to a rack railway, so I installed myself on Mont Revard and there I sketched out practically the whole of the music for *Hélène*, which I then finished off in Paris.

That is how one always ought to work: in calm and silence, far away from distractions and interruptions, refreshed by grand views of Nature and surrounded by flowers and scents. Under these conditions, work is more than a pleasure, it is a delight.

The analogy has been remarked upon between the appearance of Pallas in *Hélène* and that of Brünnhilde in the second act of *Die Walküre*. This analogy had not escaped me, but I was unable to avoid it.

Helen calls on her father Zeus for his help. What is he to do? Come in person? That would entail a startling apparition which would upset the balance of the story. Is he to send Mercury the messenger to her? The ancients would perhaps have accepted this because Mercury conducts the souls down to the Underworld. But for us, Hermes is a light-hearted god, both in character and appearance; it is not easy to see him as being menacing and baleful, predicting a catastrophe. On the contrary, as this role naturally falls to Pallas, the living antithesis of Venus (like Helen, a daughter of Zeus), there was no cause to hesitate.

In art, when logic dictates, you have to obey without concerning yourself with anything else. Of course it is annoying to find yourself courting comparison with one of the finest scenes in the whole of opera; but it would be even more so to back away from an analogy that you have not chosen, but which has been imposed on you by force of circumstance.

---

[3] A run of 11 performances starting on 18 May.

Helen and Paris, Samson and Dalilah, Adam and Eve—at heart, they all tell the same story: temptation triumphant, the irresistible allure of the forbidden fruit.

We may protest for form's sake, but at the same time we harbour a store of indulgence and even sympathy for the victims.

The Church itself rejoices at Adam's fall—*O felix culpa!*—which necessitated the Redemption, the basis of Christianity.

Suppose that Helen and Paris, terrified by Pallas's predictions, were to bid each other an everlasting farewell: they would take with them our esteem, but we should no longer be interested in them. Who was ever interested in Menelaus?

This state of things, which dates back to the Garden of Eden, is disturbing; there's a problem here that no one has so far managed to resolve. Maybe the civilised condition of which we are so proud, but which is very recent in the development of the human race, is merely a transitory one, a step towards a superior condition in which what now seems to us obscure will become clear, in which some things that now seem to us essential will be no more than words. Let us hope so. In the words of Carmen, that other incarnation of the same idea, one is always permitted to hope.

7

ON NOT WRITING A PREFACE

(Prefatory Letter to George Docquois,
Le plaisir des jours et des nuits,
Paris, 1907;
Autograph Ms, BNF,
Dept de la musique,
Rés F.1644 [5])

Have you thought carefully, dear friend, about the danger of what you are doing me the honour of asking? A preface for your collected verse plays! Would it be allowed? Would not any such notion make the hair stand up on the heads of all literary persons, or at least of those who still have any? Is it not generally acknowledged that writers, without knowing anything about music, are qualified to judge it, but that musicians on the contrary, however literate they may be, have no rights in the field of literature? Where have you been? How do you come to be so ignorant of the simplest facts? Because I can't believe your soul is so black as to lure me into a wasps' nest—not that that would be a serious inconvenience. Altogether more serious would be the damage that my recommendation—the recommendation of a composer!—would necessarily cause to you.

In any case I couldn't possibly do what you ask, for the reason that I have long been convinced that I understand nothing about the theatre.

The first blow landed when I was still a boy, during a performance of *Don Giovanni* at the Théâtre Italien. I already knew the work and was keyed up at the thought of seeing the terrible final scene. I cannot describe my amazement when, as this scene was about to be played, I saw the hall emptying as though by magic, and I realized that what was for me the culminatory point of the drama, the climax towards which the whole opera had been moving, was for the public of no interest!

From that moment I intuitively felt that, between the public and myself, there would often be misunderstandings. This presentiment was to be all too fully realized. How many times have I found myself, in the theatre, laughing on my own amid total silence? Or being bored to death, while all round me are convulsed with hilarity? I no longer dare to go to hysterically funny plays, ones that run to hundreds of performances, in case I dislocate something; and I frankly enjoy *Les femmes savantes*, and even *Athalie* and *Britannicus*, plays where being bored to death is the respectable thing. These thousands of little theatrical conventions—you know what I mean—which no one dares abolish because the public, apparently, couldn't do without them, they fill me with horror; and the worst of it is that this horror of banality has not turned me towards the contemporary movement, towards theatrical realism or mysticism. Wagner's operas interest me only from the musical point of view, while Ibsenism and its imitators strike me as forms of mental aberration . . .

So there we are! If I am not with the crowd nor with the elitists, that's because I don't understand anything—it's as clear as daylight. So ask someone more competent to introduce your "poetical thoughts" to the public, and leave me to enjoy in silence your fine rhymes and ingenious plots. It would be better for you, for me, and for everybody.

Yours devotedly,

C. Saint-Saëns

8

MUSICAL TRENDS

("Le mouvement musical",
Letter to the Editor of
La revue de l'art,
Paris, 12 November 1897,
Portraits et souvenirs,
Société d'édition artistique,
1899, 221–229)

D ear friend, you are asking me for a study of trends in contemporary music. That's all! Are you aware of what you're
asking? Have you considered your request with due care? I'm sure you
have, but I still wonder in my turn how such a survey would find a place
in your elegant Revue, and where I myself would find the necessary time
to undertake it. Music has undergone such an expansion—artistic and
geographic—and achieved such an importance in the world; it has developed, over the last half-century, in such an astonishing manner, that a
survey of the subject could not written without considerable research,
nor could it be condensed into a few pages: a large volume would not ex-
ceed what is required. It would furthermore be a more suitable task for a
historian who combined competence with total disinterestedness, someone who could rise above factional quarrels and fashionable caprices, and
even conceal his personal views, if necessary. Is it reasonable to ask a composer now reaching the end of a long career to embark on such a task?
Would he not be suspected of unwittingly favouring the past to the detriment of the present and, even given that he did not do so deliberately, would
the result not be to undermine the reader's confidence?

I won't risk giving an answer to these questions, since it strikes me as
likely to be rather unfavourable; and if I set my foot nonetheless on dangerous ground, it is with the intention of not venturing far and of retreat-
ing to my tent at the earliest opportunity.

Let us try, to begin with, to gain an overview.

One important factor dominates the modern musical world: the emancipation of instrumental music, hitherto an underling of vocal music, and now suddenly taking flight, revealing a new world and setting up as a rival to its one-time dominatrix. Ever since the revolution that had Beethoven as its hero, the two powers have continued to battle without respite, each inhabiting its own domain: the opera and oratorio for one, the symphony concert and chamber music for the other. The struggles were fierce. Then as both sides suffered defections here and there, the combatants gradually mingled, with the result that now confusion is everywhere; the occasional tentative punch is still landed, but the public appear to have lost interest in the fight; they rush from the operetta to the symphony, from the Wagnerian drama to old-fashioned opera, from German conductors to Italian singers. This bizarre eclecticism leads to composers being removed from any kind of protection; for them it is total liberty with its advantages and dangers: and the dangers are great.

It is important to point out that the public's taste, whether good or bad, is an invaluable guide for the artist, and when he has genius—or simply talent—he always finds ways of doing good work while conforming to that taste. It is an entirely novel idea to suggest that the artist should consult nothing but his own will, and should obey nothing but his own caprice. The problem is not a serious one for geniuses: they are forgiven for sometimes demanding of their performers or their listeners efforts that go beyond what feeble human nature can support. But for the rest! . . . those who would make good progress with the help of an arm or a stick, and who now realize with terror that they have to fly, as though they had wings! And they do not admit, they never will admit, poor devils, to their baffling situation. They dash forward, proceeding by irregular jumps and pitiful somersaults; and these are valuable energies that are wasted and, all too often, attractive talents that go astray, lost in quagmires from which they will never escape. Imagine Marivaux trying to ape Shakespeare: he would never have written anything worthwhile, and we should not have *Les fausses confidences*.

In a well-regulated musical empire, the theatre and the concert hall would be two entirely distinct musical kingdoms, settled in their ways as they are varied in their customs, one might almost say enjoying different climates. While music is queen in the concert hall where everything is arranged to promote her glory, in the theatre she is merely one of the elements of an ensemble: there she is often an underling, sometimes a slave. In days gone by she used to avenge herself for these humiliations by means of the overture, an intrusion of the concert hall into the world of the theatre: the overture with pretentions, developed at length and separated from the rest of the work like a triumphal arch in front of a city gate. This conception of the overture is tending to disappear now that the symphony, inserting itself into the tissue of theatre music, is monopolizing interest to the detriment of the voices and the dramatic action. This treacherous invasion by concert music has led theatre music to take revenge in its turn by profiting from its symphonic transformation to return to the concert hall and to drive out from it the symphony proper and the oratorio. So, properly speaking, neither concert music nor theatre music exists any more, but instead a hybrid, universal genre, a compromise that leaves nothing in its rightful place. This is not the progress that we had reason to hope for when, fifty years ago, the musical world began to ferment; it is a crisis, a chaos from which very probably, in the future, a new order will arise.

It would however be quite easy to shut theatre music out of the concert hall, now that new forms have appeared and we are no longer condemned to do the unending round of symphony, overture and concerto. Berlioz and Liszt, each in his own way, have opened up new paths, and if composers have been over-hesitant in following them, sticking to lightweight stuff such as *airs de ballet* under greater or lesser disguises (an atavistic phenomenon demonstrating that the origins of instrumental music lay in the dance, as Wagner has rightly pointed out), there have been some outstanding exceptions and, over a period, a whole repertoire of individual and interesting works has come into being that are destined, sooner or later, to achieve the recognition they deserve. The secular or semi-sacred oratorio, already embraced by Handel in works such as *Alexander's Feast, Acis and Galatea* and *Allegro e pensieroso,* again saw the light, in a most unexpected fashion, under the slightly strange title of *ode-symphony* with Félicien David,[1] and later with even greater éclat in Berlioz's *Faust* and *Roméo;* and these works have been followed by many others of the same sort, which needed only a little encouragement for them to survive. This encouragement has not been bestowed; it is operatic fragments that have attracted the public's favour. In all this we must make an exception of England, which through its permanent institutions of regular festivals observes the cult of the oratorio, both ancient and modern, and in this way preserves a fortress unbreachable by anarchy; but outside this fortress, anarchy reigns there as elsewhere.

We shall, with regret, pass over the question of chamber music. This exquisite form of music, created to be heard in intimate surroundings, is denatured and prostituted by being exhibited in public and by aiming for the

---

[1] *Le désert,* first performed on 8 December 1844, gave him the unjustified reputation of having introduced exoticism into music.

sort of noisy acclaim for which it was decidedly not intended. Meanwhile amateurs, finding it more convenient to "tickle the ivories" rather than learn an instrument seriously, have abandoned the violin and cello for the everlasting piano: both of these tendencies have led to the decay of that source of delicate delights, which must now give way to the preference for violent emotions and nervous shocks—a preference wrongly interpreted as progress. Happily, there is some hope that a renaissance is under way and that, with the public discovering a taste for string instruments, there will be a return to the string quartet, which is the basis of instrumental music.

The West enjoys poking fun at Oriental immobility. The Orient could quite reasonably return the compliment and mock the West's instability, its current incapacity to retain a form or a style for any length of time, and its mania for hunting out the new at any price, without rhyme or reason.

At the end of the last century opera had discovered a charming format, seen in the works of Mozart, which was highly flexible and which it would have been sensible to hold on to for as long as possible. It consisted of: *recitativo secco*, more spoken than sung, used for "clearing up" bits of the plot, accompanied by a harpsichord or piano supported by a cello or double bass, or simply by these two string instruments, with the cello supplying the harmony by means of arpeggiated chords; *recitativo obbligato*, accompanied by the orchestra and surrounded by ritornellos; arias, duets, trios etc.; and large ensembles and finales in which the composer allowed himself free rein. Mozart showed how it was possible, even in arias, duets and other numbers, to shape the music exactly to the situation and to escape the monotony of a regular framework. Nowadays, as we know, fashion dictates that entire acts are cast in bronze, in a single gesture, without arias or recitatives or "numbers" of any kind; the musical world is full of young composers straining to wield this club of Hercules. It would perhaps have been wiser to leave it to the man who wielded it first, with a vigour known to him alone; but as they want to appear as strong—what am I saying?—even stronger than Hercules himself, they disguise their impotence beneath an extravagance that bears the labels of modernity and conviction. I needn't go on. As I said at the start, I'd be afraid of not being a good judge in this affair. But I should just like to point out that the public does not seem to take much interest in these exercises and that, even if it admires Hercules without always understanding him, out of trust because it instinctively feels itself in the presence of an unquestionable force, it seems to react much more coldly to his imitators and successors.

I shall bring to an end here, if you will allow me, these reflections on the music of our time. That is not to imply that there is not a great deal still to be said; but for that I should have to embark on technical matters, and I should be very concerned about boring your readers. And then, to be perfectly honest, I'm not greatly drawn to these kinds of dissertations: as I see it, in the field of art, theories are of no great value, works are everything.

9

IN DEFENCE OF OPÉRA-COMIQUE

("La défense de l'opéra-comique",
Portraits et Souvenirs,
Société d'édition artistique,
1899, 169–176)

A striking book could be written on *intolerance in art*. This disease, which is not an invention of our times, is currently attacking the charming genre of opéra-comique: as the need for action to deal with this is becoming urgent, I take the task upon myself, at the risk of further talk about my versatility, comparable to that which consists of getting up in the morning and going to bed in the evening, or of clothing oneself lightly in summer and warmly in winter—activities none of which are generally considered causes for scandal.

In the first blush of my youth, I used to be very fond of that old opéra-comique, despite my cult of Bach fugues and Beethoven symphonies. To pay visits in turn to the Temple where I used to make my devotions and to the friendly House with its naïve and slightly bourgeois enjoyments, seemed quite natural to me as it did to many others. These days nobody leaves the Temple: they live there, sleep there: but as the devil does not give up his rights, they escape secretly to go and laugh at the operetta or the café-concert. Perhaps it was better to have the opéra-comique openly accepted and supported; there at least composers could not be performed without knowing their trade, or singers without having a voice or any talent. In those days it was generally loved; we were proud of this national genre and it had not yet occurred to us to be embarrassed by it. Like ships with all flags flying, the masterpieces of this art sped on their way, their sails billowing in the wind of success.

What evenings, what triumphs! Although I came too late to hear Mme Damoreau, who was, apparently, astonishing, I had the good fortune to follow the marvellous budding careers of Miolan, Ugalde, Caroline Duprez and Faure-Lefebvre;[1] one evening I even heard *Le toréador* and *L'ambassadrice* sung by Mmes Ugalde and Miolan-Carvalho![2] The men were no less brilliant with Roger, Faure, Jourdan, Bataille and so many others . . .[3] Even those who were not great singers were invaluable for the care they took in preserving traditions, in completing an ensemble of the highest class.

All would have continued for the best if the House and the Temple had lived on good terms; but the House was sacrilegious, it disparaged the Temple and denied its gods. Mozart's operas were not "good theatre", Beethoven was not "tuneful", people who "pretended to understand" Bach fugues were *poseurs;* what's more, the House wanted to be a Temple itself, and it became necessary to prostrate yourself, to worship and to describe as "admirable" and "venerable" works that had been born with a smile, aiming only to please and charm. It was too much. Inevitably a reaction set in, poking gentle fun, even if only momentarily, at this vaudeville that had pretensions to outdo straight drama, this guitar that was putting the immortal lyre in the shade. Let's not forget that Meyerbeer, in those days, was thought to be overly intellectual!

Fashions change with time. What was too intellectual is no longer even regarded as music; as for opéra-comique, an entire army has declared war on it and will not be placated. Is this war just? That is what we are going to examine.

Opéra-comique, according to its enemies, is a false, despicable genre because the mixture of singing and dialogue is something abominable and ridiculous, and incompatible with art. Those who subscribe to this view

---

[1] Marie Miolan (1827–1895) in 1853 married Léon Carvalho who in 1856 became director of the Théâtre-Lyrique, where he staged Bizet's *Les pêcheurs de perles*, the second half of *Les Troyens* and Gounod's most famous operas, *Faust, Mireille*, and *Roméo et Juliette*, in all three of which she sang the leading roles. Delphine Ugalde (1819–1910) was a *chanteuse à roulades* who was originally intended to have the role of Marguerite in *Faust*. Caroline Duprez-Vandenheuvel (1832–1875) is recorded by Berlioz as singing a duet from *Béatrice et Bénédict* in April 1863. Constance Faure-Lefebvre (1828–1905) sang two minor roles in *Les pêcheurs* but was no stranger to more important parts.

[2] Delphine Ugalde sang the single soprano role at the premiere of Adam's *Le toréador* at the Opéra-Comique on 18 May 1849. Auber's *L'ambassadrice* was premiered on 21 December 1836.

[3] Gustave Roger (1815–1879) was a tenor whose operatic but not concert career was interrupted by a shooting accident in which he lost his right arm. Jean-Baptiste Faure (1830–1914) was the outstanding French baritone of his generation, creating the roles of Nélusko in *L'africaine*, de Posa in *Don Carlos* and the title role in Thomas's *Hamlet*. Pierre-Marius Jourdan (1823–79) sang Bénédict in the revival of Berlioz's opera in Baden-Baden in 1863. Eugène Bataille (c1845–??) was a bass who created the role of Lothario in Thomas's *Mignon* at the Opéra-Comique in 1866. In 1871 he made his Opéra debut as St Bris in *Les Huguenots*.

do not stint their praise for two works (both excellent, it has to be said) which they place above all criticism: these two are *Der Freischütz* and *Fidelio*, and they both belong to the disparaged species in question: singing alternates with dialogue, and although it is true that other hands have provided them with continuous music from one end to the other, who can say that Weber and Beethoven would approve the transformation if they could see their works altered in this way? We don't know. In both operas you find couplets and even (horror of horrors!) light, perky *vocalises*, which the pure pretend not to see: such things do violence to their souls.

This system of scenes alternately spoken and sung may appear highly irrational and displeasing to a critical ear, but the fact that it has survived so long, with such success, proves that it has its uses. It gives respite to those listeners, more numerous than you might think, whose nerves do not tolerate several hours of uninterrupted music and whose hearing becomes deadened after a certain time and incapable of appreciating any sound. It allows operas to be made out of amusing, complicated comedies whose plots cannot be developed without using a lot of words, and for these to be comprehensible they must reach the audience's ears without hindrance. Music supervenes when feeling predominates over action, or when the action becomes of particular interest: in this way certain scenes, coloured and set in relief by music, stand out strongly from the rest. All these are serious advantages; they more than compensate for the slight unpleasant shock you feel when the music stops and the dialogue begins, not to mention the contrary sensation, the delightful effect you often get when words give way to song. Without dialogue—or the very simple recitative that takes its place—"numbers" are no longer feasible; you then have to confine yourself to stories free of all complication, otherwise you will be writing works which the spectators, unless they are willing to engage in long preparatory study, will not understand at all; all the interest then devolves on to the music, and no one seems to realize that, by virtue of the law which states that extremes meet each other, you arrive, by a roundabout route, at the result you were trying to avoid: instead of going to the theatre to hear voices, you go to listen to the orchestra; that's the whole difference.

There is a move to rescue Comedy in music in the way that Drama in music has been rescued. Very well. There are of course, here and there, one or two backward spirits who wonder whether it is really by imposing fore-ordained gestures that you rescue anyone or anything; whether liberty might not consist quite simply in doing what you want, without worrying about diktats from on high; but let's put that to one side. Grand opera is Tragedy: action reduced to what is indispensable and characters strongly drawn can, if necessary, suffice. Is it the same with Comedy? Is not its essence quite different? If it renounced its secular habits, would it retain its gaiety, its lightheartedness? These are problems that only experience can resolve. The new model of Comedy in music already has two famous examples in its repertoire: *Die Meistersinger* and *Falstaff*. These huge works, singularly difficult to bring off, are sumptuous exceptions rather than models; lightheartedness is the least of their faults, and it could be that they would not have had the same success if their composers had not waited to produce them until overwhelming celebrity had opened every door.

Let us return, if we may, to opéra-comique. There is no need to set out its history, which has been told and well told; this is considerable, and it is impertinent to treat carelessly and slightingly a genre that has produced so many famous works. Starting as a simple play with little songs in *Le devin du village*,[4] it was already dramatic and extremely musical in *Le déserteur* and *Richard Coeur de Lion;*[5] but it is from Méhul that dates the modern opéra-comique, which seemed to have a fine future before it and which was declared to be a "national genre", a glorious title which people are now trying to turn into a sarcastic, even an opprobrious term! We have too readily forgotten that the truly national genre was the French Grand Opera created by Quinault, whose *Armide* had the honour of being set to music by Lully and then by Gluck;[6] this is Lyric Tragedy whose prime quality was fine declamation, a tradition faithfully upheld until the Italian invasion at the start of this century. By returning to declaimed song, to the lyric drama, France would therefore be doing no more than reclaiming its heritage in a more modern guise. Is that to say that opéra-comique has not also its strong dose of nationality? God forbid, and not everything was an illusion in this "national" art; if this form of comedy with alternating speech and song is not peculiar to France, the character we gave to it does belong to us. It is fashionable to deny this: music, we're told, has no fatherland! I'm sure we shall see, and it will not be me that organizes the demonstration.

If there is one critic in the world who makes a profession of placing Art beyond questions of frontiers and nationalities, it has to be M. Catulle Mendès.[7]

---

[4] An opera by Jean-Jacques Rousseau which premiered in 1752.

[5] Opéras-comiques by Monsigny, premiered in 1769, and by Grétry, premiered in 1784.

[6] Premiered in 1686 and 1777 respectively.

[7] Mendès (1843–1909) was a critic and litterateur who supplied librettos for Chabrier's operas *Gwendoline* and *Briséis*, Massenet's *Ariane* and *Bacchus*, and Debussy's unfinished opera *Rodrigue et Chimène*. He also translated Humperdinck's *Hänsel und Gretel* into French. According to the Goncourt brothers he specialised in "night life, intercourse and journalism". Jules Renard called him a "ruffian de lettres". Jean Cocteau insisted he looked like a turbot.

It is he who will enlighten us; listen to him:

> The gaiety of *Die Meistersinger* shares no common ground with our
> fine French humour! It is German, absolutely German, a hundred times
> more German than the dream in *Lohengrin*, than the symbolism in *The
> Ring*, and especially more than the passion in *Tristan und Isolde*. The
> humour in *Die Meistersinger* is *national*.

That is the cry of truth. German gaiety flourishes in *Die Meistersinger*
in the same way that Italian humour burst out over the whole world
through *opera buffa*; and our fine French humour produced our opéra-
comique. It was madness to try and elevate it above everything else; but
we must take even greater care not to turn up our noses at it and reject
it as worthless: that would be, as the popular jargon has it, to drop at our
feet what we have in our hands. The general public, the real public, are
not so stupid; they continue despite everything to applaud *Carmen*,
Manon, *Mignon*, *Philémon et Baucis*, and *Le pré aux clercs*, and *Le domino
noir*, when anyone sees fit to stage them; they even still applaud *La dame
blanche*, and they are right.[8]

10

THE OLD CONSERVATOIRE

("Le vieux Conservatoire",
Ecole buissonnière,
Pierre Lafitte, 1913, 39–47)

Shall I let it go without a farewell, that Conservatoire in the
rue Bergère which I cherished so dearly, as you cherish everything that takes you back to early childhood?[1] I cherished its decrepitude,
its total absence of modernism, and its air of *olden times*; I cherished that
crazy courtyard where the despairing cries of sopranos and tenors, the

---

[8] Hérold's *Le pré aux clercs* was premiered in 1832, Auber's *Le domino noir* in 1837 and
Boieldieu's *La dame blanche* in 1825, all at the Opéra-Comique.

[1] In 1911 the Conservatoire moved from 2, rue Bergère in the 9th arrondissement to
14, rue de Madrid in the 8th. In 1990 it moved again to its present location as part of the Cité
de la musique at 221, avenue Jean-Jaurès in the 19th.

rumbling of pianos, the blasts of trumpets and trombones and the arpeggios of clarinets blended together to create that ultra-polyphony towards which today's most up-to-the-minute composers strive without success; and I cherished most of all the memories of my musical education, formed in that ridiculous and venerable palace which had for years been too small to contain the mass of pupils from all corners of the world.

I was fourteen when my piano professor, Stamaty,[2] introduced me to Benoist,[3] the organ professor, an excellent, charming man, known by the nickname Père Benoist. I was made to sit on the organ stool; I was extremely nervous and the sounds I made were so extraordinary that all the pupils broke up in a great gust of laughter. I was accepted as an "auditor".

This meant that I was allowed merely to listen to the others. I took my position seriously, not missing a note, or a word from the professor; and, back home, I worked and pondered, while immersing myself in Bach's *Art of Fugue*. The other pupils were not as conscientious as I was: one day when only a few of them had turned up and Benoist had no more to say, he put me back on the stool. This time nobody felt like laughing: instantly I was received as a pupil and won the second prize at the end of the year. I would have been given the first prize, were it not for my youth and the disadvantage I would have suffered from being made to leave a class where I needed to stay for longer.

That same year Madeleine Brohan won her first prize for Comedy, with a passage from *Le misanthrope;* Mlle Jouassin played opposite her as Arsinoé. Mlle Jouassin was more experienced, but her partner's looks and voice were so marvellous that she took the prize. This led to a noisy disturbance. These days, in a similar situation, the prize would have been shared. Mlle Jouassin won her prize the following year. Everyone knows how, as she was wise enough on leaving the Conservatoire to opt for roles as a duenna, she obtained and held for many years an honoured place at the Comédie-Française.

Benoist was an entirely mediocre organist, but an admirable teacher, and a veritable constellation of players emerged from his class; he didn't say much but, as his taste was discriminating and his judgment sure, every word he spoke had its value and importance. He collaborated in a number of ballets put on at the Opéra; that gave him a lot of work and, hard as it may be to believe, he would bring "his piece" into class and

[2] Camille-Marie Stamaty (1811–1870), of Greek origin, studied the piano with Kalkbrenner and Mendelssohn. Gottschalk was another of his pupils.

[3] François Benoist (1794–1878) won the Prix de Rome in 1815 and was organ professor at the Conservatoire from 1819 until succeeded by César Franck in 1872.

would be sketching out his orchestrations while his pupils were playing the organ—not that this prevented him from listening to them critically and putting his work aside to tell them what they needed to know.

Apart from his ballets, he undertook various small tasks for the Opéra, and on this front he provided me one day with the key to an impenetrable mystery.

Berlioz mentions in his celebrated *Orchestration Treatise* how much he admires a passage in Sacchini's *Oedipe à Colonne* in which two clarinets play descending thirds with profoundly charming effect, before the words: "I knew the charming Eriphyle." Berlioz passionately exclaims: "One can almost see Eryphile chastely lowering her eyes; it's superb! In point of fact (he adds) there is no trace of this effect in Sacchini's score."

I don't know why, but Sacchini didn't use clarinets at all in his score; and it was Benoist who was asked to add them for a revival of the opera, as he told me one day in conversation . . . Berlioz had no knowledge of this; and Benoist, who never read Berlioz's *Treatise*, had no idea of that composer's admiration for the splendid thirds, which, even though not by Sacchini, are nonetheless a delightful invention.

Benoist was less successful when asked to add "salt and pepper" to Bellini's *Romeo and Juliet* in the shape of a bass drum, cymbals and over-powering brass, which at that period it was thought impossible to do without. That noise-friendly epoch also witnessed Costa's[4] similar treatment of Mozart's *Don Giovanni* in London, with the whole evening labouring under trombones that the composer purposely reserved for the end of the opera . . . Benoist ought to have turned down such barbaric employment, which did nothing to rescue the failure of an empty work, put on with much hullabaloo by a director who was refusing to stage *Les Troyens!*

When I was fifteen I went into Halévy's class. I had already been through Harmony, Counterpoint and Fugue under Professor Maleden,[5] using a method which has since been taught at the Ecole Niedermeyer[6] and has formed the techniques of MM Fauré, Messager and Perilhou, and of M Gigout[7] who is now using it in his turn. My classwork consisted in writing

[4] Sir Michael Costa (1808–1884) conducted the Philharmonic Society and the Royal Italian Opera at Covent Garden.

[5] Pierre Maleden (c1806–?) also taught Gottschalk. In 1867 Saint-Saëns dedicated to him his prize-winning cantata *Les noces de Prométhée*.

[6] Louis Niedermeyer (1802–1861) founded his Ecole de musique religieuse et classique in 1853, with the express purpose of training organists and choirmasters. Saint-Saëns taught there from 1861 to 1865.

[7] Albert Périlhou (1846–1936) studied with Saint-Saëns at the Ecole Niedermeyer and was organist at the church of St-Séverin in Paris from 1889 to 1919. Eugène Gigout

exercises in vocal and instrumental music and orchestration exercises. Among these first appeared *Rêverie, La feuille de peuplier* and many other things now rightly forgotten; the level of my compositions at the time was extremely unequal.

Halévy, then approaching the end of his career, kept on writing operas and opéras-comiques which added nothing to his fame and which disappeared from the repertoire for ever after a respectable number of performances. He was utterly absorbed in his work and was very neglectful of his class, turning up only when he could find the time. His pupils came even so and we operated a system of mutual instruction which was far less indulgent than that of the *maître*, whose worst fault was a kindliness taken to extremes. And when he did come to the class, he was unable to defend himself from interruptions; singers both male and female would come to sing to him; one day it was Mme Marie Cabel, still very young and stunning in voice and appearance; at other times it would be ridiculous tenors who wasted his precious time. When Halévy sent word that he would not be coming—which happened often—I would go off to the library, and it was there that I completed my education: the ancient and modern music I got through there is beyond imagining.

But reading music is not enough, you have to hear it. The *Société des concerts* existed, but it was Paradise, guarded by an angel with a flaming sword in the form of the porter of the rue Bergère, called Lescot, whose job it was to prevent the profane from entering the sanctuary. Lescot was very fond of me; he was an intelligent man and he understood this consuming need of mine to hear the orchestra, so he would make his rounds as slowly as he could, enabling him to wait until the last possible moment to eject me. Happily for me, a subscriber, M Marcelin de Fresne, gave me a seat in his box where I was allowed to sit for several years: I would read and study symphonies before listening to them, and I realized that there were, in the performances so famously given by the *Société*, serious errors that nobody would put up with nowadays, but which then passed unnoticed. Being naïve and ingenuous, I would sometimes point them out, and you can easily imagine what thunderbolts I summoned upon my head!

As far as the public was concerned, the great success of the *Société*'s concerts depended on the incomparable charm of their sound, which people attributed to the hall; the members of the *Société* themselves were also of this opinion and would not have allowed another orchestra to appear at the same venue. This situation continued until the day when

---

(1844–1925) was also a pupil of Saint-Saëns at the same institution, where he then taught. He was organist at St-Augustin from 1863 until his death.

Antoine Rubinstein[8] obtained permission from the Ministry of Fine Arts to give a concert there with the Orchestre Colonne. The *Société* spat fire and brimstone and threatened to suspend its concerts; the matter was resolved and it was then discovered, to general amazement, that another orchestra in this same hall produced a quite different sound, and that the sonority so greatly relished was a function of the illustrious *Société* itself, of the quality of the instruments played and of the mellowness of the performances.

This is not to say that the hall is not excellent. It is not large enough to cope with the great expansion in modern music. But what a marvellous place for the numerous concerts given by virtuosos, both singers and instrumentalists, with orchestra, and for concerts of chamber music! When all is said and done, the hall in which France was introduced to the masterpieces of Haydn, Mozart and Beethoven—an introduction with such profound consequences—is a historic site.[9]

Any number of improvements, during these last years, have been introduced into the running of the Conservatoire; but, on the other hand, some old institutions have disappeared that we may reasonably claim to miss.

In Auber's time, the Conservatoire contained a boarding school where young singers, arriving from the provinces at 18, used to find bed and board and a regular lifestyle that was a bulwark against the temptations of the great city—temptations which are so dangerous for voices that are still fragile. From this boarding school have come singers such as Bouhy, Lassalle, Capoul, Gailhard and so many others who have adorned the French stage.[10]

There were also the run-throughs on stage, which were invaluable both for artists and audiences because works were performed there that were not in the repertoire. It was there that they put on Méhul's *Joseph*,[11] which had not been staged for a long time; and those beautiful choruses, sung by the fresh voices of young students, made such an impact and the whole

---

[8] Russian pianist, conductor and composer (1829–1894).

[9] The hall was also the venue for the first performance of the *Symphonie fantastique* on 5 December 1830.

[10] Jacques Bouhy (1848–1929) was a Belgian baritone who made his Opéra debut as Méphisto in *Faust* in 1871. Jean Lassalle (1847–1909) was a French baritone who made his Opéra debut as Guillaume Tell in 1872 and sang with the Metropolitan Opera from 1891 to 1898. Victor Capoul (1839–1924) was a light French tenor who made his debut at the Opéra-Comique as Daniel in Adam's *Le chalet* in 1861; he was one of the earliest singers to record. Pierre (Pedro) Gailhard (1848–1918) also made his Opéra debut as Méphisto in 1871; from 1885 he served several terms as director of the house.

[11] Premiered at the Opéra-Comique on 17 February 1807. In a revival in 1866, Capoul sang Joseph.

work was so enthusiastically received that it reappeared at the Opéra-Comique with a renewed success that is still with us today. It was there that we heard Gluck's *Orphée*, long before this masterpiece's resurrection at the Théâtre-Lyrique; it was there that we could see Méhul's *Irato*, a strange and charming work which the Opéra-Comique staged subsequently;[12] it was there that we could hear the final act of Rossini's *Otello*, in which the storm gave me the idea for the one that rages in the second act of *Samson and Dalilah*.

When the hall was renovated, the stage was removed, making these occasions impossible. On the other hand, they installed the organ, which is needed for performances of music.

Finally, in Auber's time, and even Ambroise Thomas's, the director was the chief;[13] no one had had the idea of attaching to him a committee which, while safeguarding the director's responsibility, has the strange effect of diminishing his authority. The only benefit of this new system has been the end of the incessant war waged by the music critics on the director. But what effect did this war have? It did no damage either to the director or to the Conservatoire, whose prosperity has continued to grow, to the point where a move to larger premises has long been imperative. This has happened and is now a *fait accompli*; one would hope that the opportunity will be taken to increase the number of pupils, now that there are so many applicants each year and so few are accepted.

We are infected, as is generally recognized, by a mania for reform; and there has been no lack of suggestions with regard to the Conservatoire. The regulations of foreign conservatories have been studied and there is a move to introduce them here. It's true, abroad you can find magnificent establishments set up in palaces, whose regulations have been worked out with a care that can only be admired. Do they produce better pupils than our Conservatoire? That is highly doubtful, and what is incontestable is that many young foreigners come for their education to us.

Some reformers are scandalised at seeing a school where declamation is taught being directed by a musician. They forget that a musician can also be well-read; the present director[14] combines these two qualities, and it is not likely that in the future things could be otherwise. The professors of declamation have always been the best that could be found, and M Fauré, although he is a musician, has decided to revert to the original syllabus in the case of the classes for tragedy, which were moving towards

---

[12] Saint-Saëns is probably referring to the revival of 28 May 1852.

[13] Auber was director from 1842 to 1871, when he was succeeded by Thomas.

[14] Fauré was director from 1905 to 1920.

a dangerous modernism by substituting prose drama for classical verse, from the study of which one learns so much.

Not only does this combination of music and declamation contain nothing harmful, it could be very useful, if singers and composers took advantage of it to follow courses in diction: which are, in my view, indispensable to both parties. I mean to say! Melody is despised, all that people want in opera is declamation, and the singers make works incomprehensible by not articulating the words, while composers give no directions or indications about the way these same words should be declaimed! There is a highly regrettable gap here, and a reform that needs instituting.

As you can see, I stand up against the mania for reform and I'm infected in my turn. Well, there you are. One has to belong to one's time and the contagion is not to be avoided.

11

THE ORGAN

("L'orgue", Ecole buissonnière,
Pierre Lafitte, 1913, 169–176)

[The first part of this article deals with the history of the instrument and technicalities of playing it. The final paragraphs translated below, from pages 175–176, have a more personal touch.]

I know perfectly well what there is to be said against improvisation. There are bad improvisers whose playing is of no interest. But then there are also preachers, and even deputies, who speak extremely badly. That is irrelevant. A mediocre improvisation is always tolerable when the organist is convinced of the notion that music, in church, must fit the Office and be of assistance to meditation and prayer; and if the organ, following this spirit, is a harmonious noise rather than music of any precise sort and does not produce anything worth writing down, then it follows the example of those ancient stained glass windows whose figures are hard to make out, but which we find more pleasing than modern glass. It has more value, no matter what anyone says, than a fugue by a great master, given that the criterion of the good in art is that everything should be in its right place.

It's also the case that for the nearly 20 years when I was the organist at the Madeleine I improvised practically the whole time, giving free rein to my imagination; and it was one of the joys of my existence.

But there was a legend: I was the musician of severity, austerity; and the public were led to believe that I played fugues continuously; to the point that a young girl about to be married came and begged me not to play any at her wedding mass.

It is true that another girl asked me to play funeral marches. She wanted to weep at her wedding and, as she couldn't weep to order, counted on the organ to produce tears in her eyes.

But this was a unique instance; normally it was my severity that people were afraid of; that severity was nonetheless well tempered.

One day one of the vicars of the parish began to lecture me on this point. "The congregation of the Madeleine," he said," is made up for the most part of rich people who often go to the Opéra-Comique; there they have picked up musical habits which it would be well to respect."

"My dear Abbé," I replied, "when I hear Opéra-Comique dialogue delivered from the pulpit, I shall play the appropriate music; but not before."

In those days there was gaiety in the salle Favart.[1]

[1] An alternative name for the Opéra-Comique building.

Part II

Musicians

12

MEYERBEER

*(*Ecole buissonnière,
Pierre Lafitte, 1913, 277–300)

I

Les Huguenots, Le Prophète . . . Who would have said it or thought it, that one day it would be necessary to come to the defence of Meyerbeer, whose figure once dominated all the opera houses of Europe, during a brilliant reign that was expected to last for ever!

And now it's a competition to see who can give the dying lion the well-known kick. I could cite a book in which all the composers of the past are praised without stint, and Meyerbeer alone is accused of any number of faults. The others, though, have theirs! I have already said so elsewhere, but it cannot be repeated too often: it is not the absence of faults but the presence of virtues that makes great works and great men. It is not always good to be without faults. Too regular a face and too pure a voice can lack expression; and if perfection is not of this world, that is probably because it is not made to be.

Not being of the "partial" school that claims to see everyone in terms of black and white, I shall not try to hide the faults of the composer of *Les Huguenots*. The most serious of these, and at the same time the most easily excusable, is his carelessness over prosody and his indifference towards the verses given to him—an excusable fault because the French school of his time, forgetting its ancient traditions, provided him with models. Rossini, even though he, like Meyerbeer, was a foreigner, did not take this line; he even produced fine effects from the union of the musical rhythm with that of the text, as we can see from the famous passage in the trio in *Guillaume Tell*:[1]

---

[1] This trio between Arnold, Tell, and Walter is one of the high points of Act II.

Ces jours qu'ils ont osé proscrire,
Je ne les ai pas défendus!
Mon père, tu m'as dû maudire!

If Rossini had given us two or three more operas, instead of retiring to his tent at an age when other people are beginning their careers, his shining example would have restored the old principles on which French opera had been based since Lully. Auber, on the other hand, took with him a whole generation besotted with Italian music, and went as far as to fit Italian rhythms to French words. The famous duet, "Amour sacré de la Patrie",[2] is set as if the text were "Amore sacro della patria". This can only be seen by looking at the score, because no one sings it as it's written.

Meyerbeer could therefore be excused to a certain extent, but he abused our tolerance in a similar area: in order to keep his musical form intact, even in the recitatives which are nothing other than notated declamation, he did not content himself just with accentuating weak syllables and vice versa, but actually added words, pointlessly producing unmetrical verse and transforming bad verse into still worse prose—literary abominations that a tiny modification in the music would have avoided without any damage. The verse given to composers in those days were often pretty wretched; that was the fashion. The wordsmith thought he was doing his collaborator a service by offering him snippets of verse like this:

Triomphe que j'aime
Ta frayeur extrême
Va malgré toi-même
Te livrer à moi!

But when Scribe put aside his doggerel and tried to give his poetry wings by offering Meyerbeer:

J'ai voulu les punir.—Tu les as surpassés.

the composer turned this into:

J'ai voulu les punir.—Et tu les as surpassés![3]

which was hardly encouraging.

Meyerbeer had other curious habits, notably that of giving the voices phrases that by their nature rightly belong to instruments. In the first act

[2] This tenor/baritone duet between Masaniello and Pietro in Act II of *La muette de Portici* was said to be the signal for the start of the Belgian revolution in 1830.

[3] Scribe's original line is an alexandrine. By adding "et", Meyerbeer destroys the metrics.

of *Le prophète*, for example, after the chorus have sung "Veille sur nous", instead of finishing on the last syllable and letting them breathe in preparation for an entry on the following phrase, he makes them repeat the words "sur nous! sur nous!" in unison with notes on the orchestra which are merely a ritornello.

And again, in the great cathedral scene, instead of letting the orchestra play its musical transformation of Fidès's sobs, "Et toi, tu ne me connais pas," through the voices, he gives this line to the voices as well, and with words that don't fit the music.

I don't know whether I should speak of his immoderate fondness for the bassoon—an admirable instrument, no question, but one it is unwise to abuse.

But all those are trifling faults.

Meyerbeer's music, a witty woman once said to me, is like the painting on the scenery: it doesn't do to look at it too closely.

It would be hard to come up with a better summary. Being a man of the theatre, Meyerbeer aimed above all at theatrical effectiveness. Not that he was indifferent to taking care over details; since he was rich and could reimburse theatres for the extra costs he imposed on them, he would increase the number of rehearsals and try out different versions on the orchestra before making a choice. He was not one of those composers who cast their work in bronze and present it to the public saying "Thus it must remain." He fiddled about and recast his music ceaselessly, in a search for the best, which, sometimes, was the enemy of the good. Too often his searching led him to spoil a characterful idea with inferior development. Take the aria "Enfants de l'Ukraine—fils du désert" from *L'étoile du Nord*, where the picturesque jauntiness of the opening leads to a truly dreadful conclusion.

He always lived alone, with no settled home, staying in Spa in the summer and in winter on the Côte d'Azur, and visiting the major cities when business took him there. He remained outside fashionable society and lived only for his work. This he pursued without intermission for years; it was a Penelope's shroud, demonstrating certainly a great desire for perfection, even though it is not always the best way of attaining it. The seekers after success, among whom some people have tried to include this conscientious artist, do not usually behave like that.

Artist! Since the word has been written, let us pause on it for a moment. In contrast to the Glucks and Berliozes, who were more artists than composers, Meyerbeer was more of a composer than an artist, and at times he employed the most refined and learned methods to achieve an artistically mediocre result. But what right have people to criticise him for faults that they pretend not to notice in so many other composers?

He was the reigning master in the operatic empire, when the first blow against him was struck by Robert Schumann.

Being a stranger to the opera house, into which he made only one unsuccessful incursion, and not understanding that there might be more than one way of practising the art of music, Schumann violently attacked Meyerbeer, his bad taste and his Italianate tendencies, forgetting that Mozart, Beethoven and Weber drew heavily on the Italian style when they made their first forays into opera. Later, the Wagnerians wanted to clear the ground and get rid of Meyerbeer who was in the way, and so they took Schumann's sharp criticisms as being authoritative, even though, when these skirmishes first began, the relationship between the Schumann and Wagner schools was on a par with the one that separated those of Ingres and Delacroix in France. But they were united against the common enemy and the French critics went with them, ignoring the opinion of Berlioz who, after a long struggle, was admitted by them into the company of Heaven—the same Berlioz who, in his famous *Orchestration Treatise*, garlanded Meyerbeer with immortal crowns!

To digress for a moment, if there is one idea in the history of music criticism that surprises, it is its curious and openly expressed persistence in putting those two wild beasts, Berlioz and Wagner, into the same golden cage, in dressing them in the same cloth. The only thing they have in common is their great love of art and their contempt for traditional forms; otherwise they differ in every respect. Enharmony, dissonances endlessly resolving on one another, continuous melody—all these regular ingredients of "the music of the future" were abhorrent to Berlioz; he also admitted to not understanding a note of the *Tristan* Prelude, in which he was undoubtedly sincere since he thought the one to *Lohengrin*, which is conceived on quite different lines, was a masterpiece. He could not agree that the voice should be sacrificed and relegated to being simply one strand in the orchestral sound. Wagner, on the other hand, demonstrated to the highest degree a technical elegance and virtuosity that we could never find in Berlioz. The latter opened the doors of a new world for the orchestra; Wagner launched himself headlong into this unknown country and found many a new region to cultivate. But what huge differences there were in the styles of these two geniuses, in their way of treating the orchestra and the voice, in their construction of a musical phrase and in their conception of Opera!

For all the great qualities of *Les Troyens* and *Benvenuto Cellini*, Berlioz's chief glory is in the concert hall, whereas Wagner is pre-eminently a man of the theatre; and in *Les Troyens* Berlioz clearly shows his desire to follow in the steps of Gluck, whereas Wagner freely admitted his closeness to

Weber and particularly to *Euryanthe.* He may also have owed something to Marschner, but that was something he never mentioned.[4]

The more we study the works of these two geniuses, the more we see the enormous distance that separates them; to treat them as twins is one of those exercises in fantasy that critics all too often take for truth. Once, long ago, the critics even found *local colour* in Rossini's *Semiramide* . . .

Hans von Bülow said to me one day:

> —Meyerbeer who, after all, was a man of genius . . .

Not to appreciate Meyerbeer's genius is not only unfair, it is ungrateful.

In every area—operatic conception, treatment of the orchestra, handling of massed choruses, even staging—he introduced new ideas from which our operas today have profited considerably.

Théophile Gautier, who was not a musician but had a very keen understanding of music, had this to say of him:

> —Apart from his outstanding musical abilities, Meyerbeer possesses the deepest possibly instinct for stagecraft. He really gets inside a dramatic situation, he latches on to the meaning behind the words and is alive to the historical and local colour of his subject . . . Few composers have had such a complete understanding of opera.

This understanding and this concern for local and historical colour seemed to have been destroyed by the Italian school for ever. We should be grateful to Rossini for his boldness in instituting their revival in the last act of *Otello* and in *Guillaume Tell,* but it was left to Meyerbeer to restore them in all their glory.

His character is unmistakable. The combination of his German parentage, his Italian education and his French affinities formed a metal of a new brilliance and a new sonority. His style is like no one else's; his great friend and admirer Fétis, the celebrated director of the Brussels Conservatoire, was right to insist on this fact. This style is characterised above all by the importance of the rhythmic element: it is to the variety and picturesqueness of their rhythms that his *airs de ballet* owe their excellence.

Instead of the long, tiresome Overture, he gave us the short, characterful Prelude that became so popular. The Preludes to *Robert le diable* and

---

[4] Although there is no mention of Marschner in Wagner's *Autobiographical Sketch* of 1842, he does appear in some of Wagner's later writings. Despite his reservations about Marschner's music, *Hans Heiling* in particular, this opera undoubtedly influenced *Die Walküre,* as *Der Vampyr* did *Die Feen.* I am grateful to Barry Millington for this information.

Les Huguenots were followed by those to *Lohengrin, Faust, Tristan, Roméo et Juliette, La traviata, Aida* and many other lesser known ones. Verdi, in his last two operas, and Richard Strauss in *Salome* went even further along this route and suppressed the Prelude, which comes as a rather disagreeable surprise: it's a dinner without the soup.

Meyerbeer offered us the sketch, the foretaste of the famous "leitmotif". In *Robert le diable*, it is the ballad theme we hear regularly in the orchestra whenever Bertram crosses the back of the stage, informing us of his infernal character; it is the role played by Luther's chorale in *Les Huguenots*; in the Dream Scene in *Le prophète* it is the orchestra, underneath Jean's recitative, giving whispered hints of the splendours of the Cathedral Scene to come, with a low flute and delicate violin traceries above it—a remarkable effect, never achieved before.

He brought into the theatre those ensembles of wind instruments (I'm not talking of "brass") so common in the great piano concertos of Mozart: for example, Alice's entry in the second act of *Robert*, which is echoed in Elsa's entry in the second act of *Lohengrin*; or the arrival of Berthe and Fidès at the beginning of *Le prophète*, for which the composer indicated mimed action—which nobody ever does, thus rendering this delightful piece meaningless.

He introduced passages of harmony that were daring at a time when aural sensibilities were at their most susceptible (people claim these have since been developed, whereas, on the contrary, they have been blunted to the point where they tolerate the most violent discords). The fine "progression" of the Exorcism, in the fourth act of *Le prophète*, proved hard to accept; and I can still see Gounod, sitting at the piano, singing the doubtful passage and trying to convince a group of recalcitrant listeners of its beauty.

Meyerbeer developed the role of the cor anglais which, until then, had not dared to make more than the occasional, timid appearance, and introduced the bass clarinet into the orchestra; but still, in his music, these two instruments preserve their exceptional character. They are luxury objects, strangers of distinction whom we salute respectfully and who then pass on. With Wagner, they became regular members of the household and afforded him the rich colours that we know.

Was it Meyerbeer, or was it his librettist Scribe who thought up the astonishing spectacle of the Cathedral scene in *Le prophète?* It must have been the composer, because Scribe was not of a revolutionary cast of mind, and it was a real revolution, this large, brilliant procession crossing the stage, far away from the audience, and progressing down the nave of the church until they reached the choir stalls—the whole effect was splendid and impressive in its realism. Theatre directors, spending large sums on costumes, can't conceive of processions taking place anywhere except in front of the footlights, as close as possible to the eyes of the audience, and it must have been hard to counter this.

He too was responsible for the amusing idea of the skaters' ballet. At that time there was an oddball character who had invented roller skates and who, every evening when it was fine, would practise his favourite sport on the wide macadam surfaces of the place de la Concorde. Meyerbeer saw him and this gave him the idea of the famous ballet . . .[5]

The arrival of these skaters was always a charming moment, accompanied by an attractive choral passage and by the rhythm of the violins in step with the dancers. But in those days the evening began at seven o'clock, finishing at midnight, as it does now; these days it starts at eight o'clock. An hour has to be lost and everything speeded up. The chorus in question is sacrificed—cut, as theatre parlance has it. It no longer exists.

Les Huguenots has fared even worse. Meyerbeer must surely have been particularly proud of the last act, with its splendid choruses in the church and the development of Luther's chorale together with the terror at the approaching massacre; this act has been cut, mutilated and left unrecognisable, so that in some large theatres abroad it has been removed altogether.

Once, long ago, I saw it entire, and six harps accompanied the famous Trio. We shall never see these six harps again. Charles Garnier[6] did not reproduce the orchestral pit of the old Opéra exactly; instead he arranged things in the new building so that it is impossible to fit in the six harps of years gone by, or the four timpani that Meyerbeer used to create such surprising effects in *Robert* and *Le prophète*. I gather, however, that recent improvements have mitigated this disaster to some extent and that there is now room for the timpani; but we shall never again hear the six harps, whose sound filled the auditorium with a golden cloud!

To conclude, I should like to discuss the genesis of Meyerbeer's operas, which was sometimes strange, and which few people know about.

II

We would like to think that musical works spring from a composer's brain fully armed, like Minerva from the head of Jupiter; but quite often it doesn't happen like that. When we look at Gluck's long series of Italian operas, we are surprised to find there things we knew from seeing them already in

---

[5] At this point Saint-Saëns grumbles about the introduction of the English term "skating"; for him this activity of French origin remained "patinage".

[6] Charles Garnier (1825–1898) was the architect of the present Opéra, inaugurated in 1875.

the masterpieces for which he is famous, and sometimes in these transformations the same music is adapted to quite different situations: the suggestions of an attendant lady turn into the fearsome predictions of a high priest; the trio "Tendre amour" in *Orphée*, which expresses complete happiness, is shot through with melancholy accents—the music had been written previously for a quite different situation which justified these entirely. Massenet has told us that he borrowed freely from his unpublished score of *La coupe du Roi de Thulé*, as Gluck did from his unsuccessful opera *Elena e Paride*. I must confess that a ballet tune in *Henry VIII* was borrowed from the finale of a one-act opéra-comique. This little piece was finished and ready to go into rehearsal when everything was halted because I had had the audacity to contradict Nestor Roqueplan, then the director of the Salle Favart, by insisting that Mozart's *Les noces de Figaro* was a masterpiece.

Meyerbeer was keener than anyone on not letting ideas go to waste, and a study of their transformations is not without interest.

One day Nuitter, the archivist of the Opéra, heard that an important sale of manuscripts was coming up in Berlin. He went and brought back a lot of Meyerbeer sketches, including ideas for a *Faust* that the composer never completed. The remaining fragments give no idea of what the complete work would have been like. We see Faust and Mephistopheles walking through hell and, on the banks of the Styx, coming to the Tree of Knowledge, whose fruit Faust picks. From this detail we may imagine that the libretto, of unknown authorship, must have been bizarre, and it is not surprising that Meyerbeer abandoned it.

From this stillborn *Faust*, Scribe, at the composer's request, made *Robert le diable*.

An aria sung by Faust on the banks of the Styx became the "Valse infernale".

The fact that Scribe had to make use of pre-existing sketches—the incoherent material of this incomprehensible text—explains how he came to create the enigmatic character of Bertram, half man and half devil, and invented as a substitute for Mephistopheles, who had to be made unrecognisable. The fruit of the Tree of Knowledge became the cypress tree in the third act; the fine religious scene in the fifth act, which is not linked to the plot, is a transposition of the Easter scene.

So we should not be too critical of Scribe for writing a bad libretto, considering the insurmountable problems he had to face; he even lost his way slightly, because Robert's mother, who is called Berthe in Act I, becomes Rosalie in Act III. To which one could respond by saying that when she became a nun she changed her name.

Scribe was presented with other, no less intractable problems over *L'Etoile du Nord*.

When Meyerbeer was conductor of the Opera orchestra in Berlin, he was commissioned to write an occasional work called *Le Camp de Silésie*, in which the hero was Frederick the Great and Jenny Lind the musical star. King Frederick, as we know, was a musician, composing and playing the flute, and Jenny Lind—the Swedish nightingale—a great singer; from which a combat between nightingale and flute was surely to be expected, or else the word "theatre" is meaningless. But in Scribe's libretto Frederick was replaced by Peter the Great; and to set up the vocalise competition in the last act it was necessary for the terrifying, half-savage czar to learn to play the flute.

How, with that in mind, he takes lessons from a young pastry-cook who makes his entrance with a basket of cakes on his head, and how the said cook becomes a great nobleman, there is no need to tell, any more than other details of this absurd story. It is permitted to be absurd in the theatre as long as you can disguise the fact; here, disguise is impossible. The extravagances of the libretto led Meyerbeer along insalubrious paths, and this extremely strange score is the most uneven anywhere; it contains a thousand details that are of interest to a fellow-composer, as well as moments of beauty and, here and there, passages of picturesque charm, but also childish nonsense and shocking vulgarities.

The public's curiosity for *L'Etoile du Nord* had been whetted by a long and clever publicity campaign. The work had the advantage of the exceptional talents of Bataille and Caroline Duprez and at first achieved a huge success. But since then this has become ever fainter. There were still some good performances in London with M Faure and Mme Patti, but it is doubtful whether there will be any such in the future; it is not to be desired, for the sake either of art or of the composer.

Les Huguenots may not belong to this category of works made out of bits of others, but it certainly didn't reach the public in the state the composer envisaged.

At the beginning of the first act there was a game of cup-and-ball which the composer set great store by; but he insisted that the balls must hit the sleeves of the players at precise moments indicated in the score, and the players could never manage this. This passage, which is now in the Opéra library, had to be cut.

Cut too was the role of Catherine de Medici, who was to preside over the meeting at which the Saint Bartholemew massacre is organised; the role was incorporated into that of Saint-Bris.

Cut too was the first tableau of the final act, the ball that is interrupted by Raoul, bloody and dishevelled, putting an end to the festivities with his announcement of the massacre to the terrified dancers.

But should we believe the legend according to which the great duet, the high point of the work, was improvised during rehearsals at the request of Nourrit and Mme Falcon?[7] That is rather hard to accept. The story, as we know, comes from Mérimée's *Chronique du règne de Charles IX*; this scene exists in the book, and it is impossible that Meyerbeer should not have had the idea of putting it into his opera. More probably, the theatre management wanted the act to end on the highly effective Blessing of the Daggers, and Meyerbeer, having this duet already written, only had to bring it out to please his performers. Such a splendid and impressive scene, containing so many innovations of genius, is not the sort of thing you can write in a hurry. You had to have heard this famous duet at a time when the composer's intentions and the nuances that are part and parcel of it were respected, and not replaced by the inventions in bad taste that people had the temerity to call "traditions". The real traditions have been lost, and this admirable scene has lost its beauty.

The way in which this duet ends has not been sufficiently remarked on. Raoul's phrase, "Dieu! Veille sur mes jours! Dieu secourable!" (God! Watch over my future! God, help me!), remains in suspense, and it is the orchestra that has the task of concluding it. This is the first example of a technique frequently used in modern works.

We don't know how the idea came to Meyerbeer of putting the schismatic Jan Huss on stage, under the name of Jean de Leyde—whether it came to him spontaneously, or whether it was suggested by Scribe, who turned Jan into a mythical character. All we do know is that the role of the prophet's mother was originally intended for Mme Stolz;[8] but when she left the Opéra and Meyerbeer heard Mme Pauline Viardot in Vienna, Viardot became the favoured singer and it was for her he wrote the strenuous role of Fidès. The tenor Roger, the star of the Opéra-Comique, was given the role of Jean, which he acted and sang in superior fashion; Zacharie was played by Levasseur,[9] the Marcel of *Les Huguenots* and the Bertram of *Robert*.

In spite of the violent opposition of the supporters of the then all-powerful Italian school, *Le Prophète* was enormously successful. Nowadays it is the work's faults that people notice; Meyerbeer is blamed for not obeying theories he had never heard of, and he is not given credit for his

[7] The tenor Adolphe Nourrit (1802–1839), as well as producing the opera, sang the role of Raoul, and Cornélie Falcon (1812–1897) that of Valentine. Dramatic soprano roles such as Valentine and Rachel in *La Juive*, which she also created, are still called by her name.

[8] Rosine Stolz (1815–1902), recommended by Nourrit, also deputised for Falcon in the role of Rachel in *La Juive* in 1837.

[9] Nicolas-Prosper Levasseur (1791–1871) had already sung in Meyerbeer's *Marguerite d'Anjou* in Milan in 1820 at the composer's request.

innovations, which were considerable for their time. What other composer could have painted the astonishing Cathedral Scene on such a large canvas and to such an effect? We should note the ingenuity of the paraphrase of the "Domine, salvum fac regem", the unexpected way of treating the organ, and the charming idea of the ritornello "Sur le jeu de hautbois" that leads into the children's chorus, with its lively theme, so brilliantly developed later by the choruses, orchestra and organ combined. Then there is such colour and character in the organ reprise of the "Domine, salvum" at the end of the scene, suddenly emerging from within a quite different key!

III

The history of *Le Pardon de Ploërmel* is rather strange. This work was originally called *Dinorah*, and that is how it's known abroad—Meyerbeer had a habit of changing the titles of his operas several times in rehearsal, so as to keep the public's curiosity alive.

Having had the wild idea of writing a one-act opéra-comique, he asked the well-known combination of Jules Barbier and Michel Carré for a libretto, and they came up with *Dinorah*, in three scenes and with only three characters. The music was promptly completed and delivered to Perrin, the famous director, whose pernicious influence was not slow in manifesting itself—because, in those days, the first idea of a director when you took a work to him was to demand changes.

—A single act from you, Maître, is that acceptable? What could be put with it? A new Meyerbeer opera ought to take up the whole evening.

Thus spoke the insidious director, and his words had all too great a chance of bearing fruit because the composer had an extreme form of mania for tinkering and altering. He took his score off to the Midi, where he was spending the winter, and brought it back the following spring extended to three acts, with supernumerary choruses and characters. He had written the words for all these additions himself, and Barbier and Carré had to redo them in their turn.

Rehearsals were fraught. Meyerbeer wanted M Faure and Mme Carvalho to take part; but he was at the Opéra-Comique and she was on her home ground at the Théâtre-Lyrique; so the work went back and forth several times between the place Favart and the place du Châtelet. These hesitations of Meyerbeer's were nothing but a pretext: what he in fact wanted was to postpone Limnander's[10] opera *Les Blancs et les Bleus*, which, like *Dinorah*, was set in Brittany. The two theatres each wanted Meyerbeer to settle on them, so they took turns in keeping Limnander at bay. Finally *Dinorah* appeared at the Opéra-Comique[11] where, after a long series of rehearsals demanded by the composer, Mme Marie Cabel[12] and MM Faure and Sainte-Foix[13] gave a perfect performance.

Considerable criticism has been levelled at the hunter, the reaper and the shepherds who gossip at the beginning of the third act and sing a prayer together, on the grounds that "it's not theatrical"; today "not being theatrical" is considered to be a virtue.

Meanwhile there was much talk of *L'Africaine*, which through a long period of expectation had entered the ranks of legend and mystery; where it has indeed remained. The opera's subject was unknown. All we knew was that the composer was looking for a singer and couldn't find one he liked.

Some time before, Marie Cruvelli, an Italianised German singer, had appeared at the salle Ventadour and through her beauty and sensational voice had flashed like a brilliant meteor across the operatic sky; here was Meyerbeer's Africaine. At his request she was engaged at the Opéra, where she was responsible for a striking revival of *Les Huguenots*, for which Meyerbeer wrote some new *airs de ballet* (what *Les Huguenots* was like in those days, modern audiences can have no idea). The composer of the abandoned *L'Africaine* returned to work on it and went almost every day to see this wonderful singer, when she, out of the blue, announces to him that she is quitting the theatre to become the comtesse Vigier![14]

Meyerbeer lost his enthusiasm and put his unfinished manuscript back in a drawer, where it remained until the day when, given the progress in Mme Marie Sass's[15] voice and talent, he decided to offer her the role of

[10] Baron Armand-Marie Limmander de Nieuwendhove (1814–1892) was a minor Belgian composer.

[11] On 4 April 1859.

[12] Marie-Josèphe Cabel (1827–1885) was a Belgian soprano who had also had a success in 1855 in the title role of Halévy's *Jaguarita l'Indienne*.

[13] Charles-Louis Sainte-Foy (1817–1877) was one of the Opéra-Comique's most popular tenors. It was said that "the Opéra-Comique without Sainte-Foy is a dinner without wine."

[14] Johanne Crüwell (1826–1907) was born in Germany but Italianised her name to suit her repertoire. The revival of *Les Huguenots* Saint-Saëns mentions took place on 16 January 1854. Whereas box office returns at the Opéra at that time were normally between 4,000 and 6,000 francs, this revival reached a peak of over 9,000 francs. Her final role before retirement was as Hélène in the premiere of *Les vêpres siciliennes* on 13 June 1855.

[15] Marie-Constance Sass (1838–1907) was a Belgian soprano who studied with Delphine Ugalde. She created the role of Elisabeth de Valois in *Don Carlos* in 1867.

Sélika. He got the Opéra to engage Naudin, the Italian tenor;[16] M Faure, who was due to sing Nélusko, was already on the Opéra's books.

But during the long period since the marriage of the comtesse Vigier, Scribe had died. Left to his own devices and, as we know, being all too keen on reworkings of every sort, Meyerbeer had refashioned the opera to suit himself; it had become shapeless and the composer intended to rectify this in the course of rehearsal.

As we know, he died rather suddenly, in three days, at the *rond-point* of the Champs-Elysées, in the house that is now named after him. Realizing that he was dying, and knowing how necessary his presence was for the performance of *L'Africaine*, he refused to let it go ahead; but this refusal was only verbal, he wasn't able to write it down. The public was impatient to see *L'Africaine*; and so his wishes were disregarded.[17]

When Perrin,[18] helped by his nephew du Locle, opened the packet of manuscripts left by Meyerbeer, he was astounded to find that *L'Africaine* did not exist.

—Never mind, he said; the public wants an *Africaine*, an *Africaine* it shall have.

He appealed to Fétis, Meyerbeer's great admirer, and it was he who, with Perrin and du Locle, from the tangle of sketches left by the composer managed to extract the opera we know. This involved difficulties, some incoherence, numerous things suppressed and some even added. Perrin was the inventor of that surprising map on which Sélika recognises Madagascar, where the characters were transported to justify the heroine's appellation and where, in addition, the cult of Brahminism was introduced to avoid having to take everyone to India, where Act IV should have been set.

The first performance was imminent when they realized that the work was much longer than was allowed. They took out a highly original ballet, in which we were to see a savage beating on a resonant plate; everything was chopped and shaved. In the final act, Sélika, alone and dying, was to have seen the paradise of Indra materialise in the sky; but as M Faure wanted to reappear at the end of the opera, a passage from the third act had to be fitted into the sequence of events and the Vision was suppressed. That is why Nélusko succumbs so quickly to the deadly scent

[16] Emilio Naudin (1823–1890) had been a great success in his native country; but his French suffered from a heavy Italian accent; see note 17.

[17] But his wishes were adhered to over Naudin as Vasco de Gama since, despite Naudin's Italianate French, Meyerbeer had stipulated his assumption of the role in his will.

[18] Emile Perrin (1814–1885) had managed the Opéra-Comique from 1848 to 1857, before taking over the Opéra in 1862.

of the poisoned flowers, whereas Sélika has held out so long. The ritornello to Sélika's aria, which should have been played with the curtain up
while the queen gazes at the sea and the ship that is sailing towards the
horizon, became a show-stopper, a cue for an encore, the "dernière pen-
sée de Meyerbeer".

The worst thing of all was the liberty taken by Fétis in retouching
the orchestration and, as a favour to Adolphe Sax, in substituting a saxophone for the bass clarinet Meyerbeer asked for, which meant that this
part had to be cut at the beginning of the aria "O Paradis sorti de l'onde",
because the saxophone did not sound right there. He allowed Perrin to
turn a bass solo into a unison chorus, "the bishops' chorus", where
the twisting vocal line and wide range are unsuitable for choral rendi-
tion. And there are some barbarous modulations that must certainly be
apocryphal . . .

What *L'Africaine* would have been if Scribe had lived and completed it
with Meyerbeer, we can never know. The work as it appears now is illogi-
cal and unfinished; some of the words are plain "monstrosities" of a kind
Scribe would not have countenanced, such as these lines from the great
duet:

> O ma Sélika, vous régnez sur mon âme!
> —Ah! ne dis pas ces mots brûlants!
> Ils m'égarent moi-même . . .
>
> (O Sélika mine, you reign over my soul!
> —Ah! do not speak these burning words!
> They bewilder me myself . . .)

This disjointed score on an impossible libretto nonetheless had its
admirers, fanatics even, such was Meyerbeer's prestige at the time it appeared. We should not forget indeed that there are some fine passages in
this chaos. One of them is the religious ceremony in Act IV, with the Brah-
man's recitative accompanied by pizzicato basses. But this number is not
popular in theatres today: it is either cut, or else played without conviction, which deprives it of its impact and majesty.

The question was raised at the beginning of this essay of ingratitude towards Meyerbeer. For France this ingratitude is doubled, because he loved
it. This man, who had only to say a word for every theatre in Europe to
open its doors to him, ranked them all behind the Paris Opéra and even
the Opéra-Comique, whose chorus and orchestra left something to be desired. When he wrote for Paris, after the productions of *Margherita d'Anjou*

and *Le Crociato* in Italy, he had to adapt to French taste,[19] following Rossini and Donizetti—who wrote *La Fille du Régiment* for the Opéra-Comique, a military, patriotic opera, from which the resounding "Salut à la France!" travelled round the entire world. These days foreigners don't take the same trouble, and in France we applaud *Die Meistersinger* which ends with a hymn to "sacred German art". That's progress.

Finally, a word about a less well-known score, *Struensée*, written for a play whose feebleness prevented the music from having the success it deserved; because here the composer showed himself to be more "artistic" than anywhere else in his output. It came very near to being performed at the Odéon, with another work written by Jules Barbier on the same subject. The overture used to be played once in the concert hall, like the one to *Guillaume Tell*. These overtures, though, are not to be looked down on: Rossini's with its amazing new idea of five cellos, its storm, with such an original beginning, and its delightful pastorale; Meyerbeer's with the beautiful sonorities of its exposition and its central fugal development. They say it all lacks elevation and profundity; it's possible, but composers do not always have to descend to hell and reach for the heavens, and there is certainly more music in these overtures than in Grieg's *Peer Gynt*, which has been so remorselessly dinned into our ears.

Let us conclude there, with Meyerbeer's theatre works; the rest of his music demands a separate study and would take us beyond the bounds of this essay. I hope these lines may right unnecessary injustices and bring to the attention of more refined spirits, if they are kind enough to read them, a great composer whom the general public has never ceased to listen to and applaud.

[19] *Margherita d'Anjou* was premiered in Milan in 1820, *Il crociato in Egitto* in Venice in 1824. His first opera for Paris was *Robert le diable*, premiered at the Opéra on 21 November 1831.

13

ROSSINI

(Ecole buissonnière,
Pierre Lafitte, 1913, 261–267)

It is hard for us today to grasp Rossini's position in the Paris of 50 years ago. He had long retired from active musical life, but he enjoyed more renown in his splendid retirement than others in the midst of their careers. The whole of Paris was eager for the honour of being admitted to his magnificent apartment with its high windows, which you can still see on the corner of the chaussée d'Antin. Since the divine personage never went out in the evening, his friends were always sure of finding him there; and from time to time the most varied groups of people mingled at sumptuous parties, at which the most brilliant singers and the most famous virtuosos could be heard.

The Master was surrounded by base flattery, but he remained untouched by it, knowing what it was worth, and he dominated his usual entourage from the heights of a superior intelligence that he did not deign to reveal to just anybody.

How did he come by such fame?

His operas, apart from *Le Barbier, Guillaume Tell* and a few performances of *Moïse,* belonged to the past. People still went to see *Otello* at the Théâtre-Italien, but it was to hear Tamberlick's top C sharp! . . . Rossini was so much of a realist as to try and prevent *Semiramide* entering the repertoire of the Opéra.[1]

And still the Parisian public made him into a cult figure!

This public—by which I mean the musical public, or those who called themselves that—was then split into two rival camps: the lovers of *melody,* who made up the greater part and included all the music critics, and the subscribers to the Conservatoire concerts and to the Maurin, Alard and Armingaud quartets, who were devotees of so-called learned

---

[1] In vain: it was premiered there on 9 July 1860, with limited success, and withdrawn after its 34th performance on 27 March 1861.

music, though categorised by the others as "poseurs" who pretended to admire music about which they understood less than nothing.

There was no *melody* in Beethoven; some of them even claimed there was none in Mozart. It could only be found in the Italian school, of which Rossini was the head, and in the school of Hérold and Auber that derived from it. For all the *melodists*, Rossini was a citadel, a symbol round which they gathered in serried ranks, while at the same time ignoring his music, which they allowed to fall into oblivion.

From several things Rossini said to me in confidence I realised that this oblivion pained him. It was a justified but over-justified reaction to the earlier workings of fate which had ordained that Rossini, I'm sure through no will of his own, was used as an engine of war against Beethoven, first in Vienna, where the success of *Tancredi* [in 1816] buried the ambitions of the composer of *Fidelio* for ever, and then in Paris, where people attempted to resist the growing encroachment of orchestral and chamber music in the name of *Guillaume Tell!*

I was about 20 when M and Mme Viardot introduced me to Rossini. He invited me to his small evening parties and greeted me with his usual bland amiability.

After a month, when he saw that I wasn't asking for performances either as a pianist or as a composer, his attitude towards me changed.

—Come and see me in the morning, he said, and we can talk.

I was quick to accept this flattering invitation, and I found a quite different Rossini from the one that appeared in the evening, in the highest degree interesting, open-minded, and full of ideas which, if not advanced, were at least far-ranging and lofty. He gave proof of this by defending the notorious Mass by Liszt, which had met with almost unanimous hostility when it was premiered in the church of Saint-Eustache . . .[2]

—You've written a *Duo* for flute and clarinet, he said to me one day, for MM Dorus and Leroy.[3] Would you ask these gentlemen if they would agree to come and play it here one evening?

Those two great artists did not need to be asked twice.

And then an extraordinary thing happened.

As there was never a written programme for these evenings, Rossini made it known that the *Duo* was by him.

You can imagine the scale of the success under such conditions!

[2] Almost certainly the *Gran Mass*, written in 1855, the year Saint-Saëns turned 20.

[3] The flautist Louis Dorus (1813–1896) won a first prize at the Conservatoire in 1828. He was first flute at the Opéra from 1835 to 1866. Adolphe Leroy (1827–1880) was first clarinet for the Société des Concerts for some 10 years from 1849. In 1857 Berlioz asked him to try out the famous solo accompanying Andromache's "pantomime" in Act I of *Les Troyens* and found him "a virtuoso of the first order, but cold". He succeeded his teacher Klosé as professor of clarinet at the Conservatoire in 1868.

When the piece had been encored, Rossini led me into the dining room and made me sit down next to him, taking me by the hand so that I couldn't make my escape.

Then came a procession of admirers and courtiers. Ah! Maître! What a masterpiece! What wonderful music! . . .

And when the victim had run through the gamut of congratulations, Rossini replied calmly:

—I entirely agree. But this *Duo* is not by me, it's by this gentleman here . . .

Such a combination of kindness and finesse says more about this great man than many an essay.

Because Rossini was a great man. The young people of today are not in a position to judge his works, which were written, as he used to say himself, for singers and a public who no longer exist.

—I have been criticised, he said to me one day, for the large crescendos in my overtures. But if I hadn't put the crescendos in, my music would never have been played at the Opéra.

Nowadays the public is a slave. I have even read on the programme of one institution: "all indications of disapproval will be severely quashed."

Once upon a time, and especially in Italy, the public was the master and its taste was law. They arrived before the candles were lit and they demanded the mighty overture with the mighty crescendo; they demanded cavatinas, duets and ensembles; they came to hear the singers and not to watch a lyric drama. In several of Rossini's works, and especially in *Otello*, he did much to promote realism on the stage. With *Moïse* and *Le siège de Corinthe* (not to mention *Guillaume Tell*), he spread wings whose span has not been surpassed, despite the poverty of the means at his disposal. The truth is—as Victor Hugo has triumphantly demonstrated—that poverty of means is no more an obstacle to genius than richness is an advantage to the mediocre.

Together with Stanzieri, a charming young man whom Rossini was very fond of and who died early, and with M. Diémer,[4] who was still young but already a great virtuoso, I was the house pianist. Between us, on prestigious evening occasions we often played the little piano pieces that the Master liked to sketch to occupy his spare time. I was happy to accompany the singers when Rossini did not accompany them himself; which he did admirably, because he played the piano to perfection.

Unfortunately I was not there the evening when Patti sang at Rossini's for the first time. As we know, after the performance of the aria from the *Barber* he said to her, at the end of a host of compliments:

---

[4] Louis Diémer (1843–1919) won a first prize at the Conservatoire at the age of 13 and went on to teach there. Alfred Cortot and Robert Casadesus were among his pupils.

—Who is that aria by you've just sung?

I saw him three days later: he still hadn't calmed down.

—I'm well aware, he said, that my arias need decorating; they're written with that in mind. But not to leave a single note of what I've written, even in the recitatives, really, that's too much!

And in his irritation he complained that sopranos insisted on singing this aria he'd written for contralto, whereas he had written so many arias for soprano that nobody ever sang.

The Diva, for her part, was extremely offended. But she reflected: to have Rossini for an enemy was a serious matter . . . A few days later, she came repentantly to ask his advice. It was as well for her that she did; because until then her talent, for all its sparkle and fascination, had not reached its apogee.

Two months after this contretemps, Patti, accompanied by Rossini, was singing arias from *La gazza ladra* and *Semiramide* and combining with her technical brilliance the absolute fidelity to the music that she has always observed since.

Much ink has been spilt over the premature end to Rossini's glorious career after *Guillaume Tell;* it has been compared with Racine's after *Phèdre.* But there is a considerable difference between the two situations. The failure of *Phèdre* was brutal and cruel, and underlined by the scandalous success of a mock *Phèdre* running concurrently at another, low theatre. Racine's friends, his friends at Port-Royal, were quick to make capital out of such a fine opportunity, saying he was driving himself into the ground and wasn't even successful! . . . But later, when he took his pen up again, he gave us two masterpieces: *Esther* and *Athalie* . . .

For Rossini, used as he was to triumphing, it was hard, when he knew that he had surpassed himself, to be brought up short by a semi-success, for which the extravagant phraseology of one of his librettists, M. Hippolyte Bis, was probably responsible. But from the outset *Guillaume Tell* had some very warm admirers. In my childhood I heard it mentioned constantly and, if it was not in the Opéra repertoire, musical amateurs on the other hand had, so to speak, their mouths full of it.[5]

My opinion is that Rossini fell silent because he no longer had anything to say. As a spoilt child of success, he could not do without it, and this unexpected hostility poisoned the stream that had flowed, for so long, in unquenchable abundance.

The success of the *Soirées musicales* and of the *Stabat mater* only encouraged him; and he wrote nothing more apart from those little pieces

---

[5] Saint-Saëns' contention that the work "was not in the Opéra repertoire" is hard to credit, since the records show it was given there over 200 times between 1834 and 1856.

for the piano and the voice, which are like the final vibrations of a sound that is fading . . .

Later, much later, came the Mass, which by common acclaim was given an exaggerated importance.[6] "The 'Passus'," wrote one critic, "is the cry of the wounded soul!"

This Mass is written elegantly, and of course with an expert hand, but that is all: we do not find here the pen that wrote the second act of *Guillaume Tell*.

Talking of this second act, I don't know whether people realise that finishing it with a prayer was not the composer's original intention. It's not usual to head off for an insurrection with such solemn chanting. But at rehearsals the unison phrase "Si parmi nous il est des traîtres" made such an impact that nobody had the will to go on. The original finale, which consisted simply of the brilliant, catchy overture, was suppressed.

This finale still exists in the Opéra library; it would be really interesting to restore it and to give this wonderful act its natural conclusion.

14

BERLIOZ I

("Publication de ses lettres intimes",
Harmonie et mélodie,
Calmann-Lévy, 1899, 249–255)

One thought that the matter was closed, and that we had finished once and for all with unkind remarks and unjust accusations against Berlioz. But no, it was not closed, and now, with the publication of his *Lettres intimes,* people have begun to talk once again of his venomous nature and bad character.

The thing is, Berlioz wasn't a cunning person: he was sincere, and said what was in his heart and his head without thinking about the consequences. Why didn't he behave like F[élicien] D[avid]? He never indulged in the written word and used to say nice things about everyone. But up his sleeve (or rather, in his pocket) he had his friend Azevedo who used to

---

[6] *Petite messe solennelle* (1863).

write things like this: "On the façade of the temple of Art are written in letters of gold the name of F.D; and, on the steps, someone has dumped a load of excrement called Gounod." That is how to make friends.

Wagner reviled Victor Hugo and taxed Gounod's music with being "tarts' music". He has been pardoned. Soon he will be thanked. But the young Berlioz, with his head on fire and full of Shakespeare, arrives in Italy; he sees a *Roméo* by a young composer still unknown in Paris, which understandably seems to him a ridiculous travesty of the masterpiece he admires and, in a *private letter,* he calls the composer a "little idiot". What a crime! And how right people have been to make life hard for such a disagreeable person and to hound him to the end of his days! How right they have been to wait for him to die before admiring his music, to wait until they could be rid of him before treating him to applause! To have used the term "little idiot" of a composer *who would one day write La sonnambula* and *Norma*—that is truly unpardonable, and that great newspaper the *Revue des deux-mondes* was correct in calling him one fine day "an old parrot perched on a stick". It was no more than he deserved.

Between ourselves, I think Berlioz was too fond of Shakespeare, Byron and Goethe; and he unwittingly admitted the fact. "Hamlet," he says in *Lélio*, "thou profound and melancholy conception, what damage hast thou done to me!" Elsewhere, in one of his letters, he calls Goethe and Shakespeare the "expositors of his life". When you think about it, that's a terrible word. Like the mystics who reached the point of experiencing the pains of the Passion in their own bodies, Berlioz experienced the torments of Faust, Hamlet and Manfred. He incarnated in himself these poetic creations, whose imaginary sufferings were metamorphosed in him into real ones. Was it Camille and Henriette he loved, or rather Ophelia and Ariel? At some moments it is no longer he who lives, but Shakespeare who lives in him. We are observers of a curious phenomenon of poetic mysticism, leading, like the religious kind, to serious disorders of the nervous system and to a cruel and interminable torture that slowly eats into one's existence and ceases only in death.

And it is because he saw himself as Faust and Hamlet that, in his memoirs, he painted himself in totally false colours, claiming to hate mankind—he who was moved to tears by the slightest expression of sympathy. His only hatred was for the "profanum vulgus", as with Horace,[1] and all artists and poets.

At heart he was not only sincere, he was naïve; as naïve as the great Joseph Haydn, whose naïvety he was so quick to poke fun at. Why would anyone deceive him—he who never deceived anyone? And he was taken in by compliments and applause, by a friendly reception here, by promises

---

[1] "Odi profanum vulgus et arceo" (I hate the vulgar crowd and shun it) *Odes* III, 1.

there. In his letters you can follow the whole painful story of his relations with the Opéra and put your finger on the illusions of that poor, great genius, adrift in the midst of men, like the angel in the story by Théophile Gautier. He believed *Benvenuto Cellini* would be a success, and was still believing it after the third performance, which Duprez has described in his memoirs in a way that throws a very strange light on the failure and unjust sacrifice of this work. For several years he had hopes of seeing *Les Troyens* performed on our leading operatic stage, and no one will ever know what a complete performance of that huge work in that vast theatre would have been like, with Mme Viardot in the tremendous role of Cassandra.[2]

The Opéra preferred to put on the *Roméo* [*I Capuleti e I Montecchi*] by Bellini, the composer Berlioz made fun of as a young man, which fell flat. The directors had nonetheless done a good job in commissioning Dietsch[3] to add what they called "salt and pepper", by stiffening this wretched score with trombones, cornets, piccolos, cymbals and a bass drum. Bellini's last act was replaced by the well-known scena by Vaccaï.[4] Needless expense! Wasted labour! Success eluded all these efforts. But the Opéra had not put on *Les Troyens*. Honour was satisfied.

More than one essay could be written about these letters, in which the composer gives his own account of how his works came into being. We learn among other things that the astonishing effect of the brass split into four orchestras, in the "Tuba mirum" of the *Requiem*, was invented for a fantastical drama called *The Last Day of the World*, and Berlioz provides an outline of it. We are also made privy to the inception of *Lélio*, whose finale, the "Fantasy on the Tempest", was his first attempt at a half-vocal, half-orchestral composition, which was to be fully realized in *Roméo et Juliette*.

It was *Lélio*, I may say in passing, that gave me the opportunity to meet the great man and to win his valuable friendship. This delightful work will remain the subject of my eternal gratitude.

December 1881

[2] They would have to wait until 10 June 1921, when the role of Cassandra was sung by Lucy Isnardon. Saint-Saëns attended and applauded the open dress rehearsal.

[3] Louis Dietsch (1808–1865) had a varied career, winning a first prize at the Conservatoire on the double bass in 1830, conducting the notorious performances of *Tannhäuser* at the Opéra in 1861, and then, as a colleague of Saint-Saëns, teaching at the Ecole Niedermeyer.

[4] Nicola Vaccaï (1790–1848) was an Italian composer and singing teacher, best known for his book of vocal exercises.

15

BERLIOZ II

*(*Portraits et souvenirs,
Société d'edition artistique, 1899, 2–14)

A paradox made flesh, that was Berlioz.

If there is one quality you can't deny his works, and which his most determined enemies have never contested, it is the brilliance, the extraordinary colouring of his instrumentation. When you study it with the aim of finding out how he does it, you go from amazement to amazement. No one who reads his scores without having heard them can have the faintest idea of them; the instruments seem to be organised in defiance of common sense; it would seem, to use the technical term, that it shouldn't *sound*; but it does, marvellously. Maybe there are, here and there, some obscurities in the musical style, but there are none in the orchestration; light floods in and plays around as on the facets of a diamond.

In this, Berlioz was guided by a mysterious instinct, and his procedures escape analysis for the simple reason that he didn't have any. He admits it himself in his *Orchestration Treatise* when, after describing all the instruments in detail and listing their capabilities and properties, he declares that combining them is the secret of genius and that it is something impossible to teach. Here he went too far; the world is full of composers who, without the slightest hint of genius, employ tried and convenient methods to write for the orchestra perfectly well.

His *Treatise* is itself a deeply paradoxical work. It begins with an introduction of several lines, unconnected with the subject, in which the author rails against composers who abuse the art of modulation and have a taste for dissonances, "just as certain animals do for salt or prickly plants or thorn-bushes" (what would he say today!). Then he proceeds to a study of the instruments of the orchestra and, amid some absolutely solid truths and wise advice, makes some strange assertions such as: "The clarinet is not made for the idyllic." He refused to see in it anything except a voice suit to the expression of the heroic. The clarinet can indeed be extremely heroic, but also extremely bucolic; we only have to remember the use Beethoven made of it in the Pastoral Symphony to admit the fact. The charming folksy opening of Meyerbeer's *Le prophète*, which had not been composed when Berlioz wrote his treatise, is another example that contradicts his view.

At the time this treatise appeared, Berlioz's major works were largely unpublished, and they were nowhere performed. No matter, he took it upon himself to quote passages from these same works on more or less every page! What could they teach students who had never had the opportunity of hearing them?

But anyway, the same applies to Berlioz's treatise as to his instrumentation: with all its bizarre moments, it's marvellous. It was thanks to him that my generation was educated and, I venture to say, well educated. He possessed the inestimable quality of inflaming the imagination, of creating a love for the art he taught. Whatever he did not teach, he gave you the thirst for learning it, and one learns best the lessons one has taught oneself. His musical quotations might appear pointless, but they made one dream; it was a door opened on to a new world, the distant, captivating view of the future, of the promised land. Would better results have been obtained by a policy of more precise descriptions with sensibly chosen examples, but one that was dry and lifeless? I don't think so. Art cannot be learnt like mathematics.

There is a simultaneous explosion of paradox and genius in *Roméo et Juliette*. The structure is extraordinary: nothing similar had ever been thought of. The prologue (alas, all too often omitted) and the final section are lyrical; but the latter is also dramatic, given the form of an operatic finale; the remainder is symphonic, with a few appearances of the chorus joining the first and last sections by a thin thread and holding the whole work together. It's neither lyrical, dramatic not symphonic, but a little of each: a composite construction in which symphonic writing predominates. For such a challenge to common sense there could be only one excuse: to write a masterpiece, and here Berlioz did not fail. Everything is new, personal, and of a profound originality that discourages imitation. The famous "Queen Mab" Scherzo is even better than its reputation—it is a miracle of the light fantastical and of grace. Beside such delicacy and transparency, Mendelssohn's light textures in *A Midsummer Night's Dream* sound heavy. The reason is that the elusive and the impalpable derive not only from sonority, but from style. In this context I feel that only the chorus of fairies in *Oberon* can stand comparison.[1]

Roméo et Juliette seems to me to be Berlioz's most characteristic work, and the one that deserves to find most favour with the public. Until now

---

[1] Act I of Weber's opera begins with these fairies keeping guard over the sleeping Oberon.

the most popular success, not only in France but all round the world, has gone to *La damnation de Faust;* in spite of which we should not despair of seeing *Roméo et Juliette* one day taking the victorious place it merits.

Berlioz's paradoxical nature is also evinced in his critical writings. He was, beyond all possible argument, the leading music critic of his day, despite the sometimes inexplicable oddness of his opinions; and this for all that he lacked the erudition and the knowledge of music history that should form the very basis of criticism. Many people claim that in art one should not give reasons for one's impressions. That may well be true, but in that case one has to be content with taking one's pleasure where one finds it and refusing to criticise anything whatever. A critic has to act differently, taking account of merits and shortcomings, not demanding of Raphael that he should use the palette of Rembrandt, nor of the old painters who used eggs and distemper that they should produce the effects of painting in oils. Berlioz didn't take account of anything except the satisfaction or boredom he had felt when listening to a piece of music. The past didn't exist for him; he didn't understand the old Masters whom he knew only from their scores. If he was such an admirer of Gluck or Spontini, that was because in his youth he had seen their works performed at the Opéra by Mme Branchu, the last singer to maintain their traditions.[2] He hadn't a good word to say about Lully, or Pergolesi's *La serva padrona:* "To see a revival of this piece," he said ironically, "and be there on the first night, would be a pleasure worthy of Olympus!"[3]

I still remember his amazement and delight on hearing a chorus by Sebastian Bach, which I introduced him to one day; he couldn't get over the fact that the great Sebastian had written music like that; and he admitted to me that he'd always taken him for a kind of giant brainbox, engineering tremendously clever fugues, but devoid of charm and poetry. Truth be told, he didn't know his music.

Even so, in spite of that and many other things, he was a critic of the highest order because he presented to the world that unique phenomenon of a man of genius, a man of delicate and incisive spirit and with senses that were of an extraordinary refinement, relaying sincerely impressions that were not influenced by any external preoccupation. The articles he wrote on the Beethoven symphonies and on Gluck's operas are incomparable; we should always return to them when we want to refresh our imagination, purify our taste, and wash ourselves free of all that dust

---

[2] Caroline Branchu (1780–1850) was a pupil at the Conservatoire of Pierre Garat. She made her debut at the Opéra in 1801 in Piccinni's *Didon* and went on to sing the principal roles in Gluck's *Alceste,* Spontini's *La Vestale* and Salieri's *Les Danaïdes,* three works that Berlioz particularly loved. In a letter of 1825, he called her "la sublime Mme Branchu".

[3] The force of this was presumably that the pleasures of Olympus are reserved for those not of this world.

that the daily practices of life and music lay on our artistic souls, which have so much to suffer in this world.

He has been reproached for being caustic. In his case this was not malevolence, but rather a kind of naughtiness, an unquenchable comic verve that he gave out in conversation and was unable to control. As I see it, the only person against whom this verve was exercised with any persistence in a number of facetious articles was Duprez,[4] and frankly the great tenor deserved to be speared with the odd arrow or two. Did he not recount, in his *Memoirs,* how he had strangled *Benvenuto Cellini,* for which was Berlioz supposed to be grateful? Maybe he would have been a more loyal supporter of the work if Berlioz had persuaded him with the resounding arguments Meyerbeer used to get him to prolong the run of *Les Huguenots,* as the great singer also recounts in his book, with an unwitting candour calculated to blunt the claws of the fiercest critic.[5] Anyone would think, reading this, that *Les Huguenots* was not already flying under full sail and being carried along by the current, as in our own day. The public are surprised sometimes that modern works find it so difficult to break into the Opéra repertoire: perhaps that has to do with the fact that not all composers have an income of a hundred thousand pounds. I say "perhaps", not wishing to be dogmatic about it.

Berlioz was unhappy owing to his ingenuity in creating suffering for himself, in aiming for the impossible and in wanting it despite everything. He had this completely false idea (and one that is unfortunately, thanks to him, widespread throughout the world) that the composer's will should not have to take notice of material obstacles. He preferred to ignore the fact that the composer's situation is not the same as that of the painter, who is free to cover his canvas with inert matter, and that the composer has to take account of performers' fatigue and their greater or lesser capabilities; and, in his youth, he demanded of orchestras far inferior to those of today efforts that were truly superhuman.

While there inevitably are, in all music that is new and original, difficulties that are impossible to avoid, there are others that one can spare performers without damaging the work; but Berlioz did not get involved with such details. I have seen him conduct twenty or thirty rehearsals

---

[4] Gilbert-Louis Duprez (1806–1896) made his Paris debut at the Odéon in 1825, singing Almaviva in Rossini's *The Barber of Seville,* and his debut at the Opéra in 1837, singing Arnold in *Guillaume Tell.* He abandoned the role of Cellini after three performances. In his Memoirs he writes that "Berlioz's talent . . . is not exactly melodic" and that in *Benvenuto Cellini* the composer's inspiration was "strange to my Italianate ears".

[5] After the 60th performance, Meyerbeer bet Duprez the sum of his composer's rights that the run would not extend to the 80th. It reached its 100th on 10 July 1839, with Duprez singing Raoul.

of a single piece, tearing at his hair, breaking batons and desks, without achieving the desired result. The poor musicians even so were doing what they could; but the task was beyond their powers. This music had to wait until the technique of our orchestras improved before it could reach the ears of the public.

Two things caused Berlioz serious distress: the hostility of the Opéra, rejecting *Les Troyens* in favour of Bellini's *Romeo*,[6] which was a flop; and the coolness towards him of the Société des concerts. We know the reason for the latter since the publication of Deldevez's book on the Society's history;[7] it was due to the influence of its conductors. This influence was only right and proper in the case of Deldevez, who was a serious and learned musician and deserved to be regarded with respect. Maybe his understanding was limited to classical music, the only kind he had studied in depth; maybe his antipathy to Berlioz's music was purely instinctive.

Far worse was the case of his predecessor Girard,[8] a musician very inferior to Deldevez and a conductor whose leadership, vastly overpraised, introduced a mass of bad habits into the performing style, happily corrected by his successor. A brief anecdote will give an idea of his character and the comprehensiveness of his understanding. One day he wanted to programme one of my works and he sends me a note asking me to go and see him. I rush off and I find, as soon as the conversation begins, that he's changed his mind; I had no mind to object, being then a callow youth of no importance. But Girard took the opportunity to give me a lesson in musical ethics, telling me, among other things, that one shouldn't use trombones in a symphony; "but," I replied timidly, "I think Beethoven in the *Pastoral Symphony* and in the C minor Symphony . . ." "Yes," said he, "'that's true; *but perhaps he'd have done better not to.*" You can imagine, with such principles, what he must have thought of the *Symphonie fantastique*.

As we know, this retrograde attitude has entirely vanished from the rue Bergère,[9] where Berlioz is now held in high esteem, and the famous

---

[6] *I Capuleti e I Montecchi* was premiered at La Fenice in Venice on 11 March 1830. For the performance at the Opéra on 7 September 1859 the opera was supplemented by a final act taken from Vaccaï's *Giulietta e Romeo*. It was dropped from the repertory after 11 performances.

[7] Edouard Deldevez (1817–1897) was a pupil of Reicha and Halévy and won a *premier prix* for violin at the Conservatoire in 1838. From 1859 he was conductor at the Opéra and at the Conservatoire.

[8] Narcisse Girard (1797–1860) won a *premier prix* for violin at the Conservatoire in 1820. He became conductor at the Opéra-Comique in 1830 and conducted the Berlioz concert in 1834 at which *Harold in Italy* was performed for the first time. Berlioz was unhappy with his conducting and never used him again.

[9] The Société des concerts held its concerts in the hall of the Conservatoire on the rue Bergère.

Society has managed to partake of current musical developments without sacrificing any of its unique qualities.

The public began to warm to Berlioz during the last years of his life, and *L'enfance du Christ*, through its simplicity and sweetness, fought a successful battle against the prejudice that wanted to see in him nothing but a noisemaker and a purveyor of mayhem. He died not, as had been said, of human injustice, but of a stomach ailment caused by his obstinate refusal to take any of his doctors' advice or follow a sensible diet. I saw this at first hand, without being able to do anything about it, on a journey for musical purposes that I had the honour to make with him. "An extraordinary thing is happening," he said to me one morning: "I'm not in pain." And he told me of his agonies, his continual stomach cramps, and the prohibition he was under against taking any kind of stimulant or departing from his prescribed diet, on pain of terrible suffering that would only get worse. But he followed no diet and consumed whatever he felt like, without thinking of the morrow. That evening we were at a banquet. As I was sitting near him, I did all I could to dissuade him from the coffee, the champagne, the Havana cigars—it was all in vain, and the next day the great man was twisted in knots by his usual torments.

As well as total admiration, I also had a lively affection for him, born of the kindness he had shown me and of which I was understandably proud, as well as for the personal qualities I had found in him, in complete contrast as these were to the reputation he had in the outside world, where he was regarded as proud, embittered and unkind. He was, on the contrary, a good man, good to the point of it being a weakness, grateful for the slightest signs of interest one showed in him and marked by an admirable simplicity that added yet more weight to his mordant wit and jokes, because they never smacked of that searching for effect, that wish to astonish which often spoils so many good things.

People will no doubt be surprised to learn where Berlioz's reputation for malevolence had its origin. He was pursued, in certain quarters, with an implacable hatred because of an article on Hérold, unsigned, whose authorship had been attributed to him.

Well, here is the end of a piece in the *Journal des débats* of 15 March 1869, shortly after Berlioz's death:

> . . . However I do have to tell you . . . that it was wrong of certain critics to reproach Berlioz with having spoken ill of *Le pré aux clercs*.[10] It was not Berlioz, it was someone else, an ignorant young man, full of self-confidence in those days, who, in a wretched article, savaged

[10] Hérold's opera *Le pré aux clercs* was premiered at the Opéra-Comique on 15 December 1832. It reached its 1,000th performance there in 1871 and had had over 1,600 by 1949.

Hérold's masterpiece. He would regret it all his life. And this ignoramus's name (I blush to tell you!), it must be confessed, was monsieur Jules JANIN.[11]

So Janin, who lived so to speak side by side with Berlioz, since they wrote each week for the same paper, waited until he was dead to absolve him of a misdeed that weighed on him all his life, and of which he, Janin, was the culprit! What can you say of such behaviour? Was it not charming, and did Janin not deserve his reputation as an excellent fellow? One is speechless. Janin was fat and Berlioz was thin; but that was no reason for the first to pass as good and the second as unkind. What sentiment provoked the celebrated critic to publish this tardy revelation? A crisis of conscience? A need to bring his crime into the light of day so as to enjoy it more fully? . . .

Berlioz has been reproached for his lack of love for mankind, admitted by him in his *Memoirs;* in this he joins the family of Horace who said "Odi profanum vulgus",[12] and of La Fontaine who wrote: "Que j'ai toujours haï les pensers du vulgaire!"[13]

With his superior nature, Berlioz could not love the vulgarity, the grossness, the ferocity and the egoism that play such a considerable role in the world and of which he had so often been a victim. One should love the humanity of which one is part, and work if one can to make it better and help it progress; that is what Berlioz, in his sphere of activity, did as much as anyone, by opening new avenues for art, and by preaching throughout his life the love of the beautiful and the cult of masterpieces. One can ask no more of him; beyond that lies the work not of an artist, but of a saint.

[11] Gabriel-Jules Janin (1804–1874) was a prolific writer and a central contributor to the Journal des débats from 1829 to 1873. According to Sainte-Beuve, he wrote "as often as he could to the side of, above and around his subject".

[12] See ch 14 n 1, p. 79.

[13] "How I have always hated the thoughts of the mob!"

16

LISZT I

(Harmonie et mélodie,
Calmann-Lévy, 1899, 155–172)

Those people who take an interest in music may still remember a concert that was given a few years ago in the hall of the
Théâtre-Italien, conducted by the writer of this article. The programme
was entirely made up of orchestral works by Franz Liszt, a man routinely
described as "the great pianist", so that people can avoid recognizing that
he is one of the great composers of our time.

In the musical world, this concert caused a certain stir; though very
little among the general public, which has still not come round to showing an interest in Liszt's music. Liszt the composer is for many people the
equivalent of Ingres the violinist or M. Thiers the astronomer.[1] So the
public, which would have arrived in crowds to hear Liszt play ten bars on
the piano, showed little enthusiasm, as was to be expected, for coming
to hear the *Dante Symphony,* "The Shepherds at the Crib" and "The Wise
Men", orchestral movements from his oratorio *Christus,* and other pieces
which, if written by someone less famous who played the piano not particularly well, would certainly have excited their curiosity. One has to say
also, to be fair, that the concert had been very badly publicised. While
Estudiantina española[2] was taken up by every advertisement and every
possible hoarding, the Liszt concert drew the short straw and at no time
found a place among any of the theatre notices. A few days later, a pianist
gave a recital at the Théâtre-Italien and was granted this favour. Theatres
have these mysterious ways, which are inexplicable to mere mortals.

But Liszt's name did appear here and there in enormous letters at the
very top of the advertisement columns, which human eye couldn't reach
without the aid of a telescope. It was enough to ensure that our concert

---

[1] Adolphe Thiers (1797–1877) was better known as prime minister in 1836 and 1839,
and then as first president of the Third Republic in 1870.

[2] This group of Spanish singers and guitarists was a sensational success when it appeared in Paris in March 1878.

did not take place in an empty hall. The musical press had been invited, turned up in force, and were fairly well disposed; but the quality of the works on which they were asked to give their opinion seemed to escape them utterly. They found, in general, that Liszt's music was well written, that it was free of the bizarre features they had expected to encounter, and that it did not lack a certain charm. That was all.

If that had been my opinion of Liszt's compositions, I should certainly not have taken the trouble to get a huge orchestra together and rehearse it for a fortnight in order to play them. I should also like to say a few words about these works that are still so little known and which seem to me to have a bright future.

It is not long since orchestral music had only two forms at its disposal: the symphony and the overture. Haydn, Mozart and Beethoven didn't write anything else; who would dare to depart from their example? Neither Weber, nor Mendelssohn , nor Schubert, nor Schumann dared to.

Liszt dared.

To dare, in art, is the most terrible thing in the world. In theory, I agree, nothing is simpler. There are no laws against the arts and artists are free to do whatever they like; who is there to stop them?

In practice, everything stops them—everybody and themselves. The new forms that people ask for and desire, or at least appear to, inspire terror and repulsion. In order to accept new forms and grasp their meaning the mind has to make an effort: those people willing to make this effort are rare. The favourite option is to curl up inside one's idleness and routine, even if it means dying of boredom and repletion.

Liszt realized that, if you wanted to impose new forms, you had to make them seem necessary—in a phrase, to provide a motive. He set out resolutely on the path that Beethoven, in the *Pastoral* and *Choral Symphonies*, and Berlioz, in the *Symphonie fantastique* and *Harold en Italie*, had pointed out rather than opened up; for even if they had expanded the framework of the symphony, they had not destroyed it, while Liszt created the symphonic poem.

This brilliant and influential creation will be his title to immortality and, when time has removed the vivid trace of the greatest pianist who ever lived, it will inscribe on its roll of honour the name of the man who set instrumental music free.

Liszt didn't only bring into the world the idea of the symphonic poem, he himself developed it and, in his 12 examples, demonstrated the main forms that this idea can embrace. But before speaking of the works themselves, let me say a few words about their animating principle, the principle of *programme music.*

For many people programme music is an innately inferior genre. On this subject a host of things has been written which I am unable to understand.

Is the music, in itself, good or bad? That's the crux. Whether or not it is *programme* music, that won't make it better or worse.

It's exactly the same as in painting, where the subject of a picture, which is all that counts for the general public, is of no importance, or very little, for the lover of pictures.

There is more: the charge that has been brought against music of expressing nothing by itself, without the help of words, applies equally to painting. A picture will never represent Adam and Eve to an observer who doesn't know the Bible; it will only represent a naked man and woman in the middle of a garden. But observers or listeners happily go along with this fraud of adding the interest and emotion of a subject to the pleasure of their eyes and ears. There is no reason to refuse them this pleasure, nor is there any to grant it. There is complete freedom: artists make use of it, and they are right to do so.

What is incontrovertible is that, in our era, the public's taste orientates it towards paintings with a subject and music with a programme, and that its taste, in France at least, has led artists in this direction.

For the artist, programme music is only a pretext for exploring new paths, and novel effects require novel means—something that has never pleased the race of conductors and choirmasters, who infinitely prefer what they are used to and a peaceful existence. I should not be surprised if the resistance to the works we are speaking of were to come, not from the public, but from conductors, out of their reluctance to grapple with the manifold difficulties with which these works are studded. However I shall not go so far as to insist on this.

. . . [here follow descriptions of individual symphonic poems] . . .

Great efforts have been made to impose German music on the Parisian public, sometimes at inappropriate moments, and although these works may have been well written, they were also heavy and antipathetic, reflecting in miserable fashion the narrow, pedantic spirit of certain small German towns. My final wish is that a tenth of these efforts should be made for the music of Liszt, so colourful, so alive, so tuneful even; it is popular in Russia and will be so in France, once someone takes the trouble to promote it as they should.

17

LISZT II

*(*Portraits et souvenirs,
Société d'edition artistique, 15–34)

It's impossible to describe the impact, the magical prestige dis-
seminated among young musicians in early Imperial times by
the name of Liszt, so strange for us Frenchmen, with its sharp, whistling
sound like a sword swishing through the air, and cut through by its "z" as
though by a bolt of lightning. The artist and the man seemed to belong to
the world of legend.

He began by incarnating on the piano the panache of Romanticism;
then, leaving behind him the sparkling tail of a meteor, he disappeared
behind the curtain of clouds that then cloaked Germany, made up as it
was of a conglomeration of little kingdoms and autonomous duchies,
sprinkled with crenellated castles and preserving, even in its Gothic script,
a style belonging to the Middle Ages that could no longer be found in
France, despite all the efforts of poets to restore it. Most of the piano pieces
he'd published seemed unperformable by anyone except him, and were
indeed so using the old-fashioned performing techniques that called for
immobility, with the elbows tucked into the sides, limiting movement to
the fingers and forearms. We knew that at the court of Weimar he had
turned his back on his earlier successes and was engaged on works of serious composition, dreaming of a renovation of art—about which circu-
lated the most disturbing rumours, as is always the case when anyone has
the intention of exploring a new world and breaking with traditional
ideas. On their own, the memories left by Liszt's time in Paris provided
ample material for suggestions of every kind. The truth, when it concerned
him, no longer needed the support of likelihood.

There was the story of how one day, at a Conservatoire concert, after
a performance of the Pastoral Symphony, he had the audacity to play it
again on the piano, to the stupefaction of the audience—a stupefaction
that soon turned to huge enthusiasm. And how on another occasion,
being bored with the docility of his listeners and tired of seeing this lion,
so ready at other times to devour its prey, now licking his feet, he decided

to annoy it and took the liberty of arriving late for a concert at the Théâtre des Italiens, of going to see various beautiful ladies of his acquaintance in their boxes and enjoying jokes with them, until the lion began to grumble and roar; and when he finally sat down at the piano in front of this angry lion, its fury ebbed away utterly, leaving only roars of pleasure and devotion.

And there are any number of other stories which would not be relevant to this article. In Liszt's case there has been too much talk about his success with women, his penchant for princesses and the whole, as you might say, exterior part of his personality. It is high time to look more narrowly at his serious side and the considerable role he played in contemporary music.

Liszt's influence on the development of the piano was immense. The only thing I can find comparable is the revolution wrought by Victor Hugo on the workings of the French language. This influence is more powerful than Paganini's on the violin, because that has remained confined to the inaccessible regions where he alone could survive, while Liszt, starting from the same point, has deigned to descend to negotiable paths where he can be followed by anyone who takes the trouble to work seriously. To recreate his piano playing would be impossible; as the amazing Olga Janina[1] says in her curious book, his fingers were not human fingers. But nothing is easier than to walk along the path he laid out and, in fact, everybody does walk along it, whether they realize it or not. The great advances in sonority and the techniques for obtaining it, which he invented, have become an indispensable element and indeed the basis of modern performance. These techniques are of two kinds: those concerned with the activities of the performer, a particular kind of gymnastics; and those to do with the way of writing for the piano, which Liszt completely transformed. At the opposite extreme from Beethoven, who disregarded the limits decreed by physiology and imposed his tyrannical will on reluctant, exhausted fingers, Liszt takes them and exercises them in accordance with their nature, in such a way as to obtain from them, without violence, the maximum effect they are capable of producing. His music may at first sight terrify the timid, but really it is less difficult than it looks and, with practice, truly trains the hand and produces rapid progress in manual talent. We also owe to him the invention of picturesque writing in music. By ingenious and infinitely varied means, the composer uses this to indicate

---

[1] In her hysterical and wholly unreliable autobiographical novels, *Souvenirs d'une Cosaque* and *Les amours d'une Cosaque* (Paris, 1875), published under the name Robert Franz, the 23-year-old Olga Janina also relates that she and the 60-year-old Liszt had an affair in 1871, and that she threatened to shoot him and poison herself.

the character of a passage and even the way one should set about playing it. These elegant measures are today in widespread and general use.

Most important of all, he has introduced orchestral sonorities and combinations into piano music in as complete a manner as possible. His procedure for achieving this aim—a procedure not within the capabilities of everyone—consists in making his transcriptions free rather than literal versions of the original. Seen and practised in this light, transcription becomes a highly artistic enterprise; Liszt's adaptations of the Beethoven Symphonies—especially his two-piano transcription of the Ninth—may be regarded as the masterpieces of the genre. To be fair, and make acknowledgment where it is due, it must be said that piano reductions of the nine Symphonies had already been attempted by Kalkbrenner, who should be honoured for his efforts, even if the task was beyond him. It is likely that they prompted Liszt to undertake his colossal achievement.

As the uncontested incarnation of the modern piano, Liszt has, for that very reason, seen calumny hurled at his music, which is treated disdainfully as "pianist's music". The same pejorative term could be applied to the works of Schumann, whose soul was the piano. If this has never been the case, it is because—try though he might—Schumann never left the heights of "respectable" music to enjoy himself producing picturesque illustrations based on operas of every land; while Liszt, unconcerned by what anyone might say, proceeded on a random, copious scattering of pearls and diamonds from his overflowing imagination.

It should be said in passing that there is a certain amount of pedantry and prejudice in the contempt often levelled at works like the *Don Juan Fantasy* or the *Caprice on the Waltz from Faust:* there is more talent and true inspiration in them than in many works of serious appearance and pretentious nullity (of which there is never any lack). People seem not to realize that most well-known overtures, such as those to *Zampa, Euryanthe* or *Tannhäuser,* are in fact no more than fantasias on themes from the operas they introduce. If you take the trouble to study Liszt's *fantaisies,* you will see the extent to which they differ from any run-of-the-mill potpourri, where themes from the opera are taken at random, merely as a canvas for arabesques and decorative festoons. You will observe how the composer has managed to get to the marrow of any bone he finds, and how his penetrating intelligence has discovered the most deeply hidden artistic nucleus among all the vulgarities and platitudes, and fertilized it; how, if he is dealing with a masterpiece like *Don Giovanni,* he throws light on its chief beauties and gives a commentary on them that helps us to understand them and to appreciate to the full their supreme perfection and undying modernity. As for the ingenuity of his pianistic figuration, it is prodigious and he has the admiration of everyone who plays the instrument. But not enough, in my view, has been made of the fact that even in the slightest of his arrangements the composer's hand can be felt; the great musician's sensitive ear is always in evidence, however fleetingly.

For a pianist like that, who could evoke the soul of music through the piano, the term "pianist" ceases to be an insult and "pianist's music" can equally be called "musician's music". In any case, who in our time has not felt the powerful influence of the piano? This influence dates from before the piano itself, with Bach's *Well-Tempered Clavier*. From the day when equal temperament made sharps and flats synonymous and allowed the use of all the keys, the spirit of the keyboard made its entry into the world (the invention of the hammer mechanism was secondary from an artistic point of view and merely led to the progressive development of a sonority hitherto unknown to the harpsichord and of immense material resources).

This spirit turned into the destructive tyrant of music through the uncontrolled propagation of heretical enharmony. From this heresy practically the whole of modern music has been derived. It has been too fruitful for us to be allowed to deplore it; but it is nonetheless a heresy, destined to vanish on some distant but fateful day, because of the very evolution that gave it birth. What will be left then of the music of today? Perhaps only Berlioz who, never having been a pianist, had an instinctive repugnance for enharmony; in which he is the very opposite of Wagner, who was enharmony made flesh and the musician who drew the ultimate consequences from this principle. Even so, the critics and, consequently, the public still put Wagner and Berlioz in the same basket. This forced promiscuity will be the astonishment of future generations.

Without wishing to dwell unduly on the whole host of *Fantaisies* Liszt wrote on operatic themes, I must mention his "Illustrations of *Le Prophète*". But even this is surpassed by a brilliant and unlooked-for masterpiece, the Fantaisie and Fugue for organ on the chorale *Ad nos, ad salutarem undam*. It is a transitional piece, lying between the composer's more or less free arrangements and his original works. This gigantic, 40-minute piece is original in the sense that the theme it's built on does not once appear in its entirety, but circulates in a latent manner, like sap in a tree. The organ is deployed in an unusual fashion that notably increases its resources, and the composer seems to have foreseen intuitively the instrument's recent developments, just as Mozart looked forward to the modern piano in his Fantasy and Sonata in C minor. A performance of this work demands a colossal organ that is easy to manage, and a player expert on both organ and piano; which explains why chances to hear good performances are fairly few and far between.

The *Soirées de Vienne* and the *Hungarian Rhapsodies*, even if their themes are borrowed, are truly original and demonstrate the most refined talent; the *Rhapsodies* can be seen as illustrations for the strange book Liszt wrote on gipsy music. It is quite wrong to regard these merely as showpieces.

They offer a complete reconstitution—one might say a "civilization"—of the music of a race, which is of the greatest artistic interest. The composer was not interested in the pianistic difficulties, which didn't exist for him, but in the picturesque effect and the lively reproduction of the bizarre gipsy orchestra. Come to that, virtuosity is never an end in any of his piano music, but a means. Failure to realize this leads people to go against the meaning of his music and render it unrecognisable.

It is a strange fact but, apart from the magnificent Sonata, that bold and powerful work, it is not in his original works for piano that this great artist and pianist invested his genius. Schumann and Chopin easily outstrip him on this terrain. The *Méditations religieuses* and the *Années de pèlerinage* may contain some beautiful, exquisite passages, but every now and then the wings break against some invisible ceiling and the composer seems to be consumed in his efforts to reach an unattainable ideal. From this stems a malaise that it is not easy to define: a painful anguish leading to irrepressible fatigue. Exception must be made for the *Scherzo* and *March*, a stunning, vertiginous infernal hunt, but unfortunately very hard to play, and the triumphant E flat Concerto; but here the piano is joined by the orchestra and is no longer self-sufficient. That is also the case with the *First Mephisto Waltz*, written initially for the piano with the intention of adding an orchestra, as he did indeed later.

Liszt did not perhaps attach as much importance to his *Etudes* as to some of his other piano works but, as with Cramer and Clementi, it is in these particularly that one finds the first-rate composer. One of them, *Mazeppa*, was easily transferred from piano to orchestra and became one of the symphonic poems.

With these well-known poems, the subject of such differing opinions, and with the *Dante* and *Faust Symphonies*, we find ourselves in the presence of an entirely new Liszt, the great, the real Liszt of Weimar, whom the smoke of incense burning on the altars of the piano had kept hidden too long. He set his foot firmly on the path opened up by Beethoven in the *Pastoral Symphony*, and deserted the cult of pure music for what is called "programme" music, which claims to paint clearly delineated feelings and personalities; hurling himself recklessly into harmonic neologisms, he dared to do what no one had dared before him and if, to use one of his friends' curious euphemisms, he sometimes "exceeded the bounds of the beautiful", he also made useful and brilliant discoveries in this field. He broke the mould of the old symphony and the venerable overture, and proclaimed the reign of music that was freed from every discipline, bar only the one the composer was happy to create for the setting in which he had chosen to find himself.

In contrast with the orchestral sobriety of the Classical symphony, he set up the opulence of the modern orchestra and, just as he had used his prodigious ingenuity to introduce this opulence into piano music, he transposed his virtuosity on to the orchestra, thereby creating a new orchestration of unexampled richness, while profiting from the unexplored resources made available by developments in instrument making and by the increased technical abilities of orchestral players. Wagner's instrumental writing is frequently cruel; it takes no account of the exhaustion brought on by superhuman efforts and sometimes demands the impossible—one does the best one can. Liszt's writing incurs no such criticism. It demands of the orchestra everything it can give, but no more.

Instrumental music had traditionally been devoted to the exclusive cult of an impersonal form and beauty. Liszt, like Berlioz, converted its aim into that of "expression". Not that he neglected its earlier objectives. Where could you find purer forms than in "Gretchen", the second movement of the *Faust Symphony*, or in the "Purgatoire" of the *Dante Symphony*, or in *Orphée?* But it is in the truth and intensity of expression that Liszt is truly incomparable. His music speaks, and to avoid hearing its words you have to stuff your ears with the cotton wool of prejudice, which unfortunately is always to hand. His music describes the indescribable.

Maybe he made the mistake—an excusable one, in my view—of believing too firmly in his own music and wanting to impress it on the world too quickly. The attraction of an almost magical prestige and a seductiveness that few men have possessed to the same degree meant that he had gathered round him and enthused a whole circle of ardent young spirits who asked nothing better than to set out on a war against ancient formulas and to preach the good word. These hotheads, undaunted by any exaggeration, regarded all the Beethoven symphonies except the Ninth as "tattered old boots", and other works in the same fashion. Instead of persuading the great mass of musicians and critics, they inspired them with disgust.

It was while these polemics were at their height and he was proudly battling away with his tiny but determined army, that Liszt fell in love with the works of Wagner and triumphantly produced on the Weimar stage his opera *Lohengrin*, which had been published but which no theatre had dared take on. In a pamphlet, *Tannhäuser and Lohengrin*, which made a great splash, he became the mouthpiece of the new doctrine; he used all his influence to spread Wagner's music and get it played in theatres that had so far jibbed at doing so; as to the opposition he faced and the efforts he had to make, it would be hard to imagine them. We may surmise that since Liszt felt himself not powerful enough to lift the world all on his own, he had dreamt of forging an alliance with the great reformer in which each of them would play his part, one reigning over the opera house, the other over the concert hall; because Wagner openly claimed that he wrote complex works in which music was, so to speak, no more than the root, combining with poetry and staging to form an indivisible whole.

But Liszt, being generous-hearted and ever ready to devote himself to a good cause, had not counted on the invasive spirit of his gargantuan, dangerous protégé, who was incapable of sharing world power even with his best friend. Since the publication of the Liszt/Wagner correspondence, we now know the outcome. The artistic movement founded by Liszt was turned against him and his works banished from the concert hall, to make way for Wagner's; and because these, according to Wagner's own theories, had been written specifically for the theatre, they could not be given outside it without becoming unintelligible. The pro-Wagner critics turned back to the arguments of the classical school and undermined the very basis of Liszt's work by preaching the dogma of pure music and declaring descriptive music to be heretical.

But it is obvious that one of Wagner's great strengths and one of his most powerful means of working on audiences is precisely the development of descriptive music pushed to its furthermost limits. He achieved nothing short of a miracle by managing to conjure up sea noises during the whole of the first act of *The Flying Dutchman* without interrupting the dramatic action. He created a whole world of similar passages.

How can this contradiction be solved?

—Quite simply, and ingeniously. "Yes," the rubric runs, "music has the right to be descriptive, *but only in the opera house.*"

What a miserable sophism! On the contrary, thanks to the staging and noises off, music in the opera house could perfectly well be given over exclusively to the expression of feelings.

What then do the overtures and extracts from Wagner's works that are played in the concert hall become, if not descriptive incidental music, or "programme" music? What else is the prelude to the third act of *Tannhäuser,* which claims to tell us everything that is happening in the interlude—the story of the pilgrimage to Rome and the Pope's curse? What is the meaning of the protection the Wagnerians have given Berlioz, who wrote not a single note of "pure music"?

But enough on this subject. The spectacle of ingratitude and bad faith is too distasteful to warrant lengthy attention.

Let us rather ascend to the luminous heights of Liszt's music and, leaving regretfully aside other highly interesting works such as marches, choruses and *Prometheus,* let us consider the large religious compositions in which he has put the purest essence of his genius: the Masses, the Psalms, the *Christus* and the *Legend of Saint Elisabeth.* In these serene regions the "pianist" disappears. Here a rightful place with room for development is found for his strong tendency towards mysticism, which from time to time shows itself elsewhere, even in the piano pieces where it occasionally produces a strange effect (as in *Les jeux d'eau de la Villa d'Este* where innocent cascades finally turn into the Fountain of Life, the source of grace, with accompanying texts from Scripture). There has been widespread astonishment at the consummate skill with which Liszt handles vocal parts and at the absolute correctness of his Latin prosody, which he studied in depth. This fantasist sets the liturgy impeccably. The smells of incense, the charms of stained glass, the gold of the sacred vessels, the incomparable splendour of cathedrals are all reflected in his Masses, with their profound feeling and seductive charm. Take the "Credo" of the *Gran Mass*, with its magnificent layout, its fine, bold harmonies, its strong colours and its dramatic but never theatrical impact—born of that special drama belonging to the Holy Mysteries and accepted by the Church; this movement alone would be enough to place its composer in the front rank of musical poets. Anyone who cannot see it must be blind!

In *Christus* and *Elisabeth*, Liszt created a kind of oratorio quite different from the Classical model, split up into different, independent tableaux in which the picturesque predominates. *Elisabeth* has the freshness and naivety of the legend on which it is based and, listening to it, we may regret that the composer never wrote for the stage; he would have brought to it a character of his own, namely a great feeling for drama and a respect for the resources of the human voice, both too often absent from celebrated operas that we all know. *Christus,* which I believe the composer thought of as his major work, is on an exaggerated scale and goes some little way beyond the limits of human patience; endowed with grace and charm rather than strength and power, *Christus* overall seems rather monotonous. But it falls naturally into separate sections, so it is possible to perform individual movement without doing violence to the music.

Seen in its totality, Liszt's output appears vast, but unequal. We need to make choices from among the works he has left us. Of how many great geniuses can this be said, without in any way lessening their great genius! Corneille is not diminished by *Attila*, nor Beethoven by the *Triple Concerto*, nor Mozart by the Variations on *Ah! vous dirai-je, maman*, nor Wagner by the ballet from *Rienzi*. If there are failed works in Liszt's catalogue, at least there is not a single one, however insignificant, that does not bear the mark of his style and the imprint of his personality. His main failing is that at times he lacks moderation, doesn't stop in time and loses himself in digressions and otiose, boring elaborations; he knew this and preempted such criticism by indicating cuts in his scores. It is possible to find more effective ones than those indicated by him.

Melody flows abundantly in his music—rather too much so for German taste and for those who follow that country's approach and express a real contempt for any truly *cantabile* phrase that is developed regularly;

their only delight is in polyphony, however heavy, sluggish, inextricable and dull. No matter, in certain circles, that the music is bereft of charm, elegance, ideas even and true technique. It is a taste like any other and therefore not a subject for discussion. But the melodic richness of the works we are considering is matched by an equal richness of harmony. In his bold exploration of new harmonies, Liszt surpassed by a long way anything that had been done before him. Wagner himself never reached the audacious extreme of the Prelude to the *Faust Symphony*, which is written in an unknown tonality, even though nothing offends the ear and it would be impossible to change a single note.

Liszt has the invaluable advantage of characterising a race. Schumann is the soul of Germany, Chopin is the soul of Poland; Liszt is the soul of the Magyars, made up of a brilliant mixture of pride, native elegance and savage energy. These qualities were marvellously enshrined in his supernatural playing in which one found the most varied talents, even those that seemed to be mutually exclusive, like absolute correctness and utterly unbridled imagination. Protected by his patrician pride, he never gave the impression of being *a man who plays the piano.* He looked like an apostle when he was playing *Saint François de Paule marchant sur les flots,* and you seemed to see, you really did see the spray of the wild waves flying around his pale, impassive face, with its eagle gaze and keen profile. From violent, brassy sonorities, he would pass on to dreamlike wraiths of sound; whole passages were as though spoken in parenthesis. The memory of hearing him is a consolation for no longer being young! Without going so far as to say, with M de Lenz,[2] that "anyone who had as much facility as he had would *for that very reason* be set apart", it is a fact that his prodigious technique was only one ingredient of his talent. What made him the performer of genius was not only his fingers, but the musician and poet that resided in him, his great heart and his fine soul. It was before all things the soul of his race.

His great heart can be discovered complete in the book he devoted to Chopin. Where others might have seen a rival, Liszt was moved to see only a friend and did his best to bring out the creative artist, where the public saw only the disarming virtuoso. He wrote French of a bizarre, cosmopolitan kind and took the words he needed from everywhere, including his imagination; our Symbolist writers of today have invented a good many more! For all that, the book on Chopin is highly remarkable and a marvellous aid to understanding its subject. The only judgment I would question is the rather severe one on the *Polonaise-Fantaisie,* one of Chopin's last works. Personally, I find it a very touching piece! Discouragement,

[2] Wilhelm von Lenz (1809–1883) studied with Liszt and then with Chopin.

disillusion, regret at leaving life behind, religious thoughts, hope and confidence in immortality, it expresses all that within an eloquent, fascinating form. Is that nothing?[3]

I am amazed at this judgment by Liszt, and perhaps it was inspired by the fear of seeming biased, of always distributing praise—a fear that I too sometimes suffer when speaking of Liszt. People have not been slow to scoff at what they call my weakness for his music. Even if the feelings of affection and gratitude he awakened in me were to interpose themselves like a prism between my eyes and his image, I would not regard that as something to be deeply regretted; but I was not in his debt, I had not felt his personal fascination, I had not even heard or seen him when I fell in love with the scores of his earliest symphonic poems, and when they pointed me along the road where later I would encounter the *Danse macabre*, the *Rouet d'Omphale* and other similar pieces; so I can be certain that my judgment has not been clouded by any external factor and I take total responsibility for it. Time, which puts all things in their place, will be the ultimate judge.

[3] In his book *Frédéric Chopin*, Liszt summed up the work as "pictures hardly conducive to art, like those of all extreme moments, all agonies, death rattles and contractions, where the muscles lose all elasticity and where the nerves, ceasing to be organs of the will, reduce man to being no more that the passive prey of pain! Deplorable visions that the artist is wise to admit into his domain only with extreme circumspection!"

18

WAGNER: THE RING OF THE NIBELUNG AND THE BAYREUTH PREMIERE, AUGUST 1876

*("L'anneau du Nibelung et
les représentations de Bayreuth,
Août 1876",*
Harmonie et mélodie,
Calmann-Lévy, 1885, 37–98)

It is not without a certain apprehension that I undertake this
article on Richard Wagner and his works.

The press has been discussing the composer of *Tannhäuser* for many
years now. Maybe I'm wrong, but it has seemed to me that every time
anything was written on this subject, the pen involved went through
strange contortions, jumping to right and left in a disturbing and un-
natural manner.

Shall I escape this curious contagion? Shall I, in this delicate exercise,
preserve my mental faculties unharmed? At all events I am no more at
risk of insanity than many others, and over some I have the advantage of
not belonging to any coterie.

First of all let us beware of that stand of principle which confounds the
question of nationality with that of art. Wagner loathes France, but what
has that to do with the quality of his music? Those writers who have for
the last fifteen years been covering him with the grossest insults find him
to be ungrateful; they could be right, because nothing has done more to
promote his fame than these unceasing attacks. Whatever the truth of
that, his hatred of France has become comical, since the day when he
penned that astonishing object entitled *Une Capitulation*—a disgusting
parody that no German theatre was willing to stage and that could never
harm anyone except its author. An insult to the conquered in the mouth
of the conqueror is hateful, but it ceases to be so when the insulter picks

the lyre of the *Unitéide*[1] up from the gutter. This passing resemblance to the archpoet and archprophet Gagne is indeed a worrying symptom.

But that is not the reason why they whistled at *Tannhäuser;* or why Fétis's *Biographie universelle des musiciens* treats *Lohengrin* as a monstrosity; or why a German doctor has written a book to prove that Wagner has been mad for years.

So let's forget the author of *Une Capitulation* and turn our attention to that of the *Ring der Nibelungen,* whose libretto was completely finished and published as early as 1863 and therefore has nothing to do with the difficulties that grew up between France and Germany.

Since the celebrated Tetralogy can be considered as being the most complete expression of the composer's system, its performance is the best occasion for studying this system and giving an idea of it.

Before beginning this enquiry, a few preliminary details about Wagnerians and anti-Wagnerians will perhaps not be out of place.

I studied Wagner's works at some length. I took the greatest pleasure in doing so and the performances of his works I have attended have made a profound impression on me, which not all the theories in the world will force me to forget or deny. Because of that I was accused of Wagnerism, and I myself believed for a certain time that I was a Wagnerian.

How wrong I was and how far this was from a true reckoning!

I got to know some Wagnerians and I realized that I was not one of them and never would be.

For the Wagnerian, music did not exist before the works of Wagner, or rather it existed merely in an embryonic state. Wagner elevated it to the status of art. J. S. Bach, Beethoven and at times Weber heralded the coming of the Messiah: as precursors, they have their value. As for the rest, they don't count. Neither Handel nor Haydn nor Mozart nor Mendelssohn wrote a tolerable note; the French and Italian schools never existed. When listening to the music of anyone other than Wagner, the face of the Wagnerian expresses profound disdain; but any old product by the master, even the ballet from *Rienzi,* plunges them into a state of exaltation that is hard to describe.

One day I was present at a truly curious scene between the master and a charming lady who was a very talented writer and a Wagnerian of the first water. The lady was begging the master to play for her an unheard-of, indescribable chord that she had discovered in the score of *Siegfried.*

---

[1] *L'Unitéide ou la Femme Messie* (1858) is a sprawling philosophico-poetic saga, published by Paulin Gagne at his own expense. The action takes place in 2000 when, so the author assures us, there are only 12 countries left in the world. God sends the female messiah of the title to save it.

—O maître, maître, that chord!

—But my dear girl, replied the master with a kindly smile, it's only the chord of E minor, *you can play it as well as I can.*

—O maître, maître, I beg you, THAT CHORD!!!

And the master, wearying of the struggle, went to the piano and struck the chord E G B. At which the lady fell backwards on to the sofa with a loud cry. It was too much for her to bear!

On the other hand, I saw a musician, a man of talent and experience, turn red, then blue, then purple at the third bar of the "March of the Gods" in *Das Rheingold*, which is written entirely in perfect major chords and in a slow tempo. At the sixth bar he was beginning to foam at the mouth and his eyes were starting out of his head: I found it impossible to finish the phrase he himself had asked me to play him.

What can one say about those people who feel their patriotism gravely threatened by the notion that at this moment Wagner is having his Tetralogy performed in a little town in Bavaria? It is true that patriotism comes in for harsh words and it would be better perhaps not to squander one of the finest sentiments of the human soul, but to keep it back carefully like a choice weapon and not use it except on certain occasions. But we must all judge this matter for ourselves.

Other people, who are also excellent Frenchmen and have proved it when required, would joyfully immolate themselves on the altar of their idol, if the whim overtook him to demand human sacrifices.

I regret that I cannot share these feelings, and I limit myself to respecting them. When all is said and done, I prefer those who bow to an evident superiority and do not grudge their admiration, even if it is given on trust, to those who denigrate out of prejudice and make a show of not understanding anything of works that many other people do understand, and which they themselves would be able to understand perfectly well if they were willing to take the trouble.

One of the most distinguished theorists of the last century, Bérardi, gave a very tidy definition of theatrical style: "This style," he said, "consists merely in speaking while singing and singing while speaking." That is to say, this style should in essence be sung declamation or declaimed song, which is the character of recitative and of singing suitable for the stage. This idea, which some modern writers have presented as being new and have taken further, has, from the beginning, been the sole guide of composers writing for the stage . . . and they used to apply this principle so rigorously that all operatic music was reduced to very simple recitative—which was, so to speak, no more than notated declamation.

As the ideal style and vocal music took on new developments, the theatre introduced all these improvements and enriched itself with their discoveries and, in our day, things have reached such a pitch that in all our opera houses everything is sacrificed to effect, and to the desire to bring out the singers' talents. This change in direction began with the Italians; then the Germans copied it and, after some resistance, the French did too. There is no need to point out to what extent the habits followed these days are contrary to the aims we should be setting ourselves.

Who wrote that? Choron, and no one would accuse him of Wagnerism.

Let us note in passing that France is the chosen land of opera. It has not been easy to persuade her that realistic stage action, good declamation and fine verses were nothing when compared to a graceful tune, decked out with a pedal point like an ostrich feather on a hat; it has not been easy to succeed in destroying the work begun by Rameau and completed by Gluck, in the midst of a fierce struggle; because the struggle was already going on and, essentially, it was the same struggle we are seeing now. Pergolesi was set against Rameau and Piccinni against Gluck. The enemies of these great men were using the weapon that is still being wielded by their descendants: "melody". When faced with the highest levels of reasoning or with the most self-evident beauties, they always countered with "melody". Rameau responded by writing "Dans ces doux asiles", Gluck with "Jamais dans ces beaux lieux"; but they also wrote the "Trio des Parques" and the "Songe d'Iphigénie", and there was dispute as to whether these last qualified as "melody". For a hundred and fifty years, "melody" has been the touchstone of musical criticism.

A man arrived on the scene recently who realized that modern opera, for all its grandeur and beauty, was built on a concept "contrary to the aims we should be setting for ourselves"; and that this concept was in opposition to the developments in poetry, music and drama. This man thought that a new form of opera, in which the music would not do violence to the words and would not hold up the action, in which the orchestra with all its modern developments would restore to music what it might have lost and would give up a part of its prerogatives for the benefit of the drama, that this form would be worthier of an intelligent and enlightened public than the one currently in use.

That is why this man has attracted such hatred; that is why for twenty years in his own country he has been branded a maniac, a cretin, a raving idiot and a purveyor of trash, why finally he has been heaped with all the insults usually reserved for composers who are misguided enough to take their art seriously and to think that music in the theatre should fit the words and the dramatic situation, and not confine itself to providing singers who are more or less capable with the opportunity to demonstrate their prowess.

Let's assume for a moment that this man has been wrong, that he has been pursuing a chimaera. Certainly it is a noble chimaera, which is not aimed at easy success or money, and which is concerned only with respect for music and for the public. There is nothing here to undermine the bases of society. How then could such an enterprise provoke feelings other than curiosity and interest? Why these restraints on an art which, by its nature, is the freest thing in the world? Why do writers, who spend their lives demanding freedom of the press, freedom of commerce, freedom of the rights of union and association, refuse a composer the right to compose music as he likes? What are the reasons behind this rage?

There are two. The first is the force of inertia.

Every work of art depends on a *convention*. But curiously it is a fact that when this convention is new, neither the artist nor the public realizes it; both of them think they are dealing with reality. That continues for a certain time, after which the convention loses its prestige, the mirage vanishes, and a new convention becomes necessary. The art changes its ground. This is what is generally referred to as the progress of art, which is not progress in the sense usually given to the word, but a simple change without which the life of art would become impossible.

Great artists, being gifted with powerfully active imaginations, quickly use up their tools, like tough workmen; they have soon worn through the convention they employ to express their ideas; they then create another one for their use and move their art to a different place, before the public, for its part, feels the need for it. There ensues a furious resistance. This is what happened to Rameau, and later to Gluck and Beethoven; it is what is happening now to Wagner. But this resistance on its own would not be enough to give this artistic struggle the bitterness that distinguishes it; for that it has to be combined with another emotion.

That emotion is the hatred of art.

The hatred of art—that is the secondary reason, but a powerful one nonetheless, for the persecution that determined and innovative artists must inevitably undergo.

It does not declare itself openly; it adopts any pretext and any mask. It is this hatred that latches on to the cause of "melody" and other touchstones. It is this hatred that stands out against symphonic writing in the opera house, supposedly in the interests of stage realism, and which goes into raptures about Italian operas in which the most elementary rules of stagecraft are ignored. It is this hatred that is niggardly with its applause for great artists and reserves its ovations for café-concert singers who have no voice and sing out of tune. It is this hatred that, in its attacks on art in all its manifestations, gradually eliminates picturesque costumes the world over, teaches the peasant to despise his lovely old carved oak furniture and his beautiful china, which he then sells off cheaply, and persuades

Japanese ladies to wear hats from the passage du Caire.[2] It is this hatred that leads the priest to whitewash his church and the municipal council to demolish the town's ancient tower. It is this hatred, finally, that works unceasingly for the triumph of the bourgeois, tradesman's spirit over the artistic one, for the victory of little ideas over great emotions.

Where does this hatred come from? I have no idea and do not wish to have. It is enough to recognize and oppose it.

Among the radical ideas for which Wagner has been criticised we must include the construction, duly carried out, of an auditorium with a new layout, replacing the various kinds of seating with uniform rows and concealing the orchestra from the eyes of the spectators.

It is rather interesting to find this idea in Grétry's *Essais sur la musique*. This is what the composer of *L'Epreuve villageoise* wrote in year V of the French Republic [1797]:

> I would like the theatre to be small, holding at most a thousand people; for there to be only one kind of seat throughout, no boxes, large or small. I would like the orchestra to be concealed so that neither the players nor their desk lights would be visible to the audience. The effect would be magical, and we know that, whatever the situation, the orchestra is never thought to be present.

I again find this question of the orchestra's invisibility in Choron's later *Manuel de musique*: "The presence of an orchestra playing under the eyes of the audience and being mixed up with them is, to say the least, as shocking as would be the sight of the machinery and the technicians working the scenery and lighting."

Concealing the orchestra is an excellent idea; but how? Wagner has found the way: he has put it in the space under the actors' feet. A long time ago M. Adolphe Sax produced the plan of an auditorium that differs from Grétry's and Wagner's in its seating layout, but which adopts Wagner's for the placing of the orchestra. This plan was nearly adopted at the 1867 Exhibition; unfortunately administrative and bureaucratic routine prevented it.

It was left to Wagner to realize Grétry's dream.

. . . [There follow details of the plot of *The Ring* and of the 1876 Bayreuth performance] . . .

Apart from the construction of the auditorium and the placing of the orchestra, the theatre at Bayreuth differs from others in more than one respect. The footlights are cleverly hidden and are totally invisible; more

[2] The passage du Caire, then as now, displayed clothes occupying the middle ground of fashion.

often than not they are lowered and the actors hardly ever move near them. Usually they stay upstage; as they are strongly lit from the flies and the wings, and as the auditorium is plunged in darkness, they are quite visible enough. There is no box for the prompter; the prompters stand in the wings or are concealed behind the scenery. Smoke plays a large role in the stage effects; torrents of white smoke simulate clouds; when lit in red, they turn into billows of flame.

The invisible orchestra represents an undoubted improvement that will, in time, be imported into every opera house with an increased efficiency born of experience. At Bayreuth the volume of the orchestra suffers overmuch. Many interesting details remain buried in the cavern where the orchestra grumbles, like the giant Fafner; but there is no doubt that this layout adds considerably to the stage illusion.

After the premiere of his Tetralogy, Wagner made a speech, the nub of which was: France has an art, Italy has an art; if you support my efforts, *Germany at last will have an art.* Not everyone found this notion to their taste, but his admirers have long known that his tactlessness is as great as his talent and don't take his comments seriously. If I were to report the ones he made about an important personage of the Imperial Court, France and Germany would be exchanging diplomatic notes.

He also claims he never intended to insult France; what then did he intend? That is what nobody, even he, will ever know.[3] To paint him as a bitter enemy of France is quite simply absurd; he only hates those people who don't like his music. They have every right not to, but they pass the bounds of understanding when they feel they have to represent the composer of works they loathe as a bloodthirsty monster.

Wagneromania is ridiculous but excusable; Wagnerophobia is a disease.

---

[3] On the subject of Wagner's attitude to France, and France's attitude to Wagner, it is perhaps pertinent to quote from the memoirs of the art dealer Ambroise Vollard, who implicates Saint-Saëns on a personal level:

> At [Téodor de] Wyzewa's house I met the editor of a music review [Revue SIM] who had got from one of Saint-Saëns's friends the story of the quarrel between that composer and Wagner. The scene took place at Bayreuth, in Wagner's house, to which Saint-Saëns's frenetic cult of the German composer had gained him access. One evening Mme Wagner asked the French acolyte to play something on the piano in Wahnfried's grand salon and Saint-Saëns launched out on his *Funeral March written in honour of Henri Regnault.* Upon which Wagner, whether as a friendly tease or maybe innocently, exclaimed: "Ah! a Parisian waltz!" And taking one of the ladies present by the waist, he began to dance around the piano! . . . (Ambroise Vollard, *En écoutant Cézanne, Degas, Renoir,* Grasset, Paris, 1938; 2/2005, 283–284).

Saint-Saëns's orchestral *Marche héroïque* of 1871 is indeed dedicated to the painter Henri Regnault—who was killed in the Franco-Prussian War.

19

THE WAGNERIAN ILLUSION

("L'illusion wagnérienne",
Portraits et souvenirs,
Société d'édition artistique,
1899, 206–220)

Before we begin, the reader should be warned that what follows is not a critique of Wagner's works or theories. It is something else. Now that that is understood, we may proceed.

I

We all know how prodigiously Wagnerian literature has proliferated. For 40 years, books, pamphlets, reviews and papers have been discussing the composer and his works without a let-up. Every day new analyses appear of works that have been analysed a thousand times, and new explanations of theories that have been explained a thousand times. It is still going on and there's no knowing when it might stop. It goes without saying that the questions have long since been exhausted; people chew over the same analyses, the same descriptions, the same doctrines. I have no idea whether the public is interested in all this; at least no one seems to be bothered by it.

So much is obvious. What are not so often remarked upon are the curious aberrations scattered through most of these numerous writings; and I do not mean those inherent in the inevitable incompetence of people who are not, as they say, one of us. Nothing is more difficult than talking about music: if it is a prickly business for musicians, it is almost impossible for anyone else—the strongest, subtlest minds go astray. Recently a "prince among critics"[1] and a bright spirit, tempted by the attractions of matters Wagnerian, opened his powerful wings and rose to the highest

[1] This "prince" remains to be identified.

summits. I was admiring his superb mastery, the boldness and sureness of his flight and the fine curves he was describing in the blue sky—when suddenly, like Icarus, he fell heavily to earth, declaring that opera "can venture into the domain of philosophy, but not of psychology". And as I was rubbing my eyes, I came upon this, that music is an art that does not penetrate the soul or circulate through its byways; that music's natural home among human emotions "is confined to great emotions, in their moments of extreme expansion and vigour".

I trust this illustrious and justly admired master will allow me not to agree with his views in this matter. I hope he will concede that perhaps I have some rights in claiming to understand to some small extent the secrets of an art in which, since childhood, I have lived like a fish in water. I have always regarded it as intrinsically powerless in the domain of pure ideas (and surely pure ideas are the domain of philosophy?), but all-powerful when it is a question of expressing emotion at every level and in the most delicate nuances of feeling. Penetrating the soul and circulating through its byways is its favourite role, and its triumph. Music begins where words end, it speaks the unspeakable, it forces us to discover in ourselves unknown depths; it renders impressions, "states of mind" that no word could express. And, it may be said in passing, that is why dramatic music has so often been able to thrive on mediocre texts, or worse. At certain moments the music is the Word, it is the music that expresses everything; the text becomes secondary and practically irrelevant.

With his ingenious system of *leitmotifs* (ghastly word!), Wagner has further extended the field of musical expression by letting us know the characters' most secret thoughts beneath what they are actually saying. This system had already been foreseen and attempted, but no one paid it any attention until these works appeared in which it became fully developed. Would you like a very simple example, one out of a thousand? Tristan asks: "Where are we?"—"Near to our final end", replies Isolde, to the same music that previously accompanied the words: "head doomed to die", which she had pronounced in a whisper, while looking at Tristan; and we understand immediately what the "final end" is that she means. Is that philosophy or psychology?

Unfortunately, like all delicate, complicated organs, this one is fragile; it only makes an impact on audiences if they can hear the words clearly and if they have a good musical memory.

But that is not the question in hand at the moment; I ask the reader's indulgence for this digression.

So long as commentators confine themselves to describing the beauties of Wagner's operas, one has no quarrel with them; and if they exhibit a tendency to bias and hyperbole, then there is nothing surprising in that. But as soon as they get down to details, wanting to explain to us how music drama differs from lyric drama, and that from opera, why music drama must necessarily deal in symbols and legends, how it must be structured musically, how it must exist in the orchestra but not in the voice parts, how in a music drama operatic music is inapplicable, what is the essential nature of a leitmotif, etc.; in a word, as soon as they begin to initiate us into all these fine things, then a thick fog descends on their style; strange words and incoherent phrases appear suddenly, like devils out of a box; in short, to put it politely, one no longer understands anything about the subject at all. There is no elucidation to be had from the historic but ephemeral *Revue wagnérienne*, which one day declared to its amazed readers that from now on it would be couched in language that could be understood; even the wisest, most sober writers cannot escape the contagion.

Being blessed by Nature with a substratum of naïvety that the passing years have failed to remove, I searched for a long time after understanding. It is not the light that is lacking, I used to tell myself, it is my eye that is at fault; I cursed my ingrained stupidity and made the most sincere efforts to grasp the meaning of these explanations; so much so that one day, continuing to find these same ratiocinations unintelligible, even from the pen of a critic whose style was normally as clear as rock crystal, I wrote to him asking whether, given the feebleness of my vision, he would turn up the wick of the lantern. He was gracious enough to publish my letter and to follow it up with a response—which responded to nothing, illuminated nothing and left things as they were. Since then I have abandoned the struggle and have been trying to find reasons behind this bizarre phenomenon.

There are probably several. It could be that the theories themselves, which are the basis for discussion, are not as completely clear as we should like. "When I reread my early theoretical works," Wagner said one day to Villot, "I can no longer understand them." It would not be surprising if other people had some difficulty finding their way through; and, as you know, what is not well conceived cannot be clearly expressed.

But that would not explain the vast superabundance of writings on the same subject, which we were discussing earlier; the vagueness of the theories could have no bearing on this. So let us consider further, and maybe we shall end up by finding other reasons behind these anomalies.

II

Victor Hugo's curious book on Shakespeare contains one chapter that deserves to be published on its own and to be put as a breviary into the hands of every artist and every critic. It is the chapter called "Art and Science".

In this chapter Hugo shows and establishes this fact: that between Art and Science, these twin lights of the world, there exists "a radical difference: Science is perfectible; Art is not."

He has come in for some criticism on the grounds that he had, in this book, intentionally written a disguised plea on his own behalf. If this were true—given the extent of his influence not only on literature but on Art as a whole, in having renewed poetry and the French language itself and refashioned them for his own use—then it would have been an ideal occasion for him to imply, by firmly establishing a law to say that Art progresses, that his own work was the ultimate in modern art.

He did the exact opposite.

Art, he says, is the region of equals. The beauty of every earthly thing is that it can be perfected; the beauty of Art is that it is not perfectible. Art walks in its own way: it moves like Science; but its successive creations, containing something immutable, remain.

Homer had only four winds for his storms; Virgil had 12, Dante 24, Milton 32, but their storms were none the finer. It is a waste of time saying "Nescio quid majus nascitur Iliade."[2] Art is not subject to diminution or expansion.

And Hugo finishes with these profound words: "As for these geniuses we cannot surpass, we can equal them. How? By being different."

Wagnerian exegesis stems from a quite different principle. For it, Wagner is not only a genius, he is a Messiah; until he arrived, Drama and Music were in their childhood and paved the way for his appearance; the greatest composers, Bach, Mozart, Beethoven, were merely precursors. There is nothing left to do outside the path he has traced, because it is the path, the truth and the life; he has revealed the gospel of perfect Art to the world.

This being so, there can no longer be any question of criticism, but of proselytism and apostolate; and we find a ready explanation of this perpetual renewal, this preaching that nothing seems able to stem. Christ and Buddha have been dead for a long time and commentaries are still made on their doctrines, people still write their biographies; that will last as long as their cults do.

But if, as we believe, the basic principle is wrong; if Wagner is only a great genius like Dante or Shakespeare (which should be enough), then the error of principle will inevitably have a bearing on the consequences; and it makes perfect sense in this case to find commentators launching themselves at times on incomprehensible arguments and coming to insane conclusions.

[2] (I know of nothing in creation greater than the Iliad), Propertius, *Elegies* II, 34.

"Every great artist," says Hugo, "recasts art in his own image." Therein lies the whole truth. That does not wipe out the past nor close the door to the future.

The *St Matthew Passion, Don Giovanni, Alceste, Fidelio*—these works have lost nothing of their value since the birth of *Tristan* and *The Ring*. There may be only four wind instruments in the *St Matthew Passion,* fewer than 20 in *Don Giovanni* and *Fidelio,* 30 in *Tristan* and 40 in *The Ring.* But such numbers are meaningless. So much so that Wagner himself, in *Die Meistersinger,* was able to return almost to a Beethovenian or Mozartian orchestra without a loss of integrity.[3]

III

Let us try and bring a cool head to these questions.

This idea of a perfect union between drama, music, acting and the decorative resources of the theatre is presented to us as being new, or rather copied from the Greeks, on the same lines as the noble Game of the Goose.[4] If you will forgive me for saying so, this idea has been the basis of opera right from the beginning; it may possibly have been badly executed, but the intention was there. And the execution was not always as bad as some people like to make out; when Mlle Falcon appeared in *Les Huguenots,* or Mme Malibran in *Otello,* or Mme Viardot in *Le prophète,* emotions reached their highest pitch; we were terrified by the gory proceedings of the Saint Bartholemew's massacre, we trembled for the life of Desdemona, we shared Fidès's amazement as she realized that the Prophet, surrounded by the full ceremonial splendours of the Church, was the son she had thought was dead . . . and we asked for nothing more.

Wagner has "recast art in his own image"; his formula has brought a new and powerful dimension to the intimate union of the different arts, which together constitute lyric drama. This is true. But is this formula the definitive answer, is it THE TRUTH?

No, it isn't, because it can't be, because there can't be any such thing.

Because, if there were such a thing, art would have reached perfection, which is not within the powers of the human spirit.

---

[3] This is true only up to a point. The orchestra for *Die Meistersinger* is larger than that for Beethoven's Ninth Symphony, adding a third trumpet, bass tuba, glockenspiel, harp and lute, as well as onstage organ, cowhorn, horns, and trumpets "in different keys with as many players as are needed". It is true that Wagner finds no use for Beethoven's double bassoon.

[4] The Game of the Goose is a board game, possibly of Greek or Egyptian origin, in which the moves are entirely governed by throws of the dice. No skill is involved.

Because, if there were such a thing, art in future would be no more than a heap of imitations, condemned by their very nature to mediocrity and uselessness.

By persistently incorporating new solutions to the problem, the different elements that make up the lyric drama will continue to move towards perfect equilibrium, but without ever reaching it.

In time past, audiences were happy to forget about the drama and to concentrate on the voices, and if the orchestra showed signs of being too interesting, then they complained and accused it of stealing the limelight.

Nowadays audiences listen to the orchestra and try and follow the myriad of intertwining parts and the seductive play of sonorities. At the same time they forget to listen to what the actors are saying and lose track of the plot.

The new system annihilates the art of singing almost completely, and is proud of the fact. So it is that the instrument par excellence, the only instrument that is truly *alive,* will never again be given the task of producing melodic phrases; it is the others, the instruments made by human hands, pale, clumsy imitations of the human voice, which will sing in its place. Surely there is something wrong here?

To go further. The new art, by reason of its extreme complexity, induces in the performer, and even in the spectator, extreme exhaustion and efforts that are at times superhuman. Through the peculiar ecstasy that comes from a hitherto unknown development of harmonic resources and instrumental combinations, it engenders extremes of nervous excitability and rapture that lie beyond the aims that art should set for itself. It overloads the brain, and threatens to unbalance it. I am not making a criticism: I am merely stating facts. One can be drowned in the ocean and killed by lightning: that does not make the sea or the storm any the less sublime.

To go further still. It is contrary to common sense to put the drama into the orchestra, when its place is on the stage. I may say that, in this case, I am entirely unconcerned. Genius has its reasons that reason does not know.[5]

All this is enough, I think, to show that this art has its faults, like everything in this world; that it is not the perfect art, the definitive art, after which it remains only to pull up the ladder.

The ladder is still there. As Hugo says, the first rung is still empty.

---

[5] An adaptation of the famous aphorism from Pascal's *Pensées:* "Le coeur a ses raisons que la raison ne connaît point."

IV

Hugo paints a picture of geniuses, and it is strange to see how naturally it applies to Wagner; at times you would say he has outlined his portrait. For example:

> . . . These men ascend the mountain, climb into the mist, disappear, reappear. We catch sight of them, gaze at them . . . The route is hard going. The escarpment looms fiercely . . . We have to make our own way, hack at the ice before walking on it, make steps with loathing in our hearts . . .
>
> These geniuses are outrageous . . .
>
> Not to offer anything people can get hold of is a negative kind of perfection. It is a fine thing to be attackable . . .
>
> Great minds are importunate . . . there is truth in the criticisms made of them . . .
>
> Strength, grandeur and brilliance are, from a certain point of view, offensive . . . They outpace your intelligence, they pain your imagination, they question and disturb your conscience, they tie your entrails into knots, they break your heart, they seduce your soul . . .

It is then possible to be great like Homer, like Aeschylus, like Shakespeare, like Dante. A great genius, but not a Messiah. The age of gods is past.

There would be no need even to mention this, were it not that there are, beneath this illusion, both traps and dangers.

A danger of imitation first of all. Every great artist introduces new procedures, and these procedures enter the public domain: everyone has the right, the duty indeed to study them and profit from them as from a source of nourishment. But that is as far as imitation should go. If you are content to follow the model step by step, not daring to depart from it, then you condemn yourself to impotence; the only works you produce will be artificial, and as lifeless as they are negligible.

Another danger is to imagine that art has made a clean sweep and entered on a wholly new career that has nothing to do with the past. It is rather like taking it into one's head to make a tree grow by cutting off its roots.

No one can engage in serious study without respecting and cultivating tradition.

> Tradition is a force, a light, a lesson. It is the depository of the most profound capabilities of a race. It assures the intellectual stability of generations through time. It distinguishes civilisation from barbarism.
>
> But its services are no longer required and its teachings are held in low esteem. People vilify and neglect the masters and, curiously, at the

same time they launch into imitations of foreigners. But in imitating them they lose their innate qualities and succeed only in acquiring their faults. They have ceased to be clear like true Frenchmen in their attempts at being profound like Norwegians or sentimental like Russians. Their only achievement has been to become obscure and tedious and, on the pretext of bringing more life and beauty into our literature, they have written books that lack not only both those qualities, but also the ancient national traditions of movement, order and common sense.

Those are the words of an eminent gentleman, M Charles Richet,[6] who probably did not have the questions we are addressing at all in mind when he wrote an article on "anarchy in literature." There is another waiting to be written on anarchy in music. Some unfortunate young persons actually believe nowadays that the rules should be thrown on to the rubbish heap and that you should invent your own rules according to your individual temperament. They go back to music's primitive condition, to polyphony in two parts. This leads some of them to write things that are without form, like the sounds children produce when they put their little paws unthinkingly on the keyboard . . .

This was not Wagner's method: he sent his roots deep down into the earth of past learning, into the nourishing soil of J. S. Bach; and when, later, he hammered out rules for his own use, he had earned the right to do so.

Another danger is the one encountered by those less perceptive Wagnerian critics—they do exist—who are not interested in any other music than Wagner's. They are unaware of everything else and, having no standards of comparison, embark on bizarre appraisals, going into ecstasies over minutiae and expressing wonder at the most common or garden features. It was along these lines that a supposedly serious writer one day informed a conductor, to whom he was giving the benefit of his copious advice, that "in the music of Wagner, *crescendo* and *diminuendo* mean making the sound louder and softer." It was like saying, "in the works of Molière, a full stop after a word tells the reader that the sentence has come to an end."

Quite an entertaining anthology could be compiled of the errors, the nonsense and silly sayings of all kinds that multiply themselves in Wagnerian criticism, under the eye of the innocent public. I leave this task to those who have more time on their hands.

---

[6] Richet (1835–1913) was a physiologist who won the Nobel Prize for medicine in 1913.

20

CHARLES GOUNOD

(Portraits et souvenirs,
Société d'édition artistique,
1899, 35–97)

There are two sides to Gounod's artistic personality: the Christian side and the pagan side, the seminary pupil and the Prix de Rome student, the apostle and the minstrel. Sometimes the two operate together, as in *Faust*, giving the work a sharply defined character; whereas in *Polyeucte* they are juxtaposed and cancel each other out by their propinquity and by the balancing claims of their charm and brilliance. The choruses in *Ulysse*, the first version of *Sapho*, and *Philémon et Baucis* show the pagan unadorned, the masses and oratorios the Christian mystic.[1]

The time has perhaps not yet come to value at his true worth the great artist who lends France distinction, and in whom one day she will take a pride. The indispensable workings of Time have not yet put this composer in his rightful place, deeply original as he was in his apparent simplicity—a Classical composer for years accused of being no more than a reflection of the old masters, whereas in fact he in no way resembles his models. His manner of writing is so different and his point of departure so far removed that we may be tempted to place him to some extent outside the tradition to which, by instinct, he was so strongly attached. While he was at the opposite extreme from the lightly coloured Italian school led by Auber, neither could he be considered as continuing the Italo-German school founded by Haydn, nor as a direct descendant of Mozart, his favourite among the masters; his similarities with Mozart are purely external and do not reach the essence of his style.

[1] The five-act opera *Polyeucte* was premiered at the Opéra on 7 October 1878; the incidental music to François Ponsard's five-act tragedy *Ulysse* was published in 1852; *Sapho* was premiered at the Opéra on 16 April 1851, and *Philémon et Baucis* at the Théâtre Lyrique on 18 February 1860.

Ultimately he had no other model except himself. Given that his technique combined archaisms and novelties, it was bound to upset the critics, and it is no surprise that from the very first he roused very different opinions, some people accusing him of living off borrowings from the past, others of writing incomprehensible music that only a handful of friends pretended to understand. Those days are long past, but the battle continues on another front; and while the general public, without looking for reasons why it feels as it does, abandons itself wholeheartedly to the charm of *Faust* and *Roméo*, the "enlightened amateurs" wonder what they ought to think of them. How would they know? Accustomed as they are to finding their opinions already made for them in their regular newspaper, they have always been disorientated. Thirty years ago attacks on Gounod accused him of Germanism, comparing him unfavourably with the triumphant, pre-eminent Italian school; now that the critics' favour has moved over to the German school, they try and make out that Gounod belonged to the Italian. Unmoved amid these vicissitudes, he has never been anything but a French artist, as French as you can find.

I

Young composers today will have difficulty imagining the state of music in France when Gounod appeared on the scene. The fashionable world was enraptured by Italian music; we could still feel the undulations of the mighty waves upon which the boat carrying Rossini, Donizetti, Bellini and the wonderful singers who interpreted and collaborated in their music had invaded Europe. Verdi's sun, still wreathed in the morning mist, was rising above the horizon. For the solid middle class citizen, the heart of the general public, nothing existed beyond French opera and opéra-comique, which included works written for France by distinguished foreigners.

Both sides subscribed to the cult, the idolatry of *melody*, or rather they used this term to describe the motif that implants itself effortlessly in the memory, that is easy to grasp immediately. A wonderful paragraph like the one that does duty for a melody in Beethoven's Fourth Symphony was not "melody", and it was possible to define Beethoven as "musical algebra" without incurring ridicule. Such opinions were still current twenty years ago. Those with a taste for curiosities might like to take the trouble of casting an eye over the article that gives its name to my book *Harmonie et Mélodie*, where they will find a fairly sharp critique aimed, not at melody itself, but at the exaggerated importance then being attributed to it [see chapter 3]. There would be no point writing such an article today, since melody is now regarded as one of those things it is impolite to mention.

Forty years ago, people spoke of *Robert le Diable* and *Les Huguenots* with a kind of sacred awe, and with unction and devotion of *Guillaume Tell;* Hérold and Boieldieu were already classics, and Auber and Adolphe Adam were rivals for the leadership of the French School. For Auber success reached the point of infatuation, and it was forbidden to point out the faults that were bound to be scattered through an output as large and hastily written as his. We know how this enthusiasm gave way to unjust neglect. This is not the place to deal with such a topic; but one may pause briefly to express regret that it was not possible to take up a halfway position between these two exaggerations. In France we hardly dare mention *La Dame blanche* or *Le Domino noir,* but these same works find an honourable place elsewhere, even in Germany, and foreigners appreciate in them a local atmosphere that we refuse to recognise. Nothing will do but Great Art! That's all very well, but since we all have to laugh occasionally, the gap left by opéra-comique has been filled by operetta. I would not wish to criticise a genre which, after all, is a genre, some specimens of which have provided a new character that is not without value, but we have to admit that the creation of this genre has not been evidence of progress, and that to write and perform works such as those that are now despised required a quite different order of talent from the frivolous works of today. The performers of old included Roger, Bussine, Hermann-Léon, Jourdan, Courderc, Faure, Mmes Damoreau, Carvalho, Ugalde, Caroline Duprez, Faure-Lefebvre[2] and many others, past masters of singing, acting and dialogue. "Those were the good old days," as people sometimes say with less justification.

Apart from the two large groups of listeners mentioned above, there was a small nucleus of musicians and amateurs who were attracted by music that was loved and cultivated for its own sake, and who secretly adored Haydn, Mozart and Beethoven, with the occasional diversion towards Bach and Handel, and those strange attempts by the prince de Moskowa[3] to revive the music of the 16th century. The Société des Con-

[2] Romain Bussine [1830–1899] was a poet and vocal teacher at the Conservatoire who, with Saint-Saëns and Duparc, founded the Société nationale de musique in 1871. In 1886 he and Saint-Saëns resigned over d'Indy's insistence on including foreign works in the society's concerts. Léonard Hermann-Léon (1814–1858) was a bass who created the role of the High Priest in Spontini's *La Vestale* in 1807. Details of Jourdan have not been traced. Joseph Courderc (1810–1875) was a house tenor for the Opéra-Comique, where he created the roles of Daniel in Adam's *Le chalet* in 1834 and Horace in Auber's *Le domino noir* in 1837. Laure Cinthie-Damoreau (1801–1863) studied at the Conservatoire and created the role of Pamyra in Rossini's *Le siège de Corinthe* in 1826, La Comtesse in *Le Comte Ory* in 1828 and Mathilde in *Guillaume Tell* in 1829. She taught at the Conservatoire and retired from the stage in 1843.

[3] Joseph Napoléon Ney, second Prince de la Moskowa (1803–1857) was the eldest son of Marshal Ney and a politician and composer. In 1843 he founded the *Société de musique vocale, religieuse et classique,* which performed renaissance and 17th-century music and pub-

certs du Conservatoire[4] and other musical societies were supported only by a few initiates, and outside these institutions it was fruitless to try and place a symphony, a trio or a quartet; audiences were completely bewildered by them. This was undoubtedly an annoying business but, from some points of view, possibly with more advantages than drawbacks. By following the natural leaning that took them towards the theatre and French works, the public was supporting the national school. Every year the Opéra and the Opéra-Comique devoured a quantity of new works; people went to first nights as assiduously as they have avoided them ever since, and every opera, unless it was a complete flop, was assured of a success born of curiosity. Every young composer who was gifted and knew his trade could expect to have an honourable career. Today the public knows everything and understands everything, and will open its noble ears only for masterpieces: and as masterpieces are few and far between and the odds are always long against a new work being a masterpiece, the public is no longer interested in new works; the French school, deprived of this indispensable nourishment, is dying of starvation. Some time ago England created the same situation in her theatres, and it would have been sensible not to imitate her. If we continue along this road, the French musical scene will soon be nothing but a museum where, after fighting on every front to win their place in the sun, works come to enjoy in peace the repose of immortality.

When (happily for art) Charles Gounod abandoned his attempt to lead a life in the Church and opted finally for a career in music, such a career was already considered to be hard to initiate. The only major concerts of serious music were those of the Conservatoire, which were closed to new composers. The only avenue open was the theatre, and here you could hope, sooner or later, to find a place: so Gounod set his sights on the theatre, and made his first approaches to the Opéra-Comique. It was at that crucial juncture that I had the good fortune to meet the young composer at the house of one of my relatives, Hoffmann the homoeopathic doctor; fashionable parties took place in his salon to which Gounod was attracted by a bevy of beautiful women, who were the doctor's patients and the composer's passionate admirers. I was then ten or twelve and he was perhaps twenty-five, and through my great musical facility and my naïvety and enthusiasm I attracted his sympathy.

In collaboration with a brother-in-law of the mistress of the house he was writing an opéra-comique and at these intimate parties he would sing

---

lished works by composers from Josquin to Handel. He also supported the creation of the Ecole Niedermeyer.

[4] This was founded in 1828 and disbanded only in 1967, on the formation of the Orchestre de Paris.

us bits of it; and already, in these hesitant pages, his budding personality declared itself—the penchant for purity, for elegance of style and truth of expression, those rare qualities that he later developed to such a high degree. Shortly afterwards he was noticed by Mme Viardot, who first persuaded Emile Augier to let him have the libretto of *Sapho* and then arranged for the doors of the Opéra to be opened for him.[5] From that moment, even if his talent did not yet bear all its fruit, we could say that it was shaped and had only to follow its evolution. It is hard to make out what he took from the instruction of his teachers, Reicha and Lesueur.[6] Reicha no doubt taught him the rudiments of his art, as he did to all his pupils, but his cold and antipoetical nature cannot have been greatly in sympathy with that of such a student. He would have found Le Sueur's mysticism more to his taste, but for every patch of gold in Le Sueur's music, how much dross and rubbish!

A more powerful influence was no doubt exerted by his time in the seminary and by his attendance as Mme Viardot's salon, not to forget the wonderful gift of the quiet but exquisite voice that Nature had given him.

In the seminary he learnt the art of speaking, of the fine, clear, polished diction required by the pulpit. No doubt it was there, while he was studying the sacred texts, that he conceived the idea of interpreting them in music, and from there sprang the source of the beautiful flood of religious music that flowed from his pen all through his life, despite the seductions of the theatre. Was it from Le Sueur or was it rather from the seminary that he got his taste for the grandiloquence and pomposity we so often find in his music? It is tempting to regard this as a fault. Fault or virtue, it is rare in music: it appears nowhere in the music of Haydn and Mozart, and very infrequently in that of Bach or Beethoven; among the moderns, we find it in Verdi and Liszt but, of all known composers, who was the most grandiloquent and pompous? Handel—certainly not a composer anyone would accuse of lacking power or true grandeur.

With Mme Viardot, we enter a different world. This famous woman was not only a great singer, but a great artist and a living encyclopaedia. She had been a friend of Schumann, Chopin, Liszt, Rossini, George Sand, Ary Scheffer[7] and Eugène Delacroix, she knew everything in literature and art, she had a deep understanding of music, kept up with all the most

[5] *Sapho* was premiered at the Opéra on 16 April 1851.

[6] Antoine Reicha (1770–1836), was a Czech composer, teacher, and theorist. He was professor of counterpoint and fugue at the Conservatoire from 1818 and his pupils also included Liszt, Berlioz, and, briefly, Franck. Jean-François Le Sueur (1760–1837) taught composition at the same establishment and many of his pupils, including Berlioz and Gounod, were successful in the Prix de Rome competition.

[7] Scheffer (1795–1858) was a Dutch painter who studied mainly in France. Puvis de Chavannes was one of his pupils.

varied trends and was at the forefront of artistic endeavour; she was a first-class pianist and in her salon used to play Beethoven and Mozart, and Reber[8] whom she greatly admired. It is not hard to imagine how such surroundings would have encouraged the flowering of an emerging talent. Gounod's natural affinity with song developed yet further: and the human voice would always be the primordial element, the sacred temple of his musical city.

II

If it were true, as M Camille Bellaigue[9] claims, that expressiveness is music's primary virtue, then Gounod's would be the finest in the world. The search for expressiveness was always his objective: that is why there are so few notes in his music, which is free of any parasitical arabesques and of any ornament to tickle the ear; every note of it sings. For the same reason, instrumental music, *pure music*, was not at all his forte; after two symphonies, the second of which was quite a brilliant success, he abandoned this path, thinking it was not for him. At the end of his career his attempts at writing string quartets did not satisfy him either.

One day, back in Paris from spending the winter elsewhere, I went to see him. I found him, as usual, at work in his magnificent studio, whose character was made more imposing by an organ on which, at his request, I had given the inaugural recital some years earlier. I asked him what he had written during my absence.

"I've written some string quartets," he replied. "They're in there."

He pointed to a cabinet placed within his reach.

"I should be very interested to know what they're like," I said.

"I'll tell you. They're bad, and I'm not going to show them to you."

I cannot convey the air of bantering good humour with which he spoke those words. Nobody has ever seen those quartets: they have disappeared, like the ones performed the previous year to which I've already referred.

As to the perpetual search for expressiveness that gripped him, he had found it in Mozart—he could even be said to have discovered it there. Mozart's music is so intrinsically interesting that it had become customary to admire it for its form and charm, without looking any further. Gounod recognised in it the intimate union of word and note, the

---

[8] Henri Reber (1807–1880), like Berlioz and Gounod, was a pupil of Reicha and Le Sueur. He was a composer and took over Halévy's composition post at the Conservatoire in 1862, the year in which he published his popular *Traité d'harmonie*.

[9] Bellaigue (1858–1930) won a first prize in piano at the Conservatoire in 1878 and became a musicologist.

absolute accord of the smallest stylistic details with the most delicate nuances of feeling. Hearing him sing *Don Giovanni, The Marriage of Figaro* or *The Magic Flute* was a revelation.

In those days it was claimed openly that Mozart's music was not "theatrical", even though every passage in his operas is modelled on the plot. On the other hand, "theatricality" was declared to be the property of those works written according to the Rossini system, in which the music develops in complete freedom, making hay of the dramatic situation, and even of the words and their accentuation; Rossini himself never took things as far. To stand out against such nonsense was to risk being taken for a dangerous subversive; the writer of these lines knows whereof he speaks, having been sent packing by Roqueplan, then director of the Opéra-Comique, for praising *The Marriage of Figaro* in his presence.

For the same reason, Gounod already had his enemies before he had written anything for the theatre: sides were taken for or against *Sapho* even before it was finished. What a premiere that was! The audience was transported by this music and, despite itself, captivated by its charm; it recovered during the intervals. The first act finale electrified the house and was wildly encored; when the enthusiasm had died down, the experts were beginning to say with a knowing air: "That's not a finale; there's no stretto!" They were forgetting that the superb finale to Act III of *Guillaume Tell* doesn't have one either. To tell the truth, there was one originally, but it was removed during rehearsals, just as a stretto in the first act of *Sapho* would have been if the composer had made any such pointless addition to the passage that forms its stunning conclusion.

The press reaction was tumultuous. It is not their custom to give instant admittance to things that depart from the common run; nevertheless, leading critics like Berlioz and Adolphe Adam treated the work according to its merits. Maybe its initial semi-success would have become a complete success if the opera had been able to continue its run. But Mme Viardot had reached the end of her contract and could only sing the title role four times. Another singer, with a fine voice and no small talent, took over the role and cut the sad figure that talent makes beside genius; there were two more performances, and then this work, which marks a milestone in the history of French opera, was left abandoned.

Much later it was revived in two acts—originally it had three. It was a mutilation. Later still, at the request of Vaucorbeil,[10] the composer and librettists stretched it out over four acts and added a ballet, and that was worse still. How could a man of the theatre like Augier have agreed to sab-

---

[10] Auguste-Emmanuel Vaucorbeil (1821–1884) was director of the Opéra from 1879 to 1884. In 1880 he supervised the French premiere of *Aida* and in the following year installed in the house a new-fangled contraption called the "telephone".

otage his work like that? With its simple plot, fitting its subject, the work required three acts, neither more nor less, and there was nothing for elegant legs to add. The success of this final revival of the remains of the initial *Sapho* gave a good idea of how popular it would have been if it had reappeared in all its original freshness and brilliance.

My close ties with Gounod date from his choruses for *Ulysse*. Ponsard,[11] like Augier, was a regular in Mme Viardot's salon, to which literary men with no interest in music were drawn by her husband, himself a distinguished man of letters well known for a much admired translation of *Don Quixote* and for writings about art that were contentious but much discussed. Ponsard had the idea of taking passages from the *Odyssey* to make a tragedy with choruses in the ancient manner, and asked Gounod to collaborate with him. The pagan nourished on classical poetry, a side of Gounod that was always quick to be incited to action, here found new food for inspiration. What more seductive subject is there in the whole of ancient literature than the *Odyssey?* And who at that time better than Ponsard for giving it a new form? Anyone interested can find a very detailed study of this *Ulysse,* in which virtues and defects tumble over each other in such a curious fashion, in the memoirs of Alexandre Dumas *père*. The great writer reckons that the best lines are precisely the ones meant for musical setting; the choruses of Nymphs, in particular, are noteworthy, and the delightful melodic lines that go with these gentle verses underline their charm. Altogether it is like nothing that had ever been written before; the young composer had discovered there a completely new little world, like a Vale of Tempé adorned with flowers, with bees buzzing and streams rippling—a place where mortal foot had never trod.

Gounod played the piano quite pleasantly, but he was no virtuoso and had some difficulty performing his scores. At his request I used to go, almost every day, and spend a little time with him, and with freshly written pages in front of us we would together decipher for better or worse— usually better—fragments of the work as it took shape. Gounod would be full of the piece and would explain his intentions to me and set out his ideas and enthusiasms. His great preoccupation was to find beautiful orchestral colours; and far from taking ready-made solutions from earlier composers, he tried to find the tonalities for his brushes directly, by studying timbres and by combining sounds in new ways. "Sonority," he used to say to me, "is still unexplored." He was right: since that time there has been a magical flowering in the modern orchestra. For his choruses of nymphs he dreamt of watery effects, and used the glass harmonica and a muted triangle, this latter obtained by covering the striker with leather.

[11] François Ponsard (1814–1867) was a dramatist of limited abilities; the Goncourts described his tragedies as resembling "a cameo antique . . . modern!"

But professional musicians know that ultimately it is above all on the music itself and on the cunning use of harmony that the character of a sonority depends. For example it is a double pedal of the third and the fifth, later developed into a triple pedal by the addition of the tonic (an invention of real genius) that lends the first chorus of *Ulysse* such charm and freshness. It is impossible unfortunately to give an idea of this in words; I ask the reader's pardon for these technical terms which only musicians will understand.

At the Théâtre-Français expectations for the work were high. A full orchestra of the best players, an excellent chorus, wonderful scenery, nothing was spared. The splendid curtain showing Raphael's Parnassus, which can still be seen at the Comédie, was painted for the occasion. In my passionate desire that my friend's music should have the success it deserved, I willed the play to be a masterpiece and refused to believe it would not be a triumph. Alas! The first performance, to which I took a medical student who was mad about music, that first performance was terrible. The audience was mostly made up of purely literary people who cared little about music and they greeted the choruses coldly; the play was boring and the rough realism of some verses shocked them. There was whispering and laughter. In the last act, one half-line ("Servons-nous de la table": "Let's use the table") provoked shouting, and I was sad to see my student friend, whom I had managed to keep under control until then, howling with merriment.

This play, bizarre but not devoid of interest, might have deserved a more patient audience. The performance was outstanding: even if Delaunay, that impeccable actor, was more used to the role of a lover and seemed ill at ease in the dull role of Telemachus, Geffroy on the other hand found ample material for showing his fine abilities in that of Ulysses. Mme Nathalie was very beautiful as Minerva coming down from her cloud in the prologue, and Mme Judith had all the discreet grace and nobility required by the role of Penelope.

After the twin failures of *Sapho* and *Ulysse* Gounod's future could have seemed in doubt in the eyes of the general public, but not for the elite who know how to set artists in their proper place: he was marked with the sign of the chosen ones.

I remember one day, when I'd been struck by the novelty of the ideas and techniques that stand out in these two works, I said to him without thinking (he was very tolerant with me) that he would never be able to do better. "Maybe", he replied, in a curious tone of voice, and his eyes seemed to be fixed on something profound and as yet unrevealed in the distance. Those eyes were already looking upon *Faust* . . .

And here I should like to pause for a moment to express my gratitude to this master who, already in full possession of his talent, was modest enough to make the schoolboy that I still was the confidant of his innermost artistic thoughts and to fill out my ignorance with his knowledge. He discussed things with me as though with an equal; which is how I became, if not his pupil, then at least his disciple, and was able to develop in his shadow, or rather by his light.

III

Among the young composer's friends there was anxiety. He needed to recoup his losses at the Opéra and for that he had to find a good libretto, a rare commodity at the best of times. Someone suggested the *Nonne sanglante* that Germain Delavigne (the brother of the celebrated Casimir) had based on an English novel,[12] I think, with the help of Scribe. This was not a happy offering; both Meyerbeer and Halévy had been initially attracted to it before withdrawing from any such collaboration; Berlioz composed two acts and then abandoned it.[13]

The fact is that the subject, for all its apparent interest, was deceptive in that it had no *dénouement*. Two lovers are frustrated in their plans by cruel parents and plan to elope. That very night is the one on which, each year, according to legend the Bleeding Nun (a young girl who committed suicide for love twenty years before and whose shroud is covered with a long smear of clotted blood) is due to appear at midnight. The lovers don't believe in the legend: no one has ever seen the nun because they always run away when they sense her coming; all they know of her is the light of her sepulchral lamp seen from afar in the galleries of the palace. The plan is for the eloping girl to disguise herself as this ghost and walk out carrying a lamp; no one will dare approach her and escape will be easy. Her lover arrives at the rendezvous first; at midnight the lamp shines out through the arches, and it is the Bleeding Nun herself who is mistaken by the young man for his fiancée and who is the recipient of his loving words and his engagement ring.

It is a frightening situation and on stage had a nightmarish impact. But what can you do with such characters from then on? The Nun took the young man to a sort of ghosts' reunion and made him swear to marry her; then she turned into a harridan and her determination to make him honour the promise extracted from him on that fatal night, her appetite for marriage having survived twenty years underground, began to seem comical.

---

[12] Matthew Gregory Lewis's *The Monk* of 1795

[13] A reconstituted version by Hugh Macdonald was performed at Montpellier in the summer of 2007.

According to the custom of the time, the libretto was decorated with verses of extreme mediocrity, and a literate person like Gounod, an innovator, or rather a renovator, dreaming, as in old French opera and in Gluck, of the intimate union of note and word, was much to be pitied in having to engage with such twaddle. Scribe has been widely criticised for producing such stuff, and quite unfairly: he *thought he was obliged* to do so. It was the general belief of the time that good poetry hindered music, and that for a composer not to have his inspiration restricted he needed common or garden words that could then be freely rearranged (today one might say "kicked around"). Audiences prided themselves on not listening to the words, an attitude that was duly noted.

What could Gounod possibly make of such a clumsy, unstylish libretto other than something unequal and incomplete? His friends even so looked forward to a great success and curiosity generally reached a high pitch. The word was that, if the *Nonne sanglante* didn't succeed, Gounod was done for. The opera had twelve performances[14] and Gounod survived, but his star suffered an eclipse. People were quick to declare that he was "empty" and that nothing of value would come from his pen ever again. Without going so far as to accept this pessimistic prognosis, I was unpleasantly surprised by certain weaknesses in this disconcerting opera, which nonetheless contained passages of real beauty. It was at this same period that Gounod tried his hand at an *Ivan le Terrible* that never came to anything! The music he wrote for this was used later in other works; for instance, the well-known march from *La reine de Saba* was originally intended for the procession of a Czarina, accompanied by conspirators muttering in the shadows. I can still hear Gounod singing "Death! Death! Death to the faithless Czarina—And let us throw her carcass to the winds!" There's no need to hide your face at this. Gluck did similar things when he scattered extracts from *Elena e Paride* over subsequent operas!

The real Gounod reappeared four years later, in 1858, with *Le médecin malgré lui.* Some time previously he had been commissioned to adapt Lully's music for *Le bourgeois gentilhomme* for a modern orchestra on the occasion of a single performance at the Opéra, and it is likely that this gave him the idea of setting Molière. He found first-class collaborators in MM Jules Barbier and Michel Carré.[15] These two men, for all that they are looked down on by today's modernists, had nevertheless been responsible for a minor revolution. After achieving some literary success, they had devoted themselves to writing librettos and demonstrated a concern for

[14] The premiere was on 18 October 1854.

[15] Jules-Paul Barbier (1825–1901) was a prolific playwright and, often with Michel Carré (1822–1872), a librettist. Together they provided texts for *Faust*, *Philémon et Baucis*, Meyerbeer's *Le pardon de Ploërmel* and Thomas's *Mignon*, among many others.

language and even a certain lyricism not usually found in this discredited genre. Their adaptation of *Le médecin malgré lui* is very tastefully done and the music is a masterpiece. What a joy it was for me to find my dear master not only in full possession of all the qualities that had originally endeared him to me, but now as a more important figure still through his incorporation of Mozart's way of orchestrating, both picturesque and sober at the same time, in which a style of old-fashioned appearance is coloured with discreetly modern sonorities, to the delight of both ear and spirit!

Molière's birthday, 15 January, was chosen for the date of the premiere. After the final scene, the backdrop was lifted and Mme Carvalho, dressed as a Muse, sang verses by Molière set to the final paragraph of Act I of *Sapho*, transposed up a semitone; she then placed a garland on the poet's bust, surrounded by the whole troupe of the Théâtre-Lyrique. The evening was a triumph: there was applause, there was laughter; Gounod had, through tact and wit, made the most daring musical pleasantries acceptable. But this success did not last, and the various revivals of this delightful work have had no more luck; the work has never "made money", as they say so elegantly nowadays. The reason is a bizarre one: it is Molière's dialogue that frightens audiences off. This same audience, though, is not frightened off by it at the Comédie-Française, and rocks with laughter at operettas whose story and dialogue are far spicier. The Man in the Street is sometimes very hard to understand!

We shall come to *Faust* shortly. But before taking a look at this famous score, it is as well to point out that we should be gaining a very incomplete idea of Gounod's genius if we confined ourselves to studying his dramatic works. His labours in the theatre have never prevented him from writing for the Church. There too he was a bold innovator, bringing to religious music not only his interesting discoveries in the way of orchestral sound, but also his preoccupation with truth of declamation and propriety of expression, applied in unusual fashion to Latin texts. Together with this went a scrupulous regard for vocal effect and a quite new atmosphere that joined divine with earthly love, under the safeguard of a breadth and purity of style.

The *Messe de Sainte-Cécile* was the composer's masterpiece in the religious genre, in the springtime of his talent; it was much talked about simply because of the impact it made—a huge impact under the vaulting of Saint-Eustache. That was also the time when he wrote the famous *Prélude de Bach;* these few bars, to which I doubt the composer attached much importance when he wrote them, did more for his reputation than everything he'd written before it. It was the fashion for ladies to faint during the second crescendo!

The first time I heard this little piece it bore but slight resemblance to what it has since become under the pernicious influence of success.

Seghers, with his powerful sound and dignified simplicity, was playing the violin, Gounod the piano, and a six-part choir singing the Latin words mysteriously intoned the underlying harmonies in the next room. Then the choir disappeared and was replaced by a harmonium; violinists treated the ecstatic phrases with those all-too-familiar procedures that turn ecstasy into hysteria; then the instrumental line became a vocal one, and the result was an *Ave Maria* that was, I'm sorry to say, more convulsed still; then the whole thing became louder and louder, the number of performers increased, and an orchestra was added, not forgetting a bass drum and cymbals. The sacred frog (why not? the Chinese have a divine tortoise) swelled and swelled without bursting, grew fatter than an ox, and audiences greeted this monster with delirium. But at least the "monster" had the crucial effect of smashing for ever the invisible barrier between the composer and the general public, who until that point had been hesitant and mistrustful.

IV

And so to *Faust*, the high point in the composer's output. The work is too well known to need describing; the only points of interest might be some souvenirs of its first performances and of its brilliant career.

Gounod's talent was becoming increasingly evident. A battle could be felt approaching; the supporters of Italian music, who were very powerful, were ready to use every means at their disposal to undermine this decisive manifestation on the part of a great composer who was threatening to put them in the shade. Goethe, and Berlioz (whose *Faust*, despite its contentiousness, already had a huge following among a certain portion of the public) loomed in the shadows like two formidable sphinxes. Among Gounod's friends as among his enemies, there was deep anxiety.

The role of Marguerite was written for Mme Ugalde, who was then one of the Théâtre-Lyrique company. It is said she preferred to sing Victor Massé's *La fée Carabosse.*[16] On the contrary, I'm fairly certain that, after rehearsing *Faust*, she was very reluctant to have to pass the role of Marguerite over to Mme Carvalho for whom the title role of La fée Carabosse had been written, and take up the latter which Mme Carvalho had sung up until then. Gounod does not mention anything about this in his *Mémoires* and we shall never know why the role of Marguerite was removed

---

[16] Victor Massé (1822–1894) won the Prix de Rome in 1844 and taught at the Paris Conservatoire from 1866 to 1880. His best-known work is the operetta *Les noces de Jeannette*. *La fée Carabosse* was premiered at the Théâtre Lyrique on 28 February, three weeks before *Faust* on 19 March.

from Mme Ugalde, who had always dreamt of premiering a dramatic role. Her voice had changed; a light soprano role no longer suited her and the brilliant creator of *Galathée* had no success in *La fée Carabosse*, which was a miserable flop. Perhaps with Mme Carvalho in the title role, the wretched *Fée* might have had better luck. Would *Faust* have been a success with Mme Ugalde? There's no way of telling, but I know, what is to the point, that in the church scene, the final trio, she was truly remarkable, and that she remained inconsolable at having missed this opportunity to present herself to the Parisian public in a new guise.

For her part, in singing *Faust* Mme Carvalho effortlessly joined the ranks of great lovers; the canary turned its back on ready-made success to engage in a perilous adventure. We know how her talent, which seemed to have given everything it was capable of, developed still further, to reach its apogee in *Faust* and *Roméo*.

The role of Faust was intended for the tenor Guardi,[17] a splendid fellow whose exceptional voice combined the qualities of a tenor and a baritone, which explains the role's peculiar tessitura and the weight it sometimes places on low notes (as at "O mort! Quand viendras-tu m'abriter sous ton aile?"—"O death! When wilt thou shelter me under thy wing?"). Unfortunately this fine voice was not reliable. At the dress rehearsal, Guardi demonstrated wonderful stage presence and a brilliant tone all through the first act, but then, in the middle of the performance, he lost his voice and had to retire from the production.

Certain details of the staging hadn't been properly thought through. In the Walpurgis Night scene, in which all the male chorus members were turned into witches, dressed in smocks and wielding broomsticks, they carried on like so many escaping hens, kicking up clouds of dust; this ballet sequence was not a success.

More work was required and they had to find a tenor. They found Barbot[18] who, if not a great voice, had great talent. He had a very good trill and agreed to take on the role only on the condition that he be allowed, at least once during the performance, to let go with a trill unrestricted. This whim had to be indulged, and the aria "Salut, demeure chaste et pure" ("Hail, innocent, pure dwelling") was crowned with a long trill, growing and then diminishing with consummate art, a trill worthy to serve as a model for all the trills in the universe, with all the effect of a charming lock of hair on a sorbet.

At last, after three weeks of extra work, came the unforgettable premiere. Everyone knows that success was slow in arriving. But it was not so for the hero, and the seductiveness of his voice, his diction and even of

[17] His real name was Hector Gruyer and he was a singing pupil of Bizet's father.
[18] Joseph Barbot (1824–1896).

his appearance conquered all resistance.[19] The corridors echoed with abuse. "It won't reach 15 performances," was the verdict of two publishers, ardent champions of the Italian school, as they shrugged their shoulders. "There's no melody," said the sceptics; "only reminiscences put together by a scholar." It was boring, it was long, it was cold. They had to cut the Garden Act because it was holding up the action . . . Oh! will anyone ever let us see Marguerite's garden again? At the old Théâtre-Lyrique on the boulevard du Temple, now so barbarously demolished, the wide, deep stage was eminently suitable for decoration and the painters had produced some masterpieces; never, since then, has *Faust* overall looked so charming. The music was interspersed with dialogue and, while we may not hanker after this initial format, it is nevertheless the case that the mixture of speech and orchestral music was extremely picturesque, especially in the scene where Mephistopheles insults the students.

Two numbers escaped the general indifference: the Kermesse, thanks to the "Chorus of Old Men", and the Soldiers' Chorus. While the Garden Act had its detractors, it also had its enthusiasts. As one charming lady put it to me, "Even if in your whole life you had only ever loved a dog, you would understand that music!"

Ten years later, when the work had become a success and was acclaimed abroad, it made a triumphant entrance at the Opéra. Would you believe that on this occasion there were still resistances to be overcome? Many people were afraid that the music would be too intimate for the vast mansion on the rue Le Peletier;[20] others, it has to be said, hoped that it would fail and that Gounod's orchestration would not stand up beside Meyerbeer's. The opposite happened. The quiet orchestra filled the hall without drowning the voices, and since then Meyerbeer's orchestra has seemed slightly shrill by comparison.

The success of the evening was the ballet. The position of this was marked in the score and it would have existed from the beginning if the Théâtre-Lyrique had had a large enough corps de ballet; it had been replaced by a rather dull drinking song, sung by Faust to a group of pretty girls lying about on beds like the courtesans in Couture's famous painting "La décadence romaine".[21] The same mimes had been making up this tableau for a decade, with the result that Mephistopheles's words at the end of the opera, "Reines de beauté/De l'antiquité" ("Queens of beauty/ Of antiquity") were becoming slightly ironic.

At the Opéra, the director, Perrin, who realised this, set up a production of unequalled splendour. Saint-Léon, himself a violinist and com-

---

[19] Though the critic Scudo referred to "his unpleasant tenor voice and Toulousain accent".

[20] The Opéra was sited here from 1821 until it burnt down in 1873.

[21] *Les Romains de la Décadence* (1847) by Thomas Couture (1815–1879).

poser, and a ballet master such as has never been known before or since, accompanied Gounod's voluptuous music with the most ingenious fairy scene you can imagine; it is sad that this aspect of the production has not been faithfully retained. There was one comic incident at the first performance. While Hélène, in the person of the statuesque Mlle Marquet, was miming to the music's noble paragraphs, she was surrounded by women carrying vases on their heads, from which poured an abundance of reddish smoke, to be wafted by a breeze from the stage into the auditorium. The audience were meant to open their nostrils enthusiastically and breathe in the perfumes with which the Greek beauty was intoxicating herself. Horrors! A ghastly smell, like that of a Bengal light, spread rapidly as far as the boxes at the back, and the pretty spectators, in total confusion, had to resort to their lace handkerchieves as a protective rampart against this disagreeable attack.

This ballet is a masterpiece of the genre—but Gounod almost didn't write it. Some months before *Faust* appeared at the Opéra, he sent our young friend the painter Emmanuel Jadin to me as an ambassador, with a delicate mission. As he began work on the ballet, Gounod was struck by scruples: he was then deeply immersed in religious ideas that prevented him from applying himself to a task so innately secular; he begged me to take it on in his place and to go and see him to talk about it. You can easily judge of my embarrassment. I went off to Saint-Cloud where I found the master concentrating on a game of cards with an abbé. I put myself entirely at his disposal, nonetheless making the objection that someone else's music in the middle of his own would not make a good impression and that, if I accepted the task offered me, it was on the express condition that he should remain completely free to rescind the agreement and to substitute his music for mine. I didn't write a note and never heard another word.

Much has been said about the way *Faust*'s librettists envisaged the role of Marguerite. Goethe made a firm mark on the subject of *Faust*, but it did not belong to him entirely; others had taken it before him and everyone can treat it in their own way: again recently, Auguste Vacquerie[22] has given it a new form. Goethe's *Faust*, which has been known for a long time in France, was popularised by the paintings of Ary Scheffer, and if the public had been presented with the real Marguerite as portrayed by the poet, they would not have recognised her. The fact is that the Gretchen of the famous poem is not some virgin found in a missal or a stained glass

[22] Vacquerie (1819–1895) was a journalist and man of letters and an admirer of Victor Hugo. He also wrote plays, of which Graham Robb, in his biography of Hugo (Picador, 1997) says "since his entire oeuvre positioned itself in orbit around Hugo's, it is difficult now to see it as anything other than a small, airless satellite."

window, the ideal of a man's dreams, encountered at last; Gretchen is Margot, and the cloth she spins could be used to make Victor Hugo's "radiant floorcloths".[23] Faust has spent his life bent over his learned books and test tubes, never experiencing love; now he is restored to adolescence and the first girl he comes across seems like a goddess. She talks to him about the house, the housekeeping and the most mundane things, and he is enchanted. It's a slice of nature: the serious man, the superior mind falls instantly in love with a slut.

This aspect of Gretchen's character struck me vividly the first time I saw a German production of fragments of *Faust* made into a play, and I was amazed that no one had written an essay on the subject (though Paul de Saint-Victor[24] has done so since). Short-lived passion, seduction, abandon, infanticide, a death sentence and madness, these are the extremely prosaic elements that make up the background on which Goethe sewed his brilliant poetic flowers. The librettists have taken over the character without changing anything; it was their right, and success, in Germany itself, gave them good reason to do so.

Mephistopheles's appearance in the church scene has played into the critics' hands. In Goethe's poem, it is not Mephistopheles but an "evil spirit"—*böser Geist*—that torments poor Gretchen. The scene may appear somewhat bizarre (evil spirits don't generally inspire remorse), but the poetry is beautiful and lends itself very well to music. If the librettists wished to include it, were they to introduce a new character, a small role for which a first-class singer would have been hard to find? It's hard to believe now, but the censors were so touchy that they almost banned this scene; for anyone who is aware of Gounod's carefulness over accents and prosody, there can be no doubt that the chorus "Quand du Seigneur le jour luira" was originally a setting of the prose sequence "Dies irae, dies illa", which the afore-mentioned censors would never have allowed to be sung in a theatre. Even today, they barely allow the sign of the Cross to be made there, while there is no embargo in profoundly Catholic Spain on turning it to comic effect.

V

As this is a general outline of Gounod's output and not a detailed analysis, you will allow me to pass swiftly over *Roméo et Juliette*, noting merely

[23] The reference to Hugo's "radiant floorcloths" presumably touches on his ability to transform base materials into something superior.

[24] Saint-Victor (1827–1881) was a journalist. In 1870 he was made inspector-general of fine arts.

that the initial triumph that was denied to Faust did not pass *Roméo* by: from the very beginning there was enthusiasm and acclaim. If *Faust* is a more complete work, we have to admit that nowhere is the composer's particular charm more striking than in *Roméo*. The time of its appearance marks the apogee of Gounod's influence; all the young ladies were singing his songs, all the young composers were imitating his style.

Some years earlier he had failed to succeed with *Mireille*. It was badly received at first, but has now recovered, albeit disfigured by modifications and mutilations of every kind. I have never been able to think of these without regrets, having known the original score in its entirety. Gounod played me each scene as he completed it and, when the whole opera was finished, sang the whole work with the gracious cooperation of the Vicomtesse de Grandval[25] in front of a few close friends; Georges Bizet and I, on piano and harmonium, did duty for an orchestra. This performance left a profound impression and no one doubted the work would be a success. But the lustrous fruit harboured a worm.

Mme Carvalho, for whom the role of Mireille had been written, had managed to expand her voice in order to make the transition from Fanchonnette to Marguerite, but she was not able to change its quality to the extent of becoming a "Valentine". Gounod liked to let me hear his works before anyone else, and the first time he sang me the scene in the Crau desert, I was terrified by the vocal abilities it called for. I said to him, "Mme Carvalho will never ever sing that." "Sing it she will have to!" he replied, opening his eyes wide to terrible effect. As I had foreseen, the singer refused before the task in front of her. The composer stuck to his guns, she gave up the role, lawyers were briefed; a writ accused the composer of asking the singer for "vociferations". Then the storm subsided: the composer cut the big scene by half and wrote the delightful rondo "Heureux petit berger!" Her role begin to diminish.

On another front the tenor was proving incapable and his role was starting to shrivel from one rehearsal to the next, like Balzac's "Peau de chagrin". The work reached the public in an enfeebled, denatured condition; and when it got to the scene in the Crau, still powerful despite its mutilations, Mme Carvalho collapsed utterly. Before that, the fine scene of the ghosts had already failed to make an effect. The Théâtre-Lyrique in the place du Châtelet was not large enough to lend itself to such illusions: when supposedly walking on the waters of the river, the deceased made uncalled-for and ridiculous crunching noises. The result was not in doubt: it was a disaster. Never since then has this misunderstood work recovered its reputation; people have made cuts here and there, changed

---

[25] Marie, Vicomtesse de Grandval (1830–1907) composed oratorios, operas, operettas, and symphonic works, now forgotten. She studied with Saint-Saëns as a private pupil.

the dénouement, suppressed or restored the supernatural scene, combined the small role of Vincenette with that of the witch Taven; I have never received again that impression of a complete, successful work which had so struck me in the composer's studio.

Habent sua fata . . .[26] and that goes for stage works as well as books!

Among those pieces marked out by an unkind Fate must be included the opera *Polyeucte*, which Gounod wanted to be his masterpiece and which caused him nothing but disappointment. He had found a wonderful Pauline in Mme Gabrielle Krauss,[27] but he never came across the Polyeucte he had dreamt of; Faure was the only singer capable of realising such a task but, being a baritone, couldn't sing a role written for a tenor. As we know, Ambroise Thomas had the courage to rewrite the score of *Hamlet* and adapt the title role to the abilities of this incomparable artist. It was suggested to Gounod that he might effect a similar transformation, but he could not bring himself to do so.

The first passage of *Polyeucte* he played me was the chorus of pagans, sung offstage, and the barcarolle that follows it. "But," I said to him, "if you make paganism so seductive, what sort of figure will Christianity cut beside it?"—"Even so, I cannot deprive it of its powers," he replied, with a look in which one could read visions of nymphs and goddesses. It transpired as I feared; the pagans, in the shape of M Lassalle, M Warot and Mlle Mauri,[28] won out over the Christians, who appeared boring. It's worth remembering that Corneille's masterpiece was a success only when Rachel and Beauvallet played it at the Théâtre-Français. In the author's lifetime the play had the reputation of being ice-cold.

As we know, the subject of Polyeucte attracted Donizetti; and although he rose above his normal style in this work, and although, given first in Italian (*Poliuto*) and then in French (*Les martyrs*), it later had some success at the Théâtre-Italien with Tamberlick and Mme Penco,[29] today it's

---

[26] "Pro captu lectoris habent sua fata libelli" (In the matter of attracting a reader books have their own destinies): Terentianus Maurus (fl. 290 a.d.), *De Syllabis*, line 1286. I am grateful to Dr Roger Brock for tracking down this reference.

[27] Marie Gabrielle Krauss (1842–1906) was born in Vienna and studied there. She sang Rachel in the first two acts of *La Juive* for the inauguration of Garnier's Opéra in 1875, Pauline in *Polyeucte* on 7 October 1878 and Gilda in the Opéra premiere of *Rigoletto* in 1885. Her beauty, clear delivery and commanding presence made her one of the stars of the period.

[28] Victor-Alexandre-Joseph Warot (1834–1906) was a popular tenor at the Opéra-Comique. He sang the role of Alvar in the premiere of *L'africaine*. Rosita Mauri (1856–1923) was a Spanish ballerina, chosen by Gounod himself for the role of the pagan dancer in the "Fête Païenne" in *Polyeucte*. In 1886 she created the role of Gourouli in Messager's ballet *Les deux pigeons*.

[29] The tenor Enrico Tamberlick, or Tamberlik (1820–1889) was famed for his high C$\sharp$ in chest voice. Rosina Penco (1823–1894) was an Italian soprano who sang Leonora in the premiere of *Il Trovatore* in Rome in 1853.

completely forgotten. It's a good story; but stageworthiness is a strange thing! In the theatre, where knowledge and study seem comical and where the most appalling crimes are not without charm, divine love is of no particular interest.

VI

"Theatres are the disreputable places of Music, and the chaste Muse we drag into them can only cross their threshold with a shudder." There is some truth in this quip, which perhaps Berlioz would never have made if the Stage had been less hostile to him: he and she could never get on together, but his poor opinion never prevented him from wanting to conquer her. We know the fruitless efforts he made to get *Les Troyens* put on at the Opéra, which was so short of new works at the time that it was reduced to adapting Bellini's *Roméo*, reinforced by Dietsch with brass and bangs on the bass drum, by express request of the Director. To have preferred such a mediocre object to *Les Troyens* will be to the eternal shame of the Imperial Academy of Music, whose glories have included *Le prophète*, *Faust* and *L'africaine*. The horror Berlioz inspired in the theatre world is hard to explain . . . As for the chaste Muse, she needs to tell herself that absolutes do not belong in this world, and that the theatre is not the place to look for them. They get close at Bayreuth; but Bayreuth is not a theatre, it's a temple.

A temple! Yes, that is the place which the chaste Muse, when she is properly recognized there, can enter without shuddering: where there is no applause, no money to be made, no worldly vanities to be satisfied, but where the beautiful is sought in and for its own self, beneath the great, mysterious, resonant vaulting that inspires respect and inclines to admiration in advance; where a stylistic breadth derives naturally from the circumstances of performance and where noble and elevated sentiments are taken as a matter of course—what could be more favourable for an artist whose nature lends itself to such surroundings!

Berlioz combined all the necessary qualities; he demonstrated this in his *Requiem* and *Te Deum*; but the nature of his gifts was bound to distance him from a genre in which the vocal element of necessity takes first place, and he was also not greatly attracted to the Church, not being a believer. Gounod, who wore Christ's monogram on his finger, was a believer to the utmost degree, if by that we may refer to the special religion of Christian artists who, fundamentally, never have any religion other than Art. Raphael and Ingres belonged to that group who follow the cult of beautiful forms and pagan nudity and who would find it hard to reconcile themselves to a purely moral beauty allied to physical ugliness. For them, Grace,

Charity is always Charis who used long ago to walk in the steps of the goddess of Cythera and has merely changed her employment.

So you won't find an ascetic in Gounod, the Roman Catholic, the regular worshipper in Saint Peter's and the churches of the Eternal City. Our modern aesthetes, in love with Flemish Preraphaelitism, would not be comfortable in his company; it is not made for them, nourished as they are on Protestantism by J. S. Bach and incapable of savouring the very special flavour of Catholicism, despite their artificial cult of Palestrina, which is a sort of musical palaeontology. You would be ill-advised to point out to them that Bach's style, as it flourishes in his German cantatas and in the *Passions*, is out of keeping with Latin texts, and that his famous B minor Mass, for all its splendours and the composer's efforts to modify his habits, is not a mass: they would not believe it and would cry "Sacrilege!" So I shall make no efforts to convince them; it would be copying those Japanese jugglers who, when they perform before European audiences, explain the meaning of their exercises in Japanese . . .

Gounod wrote for the Church all through his life, in a quantity of masses and motets; but it was at the start of his career, in the *Messe de Sainte-Cécile*, and at the end, in the oratorios *Rédemption* and *Mors et Vita*, that he reached the peaks of his achievement.

The performance of the *Messe de Sainte-Cécile* in the church of Saint-Eustache caused a kind of stupor. This simplicity, this grandeur, this serene light that shone on the musical world like the dawn, upset many people. You felt that a genius was arriving and, as we all know, such arrivals are in general badly received. It is a strange thing but, intellectually, mankind is a creature of the night, or at least of the dusk; light frightens him and you have to get him used to it gradually.

But the brilliant rays of the *Messe de Sainte-Cécile* shone down in torrents. We were first astonished, then charmed, then conquered. A bold innovation, the insertion of the text "Domine non sum dignus" into the "Agnus Dei", was a sign of the religious artist who was not content to follow received models, but profited from his ecclesiastical studies in finding the necessary authority for changes to the liturgy that an ordinary layman would not have dared allow himself.

From the musical point of view, Gounod demonstrated in this work a quality that had once been commonplace, but was now rare thanks to the exclusively dramatic and instrumental habits of modern composers: the art of writing for voices and of making vocal interest the very basis of the work, whatever the role given to instrumentation and its marvellous discoveries. Whether intentionally or not, Gounod thereby rendered immense service to his art, which had been turned from its path by powerful men of genius who had found in the orchestra a virgin forest to be cleared for cultivation, and who had forgotten that the human voice was not only the most beautiful of instruments, but the primordial, eternal one, the Alpha and Omega, the living timbre, the one that survives when the others pass by, are transformed, and die.

Vocal music is truth, instrumental music is falsehood; what admirable falsehood! If to have created it is a fault, then it is one of those faults of which we can say, as the Church says of the sin of Adam: *O felix culpa!* Happy fault, thanks to which Beethoven gave us his nine symphonies, the last of which seems to make honourable amends when, its strength exhausted and despairing of reaching Heaven, it calls the human voice to its aid!

This essay is not the place to analyse the numerous religious compositions that Gounod produced throughout his prolific and glorious career, between the *Messe de Sainte-Cécile* and the large oratorios, *Rédemption* and *Mors et vita.* These last two are of particular importance, so I shall devote my attention exclusively to them.

No one can deny Christian doctrine the virtue of being precisely that, a Doctrine: that's to say an ensemble constructed with profound skill, all of whose parts support one another firmly and whose intelligent structure commands the admiration of anyone that takes the trouble to study it.

It is this doctrine that Gounod has succeeded in compressing in *Rédemption,* or at least the most essential part of this doctrine, the one that gives the work its title.

A prologue and three sections suffice for the task.

The very short prologue relates in outline the creation of the world, the creation of man and his fall, before reaching the promise of the Redemption that is the subject of the work. Then come the three main divisions: Calvary, Resurrection, Pentecost.

"Calvary" is divided into six sections: the walk to Calvary, the Crucifixion, Mary at the foot of the Cross, the two robbers, the Death of Jesus and the Centurion.

"The Resurrection" includes first a mystic chorus:

> Mon Rédempteur! Je sais que Vous êtes la Vie!
> Je sais que de mes os la poussière endormie,
> Au fond de mon sépulcre entendra Votre voix;
> Que dans ma propre chair, je verrai Votre gloire,
> Quand la mort, absorbée un jour dans sa victoire,
> Fuira devant le Roi des Rois.

(My Redeemer! I know that Thou art Life! I know that the inert dust of my bones will hear Thy voice from the depths of my tomb, that, restored to my flesh, I shall see Thy glory, when death, engrossed one day in his victory, shall flee before the King of Kings.)

This is followed by the Holy Women at the Tomb, Jesus's appearance to the Holy Women, the Sanhedrin, the Holy Women and the Apostles, the Ascension.

"Pentecost" begins with a picture of the final age of mankind, a new golden age which, according to Christian belief, will precede the end of the world and the bliss of Eternity; then comes the scene in the upper room and the miracle of Pentecost, and finally the apostolic Hymn, a magnificent conclusion in seven sections, incorporating a résumé of the Catholic faith.

This is certainly a vast framework worthy of a poet and a composer. Even if Gounod never had any pretensions to being a poet, his text is irreproachable, continually relying as it does on Scripture and, needless to say, being admirably fitted for musical setting. Its naïvety is deliberate, but not far-fetched, and it lacks neither propriety nor brilliance.

As for the musical composition, it is impossible to give a clear idea of it in words; but it is possible to explain the ways in which Gounod's techniques differ from those of the great masters of the past; because the difference is profound. In the oratorio as it was passed on to us by earlier tradition, the work's story is told in recitatives more or less devoid of interest; from time to time the narration stops and an aria or a chorus gives a kind of commentary on what preceded it. Nothing of the sort here. Although the composer has given free rein to his rich store of melody, the recitatives are in some cases the most attractive items in the work. Those who have been lucky enough to hear M Faure singing in *Rédemption* will not have forgotten the expressive intensity of several of the recitatives, sometimes of no more than a few notes; the most striking melody is not more deeply moving.

Perhaps the most amazing movement in *Rédemption* is the walk to Calvary. It is a piece without precedent and its profound originality has, to my mind, not been properly appreciated. People have had difficulty with the deliberate vulgarity of the instrumental march, without seeing that the composer had reproduced in this large picture an effect often found in primitive paintings, where soldiers and executioners exaggerate their ugliness and brutality in contrast with the mystic beauty of male and female saints crowned with gold and adorned with precious stones. This vulgar march—the vulgarity, it should be said, is relative—is followed by the hymn "Vexilla Regis prodeunt" ("The standard of the King of Kings waves and advances in the distance"), its liturgical melody garlanded with exquisite harmonies and the most expert and delicate contrapuntal figures. The march begins again, and as it continues and develops like a long snake, the drama continues and develops in parallel, and the narrator, the distraught Holy Women, and Christ himself who is encouraging and consoling them, successively make their voices heard to most moving effect.

Then the march reaches the end of its progress and bursts out in all its power, while at the same time the liturgical hymn is intoned by the whole choir in unison; and all that is combined without apparent effort, without the movement's impact being dulled for a moment, with a complete fusion of the varying elements in a majestic unity, and with a simplicity of means that is yet one more miracle in this miraculous work!

This simplicity in the means employed and the grandeur of the results obtained, these are, together with that special, inescapable charm that is his secret, the characteristics of Gounod's style. It is what allows him sometimes to bring off striking effects with a single dissonant chord, as in the chorus "O ma vigne, pourquoi me devenir amère?" ("O my vine, why do you become bitter to me?").

This is not to criticise those geniuses who grasp music with both hands and employ its resources to the utmost. I am not one of those who, if they admire Ingres, think they have to despise Delacroix, or vice versa. To take great artists as they are and to study them according to their temperament and nature seems to me the only fair policy of criticism. That said, I may admit that my preference is for sobriety of means, so long as it does not entail poverty in the results; because, in art, the result is everything. "The laws of morality govern art," said Schumann. That's all very fine; but it's not true. In morality, the intention can justify many things; in art, the best intentions are good only for paving the way to hell. Either a work is a success, or it's a failure. The rest is of no importance.

A moment ago I mentioned the Primitive painters. It is once more to them that we have to turn to find a similar impression of naivety and freshness to that given by the episode of the Holy Women at the Tomb, crowned by the marvellous soprano solo with chorus, "Tes bontés paternelles". It is a kind of distant memory of Mendelssohn who, to be fair, we must credit with the first attempt at transforming the oratorio in the modern sense. What belongs to Gounod alone is the profound Catholic sentiment, the union of human love with religious feeling. Protestant mysticism, which is so attractive in Mendelssohn and so intense in J. S. Bach, is something else.

I have already remarked on the resplendent beauty of the final movement, which summarises the Christian faith in its seven sections. What no one can describe is the radiance and the musical majesty of this conclusion, and the solidity of the architecture whose keystone is a chorus belonging to the well-known family of *Proses*, sung at great Catholic festivals. It is the joy of the Church triumphant, the blossoming of the faithful people in their faith. This is interrupted by passages of profound gentleness, before the formidable chorus returns in still greater force, and just as we think we have reached the climax of light, a staggering succession of chords, with the bass descending 14 times by the interval of a third

while the upper part rises ceaselessly upwards, sets the seal on this daz-
zling movement.

It is the end of the work.

The oratorio *Mors et Vita* follows as a complement to *Rédemption*. It is
much simpler in conception and the whole interest lies in the music. The
Latin text is taken entirely from Scripture and from the liturgy.

First part: "la Mort"; Second part: "le Jugement"; Third part: "la Vie",
the text of which is taken from the vision of St John, the heavenly Jerusalem of the Apocalypse.

A prologue, even shorter than the one to *Rédemption*, summarises
Death and Life in a few words. "It is terrible to fall alive into the hands of
God," says the chorus. The voice of Christ replies: "I am the Resurrection
and the Life." The chorus repeats these words and that is all. The drama
begins.

This prologue looks forward to "le Jugement" which will form the second part. There are only a few notes, but the effect is terrifying; we could
say of it what Victor Hugo said of Baudelaire, that he had "created a new
frisson". Did Gounod see Hell, like Dante, in order to bring this sinister
frisson back for us? After Mozart and all the geniuses who have followed
him up to the present day, after the shattering "Tuba mirum" of Berlioz,
he found means to make our hair stand on end. It's unbelievable, but it's
true. Once again, I cannot refrain from admiring the clear and astonishing disproportion between the grandeur of the effect and the simplicity of
the means, which defies analysis.

The first part, *Mors*, is nothing but an immense Requiem, lasting two
whole hours. Interest does not flag for a moment. The composer has allowed himself considerable room to exploit that feeling for voices I mentioned earlier, and which was his speciality. Not that he turned his back on
his clever, well blended orchestration; he discovered new and particularly
happy effects by combining organ and orchestra. But the arias, ensembles
and choruses always retain pride of place in the listener's attention; there
is even a double chorus, unaccompanied in the style of Palestrina, which
rests and refreshes the ear. There is the same impression of repose and
freshness in the delightful pastorale "Inter oves locum praesta", which
sounds so attractive sung by the solo tenor.

Every vocal resource is used in this Requiem, including the fugal style
which might seem boring today, but which, when properly understood,
gives a work of this nature an authority that nothing can replace.

The "Agnus Dei" is particularly striking. After a succession of an-
guished, tormented harmonies, suddenly a soprano soars into the heights
with a wonderful phrase on the words "Dona eis requiem", a phrase that
will return. Then the movement slowly fades out in a long decrescendo
with mysterious sounds, producing an effect of impressive calm that goes

beyond the imagination. It is delight in death, the indescribable entry into eternal repose . . .

And then a mighty epilogue begins, expands and is lifted up:

> L'âme lève du doigt le couvercle de pierre
> Et s'envole . . .

(The soul lifts the stone covering with its finger and flies away . . .)

The Light has been lit, a happiness never before experienced floods the soul, now delivered from its earthly bonds; the combined forces of orchestra and organ bring the emotion to its climax.

"Le Jugement" makes up the second part. I have mentioned the terrors that spring from this music. After the sleep of the Dead, after the trumpets of the Resurrection, now the Judge appears; and it is no longer terror, but love that he brings with him. The lovely phrase of the "Agnus Dei", now developed and extended, is sung by the whole string section, joined by the chorus representing the crowd of the chosen ones comforted by the Saviour's arrival.

After so many emotional passages, we might fear that the heavenly Jerusalem could appear somewhat dull, with its azure and columns of gold and diamonds. Nothing of the kind. From the opening chords, music unfolds of such charm that we seem to be feeling the divine embrace of spring after winter. In particular there is a rascally "Sanctus"—I hope I may be pardoned the epithet—that sets the heat running through your veins. But for all that it remains sacred music, without any concession to the frivolities of the times. How has the composer managed to obtain such effects? It is his secret; it would need a mighty shrewd person to uncover it.

The final chorus, "Ego sum Alpha et Omega", reaches the extreme limits of grandiose simplicity; the lovely phrase from the "Agnus" returns, and the whole work ends with a fugue, not extensively developed, but impeccably written and extremely powerful.

The structure of the two oratorios is admirable, music aside; only a theologian could produce such a work. As to their qualities from the point of view of orthodoxy, I cannot judge, not being trained in this field. Far be it from me to want to put the matter in doubt, but instinctively I go back to the reflections I made earlier on the religious faith of artists, when I was referring to the little known history of the opera *Françoise de Rimini*, intended in principle for Gounod, and to the purely theological reason for which he refused to finish this score, for which he had already written several scenes. He had had the idea of writing an epilogue: the stage was to have been divided vertically into three tableaux, representing Hell, Purgatory and Paradise, and the two lovers were to progress from Hell to

Purgatory and from there to heaven. Gounod had written the text of this prologue himself, in excellent verse. Jules Barbier and Michel Carré, although they had no claim to be theologians, could never reconcile themselves to such a daring stroke; and after numerous discussions Gounod gave the work back to them, from where it passed to Ambroise Thomas.[30] Even if such an experience is not exactly supportive of Gounod's theological authority, I believe that no Father of the Church would have disavowed either the French text of *Rédemption,* written entirely by the composer, or the knowledgeable organization of the Latin texts that supply the structure for *Mors et Vita.*

It was a very daring enterprise to write a Catholic work in Latin for Protestant England. It is a severe work, very different from Handel's and Mendelssohn's oratorios in that it makes no concessions, either to settled habits or to religious *mores* that are undoubtedly worthy of respect. The reception was initially reserved, but then enthusiastic, and it conferred honour both on the work, which triumphed through its own power, and on the public who welcomed it. On one of those dark, rainy days that are a London speciality, I saw the huge auditorium of the Albert Hall filled right to the upper galleries with an audience of 8,000 people, silent and attentive, following the text in their programmes and listening devotedly to a colossal performance of *Mors et Vita,* given by around a thousand performers, with the hall's huge organ and the best soloists in England.

In Paris, we are still wondering what to make of the work; we puzzle as to why the "Judex crederis" is set to a love song. The work can wait: when, as time marches on, in the distant future, Gounod's operas finally come to rest in the dusty purlieus of libraries and are known only to scholars, the *Messe de Sainte-Cécile, Rédemption* and *Mors et Vita* will stand in the breach, so that future generations may know what a great composer cast his glory over 19th-century France.

VII

"What an elegant man Berlioz was!" Gounod said to me one day. It was a profound remark. Berlioz's elegance is not immediately apparent in his clumsy, maladroit writing; it is hidden in the texture, you could say in the very flesh of his music; it exists in a latent state, in his prodigious talent by comparison with which no one else's is minimised because no one else can be compared with him.

---

[30] Thomas's version was premiered at the Opéra on 14 April 1882. After its 41st performance on 12 December 1884, it disappeared from the Opéra's repertoire forever.

With Gounod it is rather the contrary: his writing, impeccably elegant as it is, sometimes conceals a certain nucleus of vulgarity; he is *common* at times, and for that very reason he found easy access to the common people—he became popular long before Berlioz, whose *Damnation de Faust* did not achieve popularity until after its composer's death. This vulgarity— if vulgarity it is—could be compared with that of Ingres (whom he deeply admired). It is like a solid basis of plebeian blood, bringing the muscles into play as a counterpoise to the element of nervousness whose pre-dominance could present a danger; it is the antidote to affectation, it is Antaeus regaining his strength as he touches the ground;[31] it is utterly distant from the triviality against which his most illustrious predecessors in opera and opéra-comique were not always able to guard themselves. He aimed high, but the constant search for expressiveness, like every-thing that partakes of realism, inevitably brought him back to earth from time to time. This very realism opened up a fruitful and absolutely new path in music. For the first time, the depiction of the union of hearts and souls was supplemented by that of the communion of bodies, the scent of loosened hair, and the intoxication of breath amid the burgeoning of spring. I have known chaste and highly intelligent people be shocked by these innovations and to accuse Gounod of having turned love in the theatre into something gross and material. How many other composers would be happy to deserve such a reproach!

He was responsible for many other innovations. To begin with, he re-suscitated techniques that had long been abandoned for no good reason, and Conservatoire students were amazed to see him restore various an-cient, discredited practices to a place of honour, such as "harmonic pro-gressions", of which the prelude to the religious scene in *Faust* offers such a remarkable example. In his desire to allow the voice all its brilliance and importance, he suppressed the futile noises that no composer in those days thought he could do without. One day, with the rashness of youth, I asked a learned professor the reason for the abuse of trombones, of bass drums and cymbals that proliferated in even his lightest music:

—But it's easy to understand, he replied: the resources are there in the orchestra; so you should use them . . .

Gounod, who had studied painting, knew that it is not obligatory to put all the colours on your palette into a picture and he reintroduced so-briety, the mother of true colouring and delicate nuance, into the theatre orchestra. He suppressed the unnecessary repetitions and exhausting

[31] In Classical legend, Antaeus was a Libyan giant, son of Poseidon and Mother Earth, and an unbeatable wrestler until Hercules realized that his strength came from contact with his mother. By holding him off the ground he was able to squeeze him to death.

longueurs that disfigure so many fine works, and in doing so attracted criticism, incomprehensible today, for shortening his phrases and pieces; people were still expecting the "reprise of the motif", and this thwarted expectation gave the illusion that the motif had been merely sketched in, because repetition had not hammered it into their memories like a nail. Instead of the conventional forms on which recitative had long been based, he invented others, staying closer to Nature, and these have now become common currency. Finally, he aimed as far as possible to reduce the number of modulations, feeling that such a powerful expressive means should not be squandered, and believing furthermore that a persistent key had special force.

—When, he said, the orchestra has been playing in C for a quarter of an hour, and the walls of the auditorium are in C and the seats are in C, then the sonority is doubled.

He wanted to "build himself a cell inside the common chord". While he was in principle sparing with his modulations, he nevertheless possessed to the highest degree that most precious of arts, which is the touchstone of the great composer. He had the keenest sense of keys and of their mutual influence, and of the ways in which harmonies interacted by attracting and repelling each other. He found new resolutions for dissonances and discovered a new meaning in certain chordal textures. He required the brass and percussion to produce sounds of unheard-of gentleness and piquancy. One day I asked him to explain the curiously mystical character of a certain bass drum stroke at the beginning of the "Gloria" of the Messe de Sainte-Cécile, and he answered:

—It's the boom of the cannon of Eternity.

Effects of an astonishingly simple kind came naturally from his pen: like the slow harp scale, that curtain of cloud that rises in the middle of the introduction to Faust, leading to the final, magical tune. It may seem almost naïve, but no one before him had ever thought of anything similar. The principles he followed were obtaining the greatest result with the least possible apparent effort, reducing the illustration of stage activity to simple indications, and concentrating the interest on the expression of feelings—principles that still run counter to the general habits of composers. And yet the very mention of them is enough for us to see they're true.

He did not espouse the system of "melodic independence", of melody chosen for its own sake with words fitted to it later as best they might; like Gluck, he preferred the system by which melody grows from declamation, modelling itself on the words and setting them in relief without losing anything of its own importance, so that the two forces grow by combining with each other instead of fighting it out. This important reform was not accepted without a struggle and for years he was criticised for sacrificing melody to "chant": this term said it all, it was the great musical cliché; without further explanation, it condemned a man to the gods of hell and everlasting calumny. And as, in addition, Gounod's discreetly colourful orchestration earned him the title of "symphonist", another word that was a scathing insult in the world of the theatre, we can see in retrospect the thorny scrub through which the composer of *Faust* had to make his way.

Adolphe Adam showed clearly, in a very perceptive article on *Sapho*, the way in which Gounod related to the ancient masters. "Today," he wrote, "we regard as a virtue what the masters of old regarded as a vice. Music for them was to be found in choruses, arias, and everything that led up to stage action. But when the action began, the music stopped and gave way to declamation. Today we do the contrary. When the stage action begins, we launch out on the music. It was to a large extent the first of these two that M. Gounod followed."

It is true that all art rests on a convention, but even so it is impossible not to see instantly what an immense service Gounod rendered by attacking head-on a system that required the actors, at the very moment a dramatic situation was set up, to stop acting and start singing as though they were in a concert hall. And he was the one accused of not having "stage sense", another deadly charge. No melody, no stage sense, and on top of that a symphonist—what was there left for him? The public, who were gradually won over by the charm and naturalness of his music and who adopted it despite all the sophisms that were hurled about their ears.

The composer, it was said, mixed up recitatives, ariettas, cavatinas, duets and ensemble pieces so that it was impossible to hear where one turned into the other. He was criticised for something that nowadays is the ultimate goal, even to the point of going beyond common sense; because if the complete freedom we now enjoy is a boon for the strong, it is a terrible danger for the weak, who drown in it and only produce things that are shapeless and incoherent. In those days, the nub of fashionable teaching was "clarity": triviality, platitude, all the most vulgar faults were allowed to pass under cover of that word. When they failed to find in Gounod either the low style they cherished or pieces slavishly toeing the official line, they accused him of lacking clarity.

How times have changed! It is no longer permissible to be clear, or melodic, or even vocal; the drama must unfold exclusively on the orchestra, and we can foresee a time when no one will write anything but pantomimes; as the orchestral contribution develops yet further, drowning the voice and making it impossible to hear the words, the most sensible thing will be to do without them altogether. The present writer recently read an article about himself—indeed a very flattering one—which claimed that he had, in the theatre, followed his policy of *completely subordinating* the melodic element to the orchestral one. He begs permission here to digress in order to protest against such an assertion. For him, melody, declamation and the orchestra are resources that the artist has a right to employ as he wishes and which he would do well to keep in the best equilibrium he can. This equilibrium seems to have been one of Gounod's main concerns; he achieved it in his own way; others will achieve it differently, but the principle will remain the same; it is the sacred Trimourti, the three-personed god who created the lyric drama.

And if one of the elements is to be more important than the others, there should be no hesitating: the vocal element must predominate. It is not in the orchestra, it is not in the Text that the Word of the lyric Drama subsists, it is in the Song: for two hundred years now this truth has reigned unopposed, and if, by dint of twenty years' unflagging labour, a remorseless army has contrived to make the opposite acceptable, it has not managed even so to impose its ideas on the mass public. This crusade has been unique in history for its violence and duration, and these ideas will be forgotten the moment it comes to an end, whether through exhaustion or for whatever other reason. We are talking here merely of theories, not of famous works that soar above every system and even, at times, exercise a superbly casual mockery of those systems of which they are claimed to be the ultimate expression.

VIII

The music of the 16th century resembles a kind of chess game in which the various pieces come and go and jump over one another, without any apparent aim except their respective relationships. No indication of tempo or dynamics is given to elucidate the meaning, and we have no idea how this music was performed. This negligence must have a cause and, if such indications are lacking, it is because in those times they did not have the importance we attribute to them today. Form, in fact, is everything in this music; expressiveness is found there only in a rudimentary state, and comes from the form itself. Gradually expressiveness made a place for itself in the music; indications of slow and fast began to appear, while those referring to dynamics were slower to arrive. But expressiveness derives always from the forms used, which become ever more complicated, and nuances can conveniently be left to the performer's taste since they don't bring more than slight modifications to the overall sound.

In J. S. Bach, expressiveness reaches powerful heights, but even here it is of only secondary importance. In Mozart, as we have already observed, it is possible to be mistaken and see only a composer where there is in fact a psychologist. In modern composers tempo and nuance have become inseparable from the idea, and means of indicating them have multiplied to excess; but they only deal with a faster or slower tempo, or a louder or softer dynamic, and attempts to penetrate further into the domain of expressiveness are feeble and unsatisfactory. In saying *molto espressivo, leidenschaftlich, avec feu, avec un sentiment contemplatif,* you haven't said a great deal, and you have to trust to the intelligence, or rather the instinct, of the performers.

Gounod's music, in which expressiveness has a role unknown before him, demands a quite different approach.

Those who had the exquisite pleasure of hearing Gounod himself perform have all agreed: his music lost half its charm when it passed into other hands. Why? Because the thousand nuances of feeling he was able to put into an apparently simple performance *were part of the idea,* and without them that idea then seemed distant and as though half obliterated.

Without being either a great singer or a great pianist, he was able to imbue certain seemingly insignificant details with an unexpected weight, and the plainness of means ceased to surprise because of the quality of the result.

It is not enough to say that, with him, the melodic line springs from declamation; this is equally true of several others, and indeed of the ancient French school. More than that, the word is like a nucleus round which the music crystallises; the form, fine as it may be, is subordinated to it and expressiveness remains the principal aim. If this point of view is misunderstood, his music is seen in a false light and takes on a quite different significance from the one the composer intended to give it. The youth of today, besotted as they are with complicated forms that border on the inextricable, are a thousand miles away from trying to find truth in vocal expression and, as they are unable to hear Gounod's music performed by the composer, have no way of understanding or loving it. Performers have already lost the key. The craze for speed, which has taken hold from one end of the musical world to the other, is fatal to Gounod's music; he prized majestic slowness above all and could not conceive of profound feeling being expressed at a rapid tempo.

I should not like to say anything to upset anyone, but still the truth forces me to state that even in Paris, where traditions ought to have survived, Gounod's music is disfigured. At the Opéra-Comique I have seen Mme Carvalho shocked by tempi in *Mireille* and *Philémon et Baucis.* At the Opéra the kermesse in *Faust,* where the details are so cunningly worked out, is now nothing but a hullabaloo, and the delightfully witty chorus of Old Men nothing but a vulgar rant in the worst possible taste; and the antique grace of the ballet has given way to a wild pandemonium. And it's the same everywhere, except when it's worse!

Gounod indeed often used to complain of the difficulty he had in communicating his intentions. He showed me one day how he wanted the overture to *Mireille* performed; it was nothing like what we know.

—It's a libel, he used to say, they make me say things I've never thought of!

Whose fault is it? Not, certainly, of those performers who have both talent and goodwill. We have to look further, to the law of nature that says: an organism is more delicate the more elevated it is. Mankind can die of an embolism, while a polyp can be turned inside out like a glove without being harmed in any way.

The truth is that for music in which the slightest nuances of expression and feeling are indispensable, a new table of indications is called for.

Be that as it may, because the necessary indications are lacking, the true nature of Gounod's dramatic works will not be revealed in future except to clairvoyants endowed with that same intuition through which he himself brought Mozart's music back to life.

As to his religious music, which by its nature is simpler and destined to be heard in conditions—large numbers of performers, large, resonant halls or churches—which will always to some extent limit the whims of conductors, the same problems for the most part do not apply. This is the main reason out of many why his fame will last. Then time, which has, as we said at the beginning, still not put this great French master in his rightful place, will lift him up on to the golden throne where he will receive the incense of future generations.

I should like to have written of the man and of his powerful charm, to have given an idea of his wit, his opinions, his habit of linking music to the arts in general, of which he saw music as only a part, of his brilliant conversation that at times reminded you of passages in Victor Hugo's novels. The composer has taken up the whole space. I leave this sketch here, with no other intention than to revive memories whose subject makes them dear to me, and perhaps to uncover one or two little known aspects of the artist I so much admired and loved, while bitterly regretting that I am such a mediocre painter for such a picture.

21

JACQUES OFFENBACH I

(Harmonie et mélodie,
Calmann-Lévy, 1899, 217–224)

Without being a great composer, Offenbach was a great musical personality. His influence on the taste of his epoch was profound, if disproportionate to the quality of his works; and, for that reason, this influence had something miraculous about it. When you see the importance operetta has assumed in the world—in the whole world— you feel you are watching the human race in the grip of a huge attack of madness, a wild, irrational dance led by a mischievous Mephistopheles, an artisan of decadence. Operetta has taken upon itself the task of belittling and cheapening everything and it has succeeded; more than that, it has given the civilised world a taste, a passion almost, for what is cheap and small. Today its work is done. It no longer even has the jocular convulsions of its youth, when it was fighting for its existence and was involved in an entertaining struggle for its place in the sun. Now it has become relaxed and bourgeois, and stretches out at its ease in the little kingdom it has gained for itself, as banal as a goldfish in its familiar bowl ... And that is what takes the place of the theatre, poetry and music for the majority of people.

Certainly the illustrious founder of operetta never foresaw its lofty destiny: and we cannot even honestly claim that he made any long, cold calculations for his nefarious work.

He was, as others have been, a victim of circumstance, and he never went looking for the path he eventually followed. His musical life had extremely modest beginnings. Some of us still remember a little Offenbach, a cellist, knowing how, by dint of his wit, to persuade people that he had talent and conducting the orchestra of the Comédie-Française, in those golden times when that theatre had an orchestra. By then Offenbach had written one or two songs, rather thin stuff, but spicy and original, and they readily won the success they deserved. But he dreamt of opérascomiques and, to judge by his later lifestyle, must have felt a furious desire to be active, which one day was to make him an extraordinary man.

M. de Villemessant[1] has recounted in his *Memoirs* how this activity, like that of many others, was paralysed by the caution of a well-known director. Offenbach was one of those people who are not prepared to wait; and in his impatience he founded the Bouffes-Parisiens. Can you imagine a director who was less timid or more forward-looking? Offenbach, with his marvellous theatrical instinct, infused new blood into the opéra-comique. Under the influence of its surroundings, his muse took on another aspect—or else his surroundings, far from promoting his talent, choked it. But, whatever the truth, opéra-comique was not killed by operetta.

Now that he was his own man, *maëstro* Offenbach (as people called him, with a slightly ironical emphasis) followed the natural inclinations of his wit and devoted himself to wild exaggerations and irreverent and malicious parodies. He had one great advantage, that of being absolutely free. As director of the theatre where his works were performed, he did not have to knuckle under to the ideas of anyone else; and at least the wrangling so familiar to all composers was spared him. An idea from outside, however good, always detracts from a work and robs it of its natural air and open character. Offenbach produced theatre clearly on his own terms, which gives one a good chance of success; and we can add to that a wonderful flair, and a knack of incorporating every artist into his scheme and getting the very best out of them, while respecting their capabilities.

At that period, before there were theatres dedicated to operetta, the opéra-comique theatres were full of specialised voices: there were *dugazons*,[2] light sopranos, and all the rest to match. Recruiting a good company was easier than it is today, and operetta's palmy days saw some true artists: Mlle Tautin,[3] for instance, whose famous virtuosity and sparkling verve contributed not a little to the success of *Orphée aux enfers* and a number of other masterpieces of lucid insanity; or Mlle Chabert,[4] whose pure voice and chaste talent were lost in that artistic madhouse; or the

[1] Hippolyte de Villemessant (1810–1879) revived *Le Figaro* in 1854 and turned it into a daily paper in 1866.

[2] A type of role named after the soprano Louise-Rosalie Dugazon (1755–1821). "The light, romantic roles she sang early in her career were dubbed 'jeune Dugazon', while the matrons she impersonated from about 1790 were known as 'mère Dugazon'" (Richard Wigmore in *The Oxford Companion to Music*, ed. Alison Latham, Oxford, 2002, 383).

[3] Lise Tautin was, according to one account, "a sentimental grisette from Brussels". James Harding describes her as "a pert-faced girl with an enchanting smile [and] pretty legs that showed to advantage in the can-can. At one moment she was coyly naïve, at another she startled with her brazenness" (*Folies de Paris*, London, Chappell, 1979, 50).

[4] Mlle Chabert has resisted all attempts at identification.

two Léonce-Désirés,[5] the delight of a whole generation; or Bache![6] ... the lanky, the interminable Bache, who first tried out his talents at the Comédie-Française, and then found them at the Bouffes-Parisiens playing John Styx in *Orpheus* and the little clerk in the *Chanson de Fortunio*.

It was the golden age of opera buffa. It was still modest and, if it had been content to rest there, there would have been no cause to speak ill of it.

There was, then, a spot in Paris containing a little theatre where you could laugh unrestrainedly. How delightful! The general public was vastly pleased; more delicate spirits discovered there spicy insults and smart new ideas which allowed them to look kindly on the vulgarities and platitudes. Louis Veuillot[7] has spoken somewhere, à propos the songs of Thérésa, of the "truffle from the gutter". Offenbach excelled at offering you this truffle, perfectly cooked in champagne, with all the depraved luxury of a first-class supper. Everyone savoured it somewhat secretly, like a forbidden fruit.

It is from the transplanting of Offenbach to the Variétés that we can date the giddy heights of operetta and the collapse of taste. When *La belle Hélène* appeared [in 1864], it sent Paris crazy and turned every head. The most respectable ladies vied with one another in renditions of "Amour divin, ardente flamme!" Pink and white children gently asked their mothers, "Maman, tourne vers moi un bec favourable!" When it was the turn of the *Grande Duchesse de Gérolstein* [in 1867], the madness overflowed and swamped the whole of Europe. The wretched little cellist of the Théâtre-Français must have swelled with inordinate pride. He was jeering at the world, and the world was at his feet. This *Grande Duchesse*, who covered kings, generals and the whole of society from top to bottom with ridicule, was adored by the very people from whom she was drawing blood with her whip. Sovereigns on their way to Paris would telegraph en route to be sure of a box, then, without a moment's rest, would rush off immediately to see the *Grande Duchesse*. There was no longer any mention of the Comédie-Française, the Opéra or the Opéra-Comique: there was no theatre in Paris except the Variétés, no actress except Mlle Schneider,[8] no composer except Offenbach.

---

[5] Léonce and Désiré were a pair of comedians.

[6] Bache was a comic actor. "Thin, immensely tall, he resembled nothing so much as a giraffe. He never smiled and always delivered his speeches in a comically lugubrious tone" (Harding, ibid.).

[7] Veuillot (1813–1883) was a Parisian journalist of right-wing, Catholic views.

[8] Hortense Schneider (1833–1920) sang in *La belle Hélène*, *La grande duchesse de Gérolstein*, and *La périchole*, and was the toast of the Second Empire. She retired after Offenbach's death in 1880.

Those glorious days are past; that fame has faded. But a power was released, which has spread and done its work. Opera buffa has been sown everywhere and has taken over everything. What was no more than a passing debauchery has become a habit. Operetta has settled down and become a good girl, and has finally taken the place of opéra-comique. This genre had to avoid the trap of being paltry, and did not always succeed. Operetta goes from the paltry to the null. That has been the profit on the exchange.

Offenbach's facility and speed of execution were unheard of. Literally, he used to improvise. His scores are written in a scrawl of microscopic notes. He had a system of abbreviations which he pushed to extreme limits, and the simplicity of his compositional techniques allowed him to make frequent use of it. Even so, he had great fertility, a gift for a tune, a sometimes distinguished harmonic style, a good deal of wit and invention, tremendous theatrical knowhow: more talents, indeed, than were required for success.

He squandered them all.

22

JACQUES OFFENBACH II

(Ecole buissonnière,
Pierre Lafitte, 1913, 301–307)

It is dangerous to prophesy.

Some time ago, in speaking of Offenbach, I did justice to his marvellous natural gifts and deplored the way he had squandered them; and I was unwise enough to say that posterity would ignore him.

Now posterity is proving me wrong: Offenbach is coming back into fashion. Our composers of today, forgetting that Mozart, Beethoven and even J.S. Bach knew how to laugh from time to time, despise gaiety and declare it to be unaesthetic; and as the dear public cannot bring itself to do without gaiety, it turns to operetta and, naturally, to the man who was its creator and prolific purveyor. The word "purveyor" is not out of place, because Offenbach was not interested in creating art; gifted as he was with comic verve and an unquenchable fount of tunefulness, his only idea was to feed the theatre of which he was simultaneously the director and, to all intents and purposes, the exclusive composer.

I have dealt elsewhere with the way in which, because he could not rid himself of his Germanic inheritance, he corrupted the taste of a whole generation with his unbalanced prosody, which was wrongly taken for originality. What's more, he lacked taste. A dreadful habit of the times was to pause on the penultimate note of a song, even if it was on a mute syllable or sounded ridiculous, simply in order to warn the public that the piece was coming to an end and to give the claque the signal to applaud. As Offenbach did not belong to that heroic race for which success is the least of concerns, he followed the fashion, and all too often charming and ingenious verses are spoilt by this crass and outdated habit.

Also, because his early education was deficient, his technique was poor. If *Les Contes d'Hoffmann* give evidence of mastery, that is because it was Guiraud's,[1] remedying the composer's mistakes in many places when he was commissioned to finish the uncompleted score.

If you put to one side his faulty prosody and these small errors of taste, there remains an output whose prodigious quantity, rich melodic invention, sparkling wit and devilish verve are comparable with Grétry's.

Grétry too was not a great composer; he too was no technician. What differentiates him utterly from Offenbach is his concern not only with prosody but with declamation, which he tried to reproduce as exactly as possible in his music. In that respect he even went too far, not appreciating that the expressiveness of a note changes according to its accompanying harmony.

And we have to accept that sometimes enthusiasm for his melodic ideas led him to forget his principles and to relegate his care over declamation to second place.

The irritating thing about Grétry is his overweening vanity—something that Offenbach, to his credit, never suffered from. In his advice to young composers, Grétry actually went so far as to write: "Those with genius will write opéras-comiques like me; those with mere talent will write operas like Gluck; those without either genius or talent will write symphonies like Haydn."

He tried, nevertheless, to write an opera like Gluck but, for all his efforts and some interesting ideas, was unable to match his formidable rival.

Although Offenbach was not a great composer, he had a surprising natural instinct and, here and there, came up with curious harmonic discoveries.

---

[1] Ernest Guiraud (1837–1892) won the Prix de Rome in 1859. He taught composition at the Conservatoire from 1881, including Debussy, Satie and Dukas among his pupils. He turned the spoken dialogue of *Carmen* into recitative.

To touch on these, I shall have to use a few theoretical terms and resign myself to being understood only by readers who are to some extent musically trained; of whom there are, I'm glad to say, quite a few these days.

In a slight work called *Daphnis et Chloé*, Offenbach risked writing a dominant 11th, unprepared and unresolved, which was extraordinarily bold for that period. To explain how bold, a brief harmony course is called for.

The first point is that in theory every dissonance has to be prepared and resolved; this is something we can't go into here, but the aim of this preparation and resolution is to soften the harshness of the dissonance, which was very much shunned in earlier times.

Let us taking as a starting point the key of C. The note C is the tonic, G is the dominant. Add two thirds, B and D to this dominant, and you have the dominant chord. Add a further F natural, and you have the celebrated dominant seventh, a dissonance that to us today sounds so gentle. Not long ago it was still thought necessary to prepare it; in the 16th century it was not even allowed; because it contains the two notes B and F, which was felt to be intolerable to the ear—the interval was dubbed *Diabolus in musica* (the devil in music).

Palestrina was the first to use it in a motet. Opinions still differ over this: some writers on harmony claim that the chord used by Palestrina only looks like a dominant seventh, a view I don't accept. Whatever the case, it is to Monteverdi that the honour is due for releasing the devil in music: it became the principle behind the whole of modern music.

Later, composers added another third, giving the bold chord G–B–D–F–A. I don't know who used it first, but I think the earliest composer to do so effectively was Beethoven, and he used it in such a way that, although this chord is now part of the standard vocabulary, it always appears in Beethoven as something new and unexpected. It is this chord that imprints its character on the second theme of the first movement of the Fifth Symphony, and lends its incomparable charm to the long, and ever surprising and moving conversation between flute, oboe and clarinets in the Andante of the same work. In his *Traité d'harmonie*, Fétis complains about this delightful passage; he agrees that the audience shiver with delight when they hear it but, in his view, the composer did not have the right to put it on paper and the audience do not have the right to enjoy it. Scholars sometimes have the oddest notions.

Then came Wagner, and with him the reign of the ninth, completely displacing the seventh. It is the ninth that gives *Tannhäuser* and *Lohengrin* that exciting character so dear to those whose chief requirement from music is the pleasure derived from an unsettling of the nervous system. His imitators leapt on this simple technique, imagining, with ludicrous naïvety, that this was an easy way of equalling Wagner; they have rendered this lovely chord banal.

If you add one more third, you reach the dominant eleventh used by Offenbach, but little since. After that there is no more to do: one third more and you get back to the fundamental, two octaves higher.[2]

But harmonic inventions are rare in Offenbach. What makes him interesting is a richness and fertility of melodic invention that has few equals. He used to improvise endlessly, and at extraordinary speed. His manuscripts look as though they were written with the point of a needle; they contain nothing otiose; he used abbreviations whenever he could, in which he was assisted by the simplicity of his harmonies. In this way he could produce his lighter works in a very short time.

One day he had the good luck to attract Mme Ugalde to his troupe. Her voice was fading, but she was still a brilliant performer and, while she was appearing in a hugely successful revival of *Orphée aux enfers,* he wrote *Les Bavards* for her.[3] His excitement at the thought of an outstanding performance led him to surpass himself and produce a little masterpiece. Its return would undoubtedly be successful, if it were possible; but for that it would need Mme Ugalde's particular gifts, which I don't see anywhere on the present scene.

One very strange thing was that Offenbach lost all his talent when he took himself seriously. This is not unique in musical history: Cramer and Clementi both wrote Studies and Exercises that are stylistic marvels, but their Sonatas and Concertos are desperately mediocre. The Offenbach works put on at the Opéra-Comique, *Robinson-Crusoé*, *Vert-Vert*, and *Fantasio,*[4] are very inferior to *La Chanson de Fortunio*[5] and *La Belle Hélène* and any number of other justly famous operettas. *La Belle Hélène* has been given several unsuccessful revivals; the reason is that the role of Hélène was written for Mlle Schneider who, apart from her beauty and talent, possessed a fine mezzo-soprano voice; the small voice of an ordinary operetta singer does not suffice. Then there are the "traditions" that have grown up: the comical aspect of interpretation has been exaggerated. In Germany the opposite has happened: someone had the idea of performing this farce solemnly in an olde-worlde setting. As was said many years ago, the best is very often the enemy of the good.

Would Offenbach ever become a "classic"? It would be unexpected. But what can we not expect? Everything is possible, even the impossible, and this is the moment for me to resist further comment: I might say things I don't intend.

[2] A curious slip by Saint-Saëns. A further third, making a 13th, is required before a final third makes the return to the tonic two octaves higher.

[3] Premiered on 20 February 1863.

[4] Premiered in 1867, 1869 and 1872 respectively.

[5] Premiered in 1861.

23

MEMORIES OF CHILDHOOD

("Souvenirs d'enfance",
Ecole buissonnière,
Pierre Lafitte, 1913, 1–10)

"Y ou have two mothers," people often used to say to me, and
indeed I did have two, the one who gave birth to me, and my
maternal great-aunt, Madame Charlotte Masson. Born Charlotte Gayard,
she came from an old family of lawyers through whom I was connected
with General Delcambre, one of the heroes of the retreat from Russia; one
of his great-granddaughters married Le comte Durrieu of the Académie
des Inscriptions et Belles-Lettres.

My great-aunt was born in the provinces in 1781 and was adopted by
an uncle and aunt who lived in Paris and had no children. The uncle was
a rich attorney who lived in style. My aunt was very precocious—she
walked at nine months—and also highly intelligent and cultured. She
remembered every detail of the customs of the *ancien régime* and enjoyed
talking about them, as well as of the Revolution, the Terror and all the
regimes that followed. After the Revolution her family was ruined and this
very young, small, slim girl took on the burden of running it by teaching:
French, the piano (the instrument was still a novelty), singing, painting,
embroidery, everything she knew, and didn't know—which she learnt in
order to teach them. Later she married one of her cousins who was a
bookseller; having no children, she invited one of her nieces to come from
Champagne and adopted her—that was Clémence Collin, my mother.
The Massons were about to retire from trade with a large fortune when
they lost everything in a fortnight in a bookshop upheaval and were left
with just enough to live decently. Shortly afterwards my mother married
my father, an office under-manager in the Ministry of the Interior. The
uncle died of shame some months before my birth on 9 October 1835, and
my father, racked with consumption, left this world on 31 December of
the same year, twelve months to the day after his marriage.

There then were these two women, widowed and in straightened circumstances, burdened by sad memories, with the responsibility of bring-

ing up a very delicate child whose existence was precarious and about whom the doctors would make no assurances. On their advice I was left out in the country with my nurse until I was two.

Whereas my great-aunt had had a serious education, it was not the same story with my mother whose studies had not been completed. She made up for this by an imagination, an enthusiasm and a facility for assimilating things that bordered on the prodigious. She often talked to me about an uncle who loved her dearly, and who went bankrupt in the cause of Philippe Egalité.[1] He was an artist, and was wild about music in particular; he had built a chamber organ with his own hands and used to play it. He would sit my mother between his knees and, while he amused himself combing her lovely dark tresses, would talk to her about art, music, painting and beauty in all its forms, so that she got it into her head that, if ever she had sons, the first would be a composer, the second a painter and the third a sculptor. So she was not in the least surprised when, on returning from my nurse, I began to listen to every noise and every sound, making the doors squeak and planting myself in front of clocks to hear them chiming. My greatest delight was the symphony of the kettle, an enormous kettle that was put in front of the drawing room fire every morning. I used to sit near it on a stool and wait with an intense curiosity for its initial murmurs, its slow crescendo full of surprises, and the arrival of a microscopic oboe whose song would gradually rise in pitch until the water boiled and silenced it. Berlioz must have heard this oboe too, because I came across it again in the "Ride to the Abyss" in *La Damnation de Faust*.

At the same time I was learning to read; and when I was two and a half I was put in front of a tiny piano that hadn't been opened for years. Instead of hammering at it any old how as children of that age normally do, I touched the notes one after the other, only letting them go after the sound had disappeared. My great-aunt taught me the names of the notes and got a tuner to come and put the piano into shape. While this was going on, I was playing in the room next door and it was observed with astonishment that I was naming the notes as they sounded.

None of these details was subsequently related to me: I remember them perfectly.

I was given Le Carpentier's method.[2] After a month I'd reached the end of it! There was no question of making such a tiny tot practise, and I used

---

[1] Louis Philippe d'Orléans (1747–1793) was a member of the royal house, but was imbued with liberal ideals, even to the point of voting for the king's execution in 1793. This did not prevent his own execution by guillotine in November of the same year.

[2] The *Cours pratique de piano* of Adolphe Le Carpentier (1809–1869) was used at the Paris Conservatoire for elementary teaching and was designed to lead up to Cramer's *Etudes*. It is still in print in 2008.

to cry in desperation when they shut the lid. They then left it open and put a stool in front; from time to time I would leave my toys and climb on it to pick out what was going through my head. Luckily my great-aunt had been well taught, and she made me hold my hands properly and not contract any of those all too common faults which are so hard to cure later. But no one knew what music to give me; the music written specially for children is in general purely melodic and the left hand part without interest. I refused to learn it. I would say contemptuously, "The bass doesn't sing."

So then they searched in the great masters, in Haydn and Mozart, to find things easy enough for me to start on. At five I was playing little sonatas quite nicely and correctly; but I would only consent to do so for listeners who were capable of appreciating them. I have read, in a biography, that I was threatened with a whip to make me play. That is completely untrue; but to persuade me, they did have to say that there was a lady in the audience who was an excellent musician and very hard to please. I did not play for the uninitiated.

As for the threat of the whip, it has to be relegated to the realms of legend, like that of father Garcia beating his daughters to get them to learn to sing. Mme Viardot told me specifically that she and her sister were never beaten by their father and that they learnt music without realizing it, as we learn to talk.

Despite my startling progress, my teacher did not glimpse what the future held for me. "When he's fifteen," she used to say, "if he can play for people to dance to, I shall be quite satisfied."

Even so, it was at that moment that I began to write music. I wrote waltzes and gallops; the gallop was then all the rage: it was rather vulgar in tone and mine did not deviate from the norm. It needed Liszt, in his *Galop chromatique*, to show what a genius can do with the feeblest of genres. My waltzes were better. Already I was doing what I've always done and writing the music straight on to the paper without trying it out under my fingers, and these waltzes were too difficult for my small hands; a family friend, a sister of the singer Géraldy, was kind enough to perform them.

Recently I looked at these little pieces again. They are quite without significance, but it would be impossible to find any fault in the way they're written and this correctness is remarkable in a child who, at that time, had no notion of the study of Harmony.

Then someone had the idea of taking me to a concert. At that time there were orchestral concerts in the Passage du Saumon. I was taken there, my mother holding me in her arms, near the exit. I had only ever heard violins on their own and I didn't find their sound agreeable; the impression made by the orchestra was quite different and I was listening in ecstasy to a phrase played by the strings, when suddenly there was an outburst of brass—trumpets, trombones and cymbals. I uttered some piercing cries. "Make them be quiet," I said, "they're getting in the way of the music!" I had to be taken out.

At the age of seven I passed from the hands of my great-aunt to those of Stamaty, who was surprised at the way my musical education had been organised.

He mentioned it in a little book in which he discussed the necessity of a good initial technique. With me, he said, there was nothing to do but perfect what was already there.

Stamaty was Kalkbrenner's best pupil and the publicist of his method, based on the *hand-guide* that he had invented; and so I was introduced to the regime of the hand-guide. The preface to Kalkbrenner's method, in which he relates the birth of his invention, is an extremely curious document. It was a bar fixed in front of the keyboard on which you placed the forearm, so as to suppress all muscular action except that of the hand. This system is excellent in training the young pianist to play works written for the harpsichord and for the early pianos, whose keys responded without demanding any effort; it is not sufficient for modern works or instruments. But that is how you ought to begin, by developing firmness of finger and suppleness in the wrist, going on progressively to add the weight of the forearm and the arm itself. But it's the fashion these days to start with the end: you learn composition from the fugues in Bach's 48, the piano from the works of Schumann and Liszt, and harmony and orchestration from those of Wagner; and all too often the result is a dog's breakfast, as with those singers who learn operatic roles and embark on a theatrical career before learning to sing, and who ruin their voices in a very short time.

It was not only firmness of finger that was acquired through Kalkbrenner's method, but also the control of sound quality through the finger alone, a precious ability that has become rare these days.

Unfortunately it was also this school that invented the perverse monotony of the perpetual *legato* and the abuse of tiny nuances, the mania for a continual *espressivo* undiscerningly applied. My natural instincts found all that revolting; I simply could not go along with it and people blamed me, saying "I would never make an effect", which bothered me not at all.

When I was ten, my teacher thought I was ready to give a concert in the salle Pleyel; with an orchestra conducted by Tilmant, I played the C minor Concerto by Beethoven and a concerto in B flat by Mozart [K.450]. There was even talk of my playing the Mozart at the Société des Concerts du Conservatoire, and we had a rehearsal. But Seghers,[3] who was later to found the Société Ste-Cécile, was then a member of the orchestra; he loathed Stamaty and took it upon himself to say that the orchestra was not there to accompany children. My mother was offended and refused to discuss the matter further.

This first concert was a brilliant success and Stamaty would have liked to see me give others; but my mother did not intend me to have a career as a child prodigy, she had higher things in mind; and she was unwilling to let me follow this path out of concern for my health. The result was a cooling of relations between my teacher and myself, which ended in a complete break.

My mother could come up with retorts worthy of Corneille. Someone criticised her one day for letting me play Beethoven sonatas, asking "What music will he play when he's twenty?" To which she replied, "His own."

The greatest benefit I got from working with Stamaty was an introduction to Maleden as a composition teacher.[4]

Maleden was born in Limoges and had kept the local accent. He was thin, with long hair, gentle and timid, and an incomparable teacher. In his youth he went to study in Germany with a man called Gottfried Weber who invented a system that Maleden brought back and perfected. He had fashioned it into a marvellous tool for penetrating the depths of music, a light to lighten its most secret corners. In this system the chords are not considered just as individual entities—chord of the fifth, sixth or seventh— but according to the degree of the scale on which they are placed; you learn that from the place they occupy, they acquire different properties, and in that way you can explain usages that have hitherto been considered inexplicable. This method is taught at the Ecole Niedermeyer; I don't know whether it is elsewhere.

Maleden very much wanted to become a professor at the Conservatoire and, thanks to some powerful sponsors, his nomination was on the point of being signed by Auber, when an access of scrupulous honesty led him to believe he should write to Auber and point out that his method differed entirely from the one taught in that institution. Auber took fright and Maleden never taught at the Conservatoire.

Our lessons were sometimes tempestuous. It happened from time to time that I did not see eye to eye with him on various questions. Then he

[3] François Seghers (1801–1881) was a Belgian violinist. It was in Seghers's house in 1852 that Saint-Saëns met Liszt. The following year Seghers gave the first performance of Saint-Saëns's Symphony No. 1 in E flat. Gounod and Berlioz were both there and were enthusiastic about the work.

[4] Pierre Maleden (b. c. 1800) also taught Gottschalk. In 1867 Saint-Saëns dedicated to him his prize-winning cantata Les noces de Prométhée.

would gently take me by the ear, twist my head and hold me down for a minute with my ear against the table; then he would ask if I had changed my opinion. When I said my opinion had not changed, he would have a think and sometimes agree I was right.

Gounod would occasionally say to me, "You never had a musical childhood." He was wrong because he didn't know the vestiges of that childhood: they are legion. Many of these attempts remain unfinished, not to mention the ones I destroyed. There is everything: arias, choruses, cantatas, symphonies, overtures; none of it will ever see the light of day. Eternal oblivion will shroud these scribblings of no general interest.

Among these masses of paper, I found some notes written in pencil at the age of four. The date on them leaves no room for doubt.

24

GEORGES BIZET

(Portraits et souvenirs,
Société d'édition artistique, 1899, 124–127)

One day, at a Châtelet concert, listening to Georges Bizet's ravishing *Scherzo*, taking part in its triumph, seeing the hall wild with enthusiasm, the audience applauding the work and its composer and crying encore with their last breath, I thought back twenty years, back to the first performance of this same *Scherzo*, badly played, unenthusiastically heard, the victim of inattention and general indifference, with no chance of being repeated;[1] because failure, in those days, for all of us young French composers, was death! Even success did not guarantee us a second hearing in those concerts whose conductor said to me: "Write masterpieces, like Beethoven, and I'll play them!"

You can easily imagine the effect of this kind of attitude, from the point of view of encouraging us and getting us to compose.

[1] If the *Scherzo* he refers to is the one Bizet submitted to the Académie des Beaux-Arts in 1861, and which was then given in public at the Concerts Pasdeloup on 11 January 1863, it has to be said that the reception on both occasions was decidedly favourable. Also, if his memory of "twenty years" is to be taken literally, for the audience to be applauding the composer at the second concert, it would have to have taken place not later than 1875 when Bizet died. But there is no known Bizet *Scherzo* dating from the 1850s.

Some years later, things had changed and we were no longer barred from the concert hall. On the other hand, the crisis in the theatre was on its way, a crisis which is still in place, even if the situation seems to be improving.

I often used to say to Bizet, "As nobody wants us in the theatre, let's take refuge in the concert hall!"

"That's all very well for you," he used to reply, "but I'm not made for orchestral works; I need the theatre and can't do anything without it."

Obviously he was wrong; a composer of that calibre has a place everywhere. He was under the influence of his education in the Conservatoire composition classes, which were aimed at the single goal of the Prix de Rome competition for dramatic music. I may say in passing that, strange as it may seem, the Conservatoire does not have a prize of its own and there is no competition for the students in the composition classes, except for the counterpoint and fugue prizes; the Grand Prix de l'Institut is the only means the pupils have of crowning their studies.

It's worth asking, now that time, the great judge, has set the glory of an apotheosis around Bizet's name, why this charming composer, this amiable, cheerful young man should have found so many obstacles in his way. For a prickly genius like Berlioz, at home on the inaccessible heights, to see the public reluctant to support him, that is in the natural order of things. But Bizet! There was youth, vigour, gaiety and good humour made flesh!

Owing to the difficulties of the times, composers have become peculiarly complicated creatures, as it were small-scale diplomats: they pretend endlessly, and pretend to pretend, as though they were acting in Marivaux's *Les fausses confidences*. And if they casually remark that it's nice weather or that it's raining, or that there's daylight at midday, you realise a long time afterwards that these insignificant words had a secret intention, a profound, hidden meaning.

Bizet was not like that at all; his life of frankness, even if it was brutal, was plain to see; he was loyal and sincere, and honest about his likes and dislikes. There was a similarity of character between him and me that brought us together. In all other respects we were utterly different and pursued different ideals: he was in search, above all, of passion and life; I was chasing the chimaera of stylistic purity and formal perfection. So our conversations never reached a conclusion; our friendly discussions had a vivacity and charm that I have never encountered since with anyone.

Bizet was not a rival, he was a brother in arms; I acquired new strength from contact with this powerful reasoning power wrapped up in endless jokes, from this well-tempered character that no disappointment could keep under. Before being a composer, Bizet was a man, and it was this perhaps, more than anything, that impeded his progress.

Truly they are culpable, those who, by their hostility and indifference, deprived us of five or six masterpieces that would now be the glory of the French school!

25

JULES MASSENET

(Ecole buissonnière,
Pierre Lafitte,
1913, 269–275)

He received a great deal of praise, without rhyme or reason: praise for his numerous brilliant qualities, praise at times for those he did not possess, and rightly so. It is the law of "de mortuis"— those who have just died should have nothing but eulogies.[1] We are prey to quite enough injustices of every sort while we are alive, and we have a right, finally, to untarnished goodwill.

So I have bided my time before speaking of him until the moment when the Académie [des Beaux-Arts] was considering replacing him, that is to say putting someone in his place; because we cannot *replace* great artists. No one has replaced la Malibran, or Mme Viardot or Mme Carvalho or Talma or Rachel;[2] no one will replace Mme Patti, Mme Bartet[3] and Mme Sarah Bernhardt; no one has replaced Ingres or Delacroix or Berlioz or Gounod. No one will replace Massenet.

Has he been put in his rightful place? Perhaps by his pupils; but they can reasonably be suspected of bias out of gratitude for his excellent teaching. Others have spoken slightingly of his music; the old tag "Saltavit et placuit" (he danced and gave pleasure) has been adapted to refer to him: "he sang and gave pleasure." The idea was to reduce his stature. But is

---

[1] Massenet died on 13 August 1912.

[2] François-Joseph Talma (1763–1826) was a tragic actor who, unusually for the time, made a point of accuracy in his costumes. Elisa Rachel (1821–1858) was probably the greatest classical actress of her era, scoring her greatest triumph in the title role of Racine's *Phèdre.*

[3] Julia Regnault, known as Bartet (1854–1941), was a member of the Comédie-Française. Proust, through the young Marcel in *Du côté de chez Swann,* ranked her as excelled only by Bernhardt and la Berma.

giving pleasure reprehensible?[4] We might think so when we look at the attraction people seem to feel for everything that is shocking and unpleasant, in all the arts and even in poetry. The appalling phrase of the Witches in *Macbeth* has become a manifesto: evil is good and good is evil. It is not enough to admire these horrors; contempt is poured on beauties that have been hallowed by time and by the admiration of centuries.

Try as they may, they will not prevent Massenet from shining as one of the brightest stars in our musical firmament. No composer has enjoyed the public's favour to the extent he did, apart from Auber—a composer he didn't like, any more than he did his school, but whom he resembles in a strange way: they both had facility, huge productivity, wit, grace and success, and both produced music that fitted their era; at the same time their music was totally different from each other's. Both of them have been accused of flattering their listeners; but isn't it rather the case that composers and audience had the same tastes, and were in perfect agreement?

Today, of course, the leaders of fashion only respect revolutionaries. It is indeed a fine thing to despise the mob, to swim upstream and compel this mob by force of genius and energy to follow you, resist as they may.

But one can be a great artist without that.

Was J. S. Bach a revolutionary, with his 250 cantatas, performed as soon as written, and a composer who was commissioned for formal occasions; or Handel, the director of a theatre where his operas were staged and his oratorios sung, and who would have gone bankrupt if he had gone against the tastes and habits of his audience; or Haydn, writing to supply the chapel of Prince Esterhazy; or Mozart, forced to write continuously; or Rossini, working for an intolerant public that would not have allowed an opera to be performed if the overture didn't have the huge crescendo for which he has been so widely criticised?

They were great composers nonetheless.

Another criticism was levelled at Massenet: he is superficial, we're told; he is not profound. And profundity, as we know, is all the rage.

It's true: he is not profound, and that doesn't matter in the slightest.

Just as the Father's house has many mansions, so there are several in the house of Apollo. Art is immense. It has the right to descend to the depths and to find its way into the secret corners of clouded and despairing souls. But this right is not a duty.

The artists of Ancient Greece, at whose works we stand amazed, were not profound; their marble goddesses are beautiful, and their beauty is enough.

---

[4] Saint-Saëns and Debussy disagreed about most things, but the sentiment here is close to Debussy's in his own obituary tribute of 14 August 1912, "Massenet n'est plus . . ." (*M. Croche antidilettante*, ed. F. Lesure, Paris, Gallimard, 1987, 208–209).

Were our sculptors of an earlier age, like Clodion and Coysevox,[5] were they profound? Is Fragonard profound? Is La Tour profound?[6] Is Marivaux profound? And do they not all do great honour to the French School?

All have their value, all are necessary. The rose, with its bright colours and its scent, is, in its way, as precious as the lofty, vigorous oak tree. Are graces and smiles negligible things? I know many people who pretend to disdain them and who, in their hearts, regret that they do not possess them!

Art needs artists of every stamp, and no artist can flatter himself that he embraces the whole of art on his own.

There are some people who, when dealing with the most undemanding subjects, preserve the gravity of a Roman emperor on his golden throne. Massenet was not like that. He possessed charm and seductiveness, and a passion that was feverish, if not profound. His melodic style is unique to himself: floating, indecisive, and nearer to recitative than to melody properly speaking. In theory, I should not be a strong supporter of it; it lacks firmness and style. But how can you resist when you hear Manon at Des Grieux's feet in the sacristy of Saint-Sulpice? How can you not be struck to the very heart by those sobs of love? How can you think and analyse when you are moved?

So an art of emotion equals a decadent art. It hardly matters. As I have insisted on showing elsewhere, decadence, in art, is often far from being synonymous with decline.

This music has one great attraction for me that is rare these days: it is cheerful. Cheerfulness is poorly regarded in contemporary music. Haydn and Mozart are criticised for it; faces are chastely turned away from the explosion of exuberance and joy that marks the triumphant ending of the Ninth Symphony. Long live misery! Long live boredom! And it is the young who are saying this. I hope they won't regret the lost years of cheerfulness when it is too late.

Massenet's facility bordered on the prodigious. I have seen him when he was ill, sitting up in bed in a most uncomfortable position and writing page after page of an orchestral score with disconcerting rapidity. All too often such facility breeds idleness: we know, on the other hand, what a huge amount of work he produced. His productivity has been held against him. But it is his cardinal virtue. The artist who produces little can, if he has talent, be an interesting one; but he will never be a great one.

[5] Claude Michel, known as Clodion (1738–1814), is famous for his small terracotta figures of classical subjects such as fauns, satyrs and nymphs. Antoine Coysevox (1640–1720) became court sculptor to Louis XIV in 1666 and was responsible for much of the decoration in the Palace of Versailles, including the Galerie des Glaces.

[6] Maurice Quentin de Latour (1704–1788) was a highly popular portrait painter. Among his portraits are those of Madame de Pompadour, Voltaire and Rousseau.

In this era of artistic anarchy, when he could have brought hostile critics round to his side by howling with the wolves, Massenet gave a demonstration of impeccable technique, managing to combine modernism with respect for traditions, at a time when it often seems to be enough to trample these under foot to qualify as a genius. Being an unequalled master of his craft, equal to every problem and privy to all music's secrets, he disdained the contortions and exaggerations that the naïve confound with musical expertise and went on his way, a way he had laid out for himself without troubling over what people might say. He took advantage, as you might expect, of the new ideas coming to us from abroad, but in assimilating them utterly he provided us with the comforting spectacle of a truly French artist, not to be seduced either by the fairies of the Rhine or the sirens of the Mediterranean. For all his virtuosity on the orchestra, he never sacrificed the voices to it, and for all his love of voices he never sacrificed orchestral colour to them. Ultimately he had the supreme gift—life, which cannot be defined, but over which the public is never mistaken, and which underlies the success of works a good deal inferior to his.

His passionate admirers can be easy in their minds: sometimes adoration is followed by oblivion; for him, it will not be oblivion, but justice, and in his case it will not be severe. Where the tree is surrounded by luxuriant vegetation and scented blooms, the ephemeral flowers will fade with time: but the tree will remain, and for many a year we shall not see its equal.

Much has been said about the friendship between us, based on the demonstrations he gave in public—but only in public. He could have had this friendship, and one as devoted and solid as any friendship could be, if he had wanted it; but he did not. He told the story—and I myself never mentioned this—of how I had arranged for one of his works to be staged in the theatre at Weimar, where they had just put on *Samson*.[7] What he did not relate was the glacial coldness with which he received the news when I brought it to him, in the expectation of a quite different reception. After that I did not press the matter and was happy to rejoice in his successes without hoping for any reciprocal feeling on his part, which I knew to be impossible from something he himself said to me on one occasion.

My friends, my colleagues were Bizet, Guiraud and Delibes; they were brothers-in-arms; Massenet was a rival. His support was only the more to be prized, when he did me the honour of recommending my works as models for his students. My reason for mentioning this question is so that it should be clearly understood that when I stand by Massenet's great

[7] The work in question was the cantata Massenet submitted for the competition to mark the 1867 Paris Exhibition, which Saint-Saëns won with *Les noces de Prométhée* (see chapter 23 n4). Perhaps Massenet felt that losing was bad enough without being patronised.

musical qualities, it is only artistic conscience that guides my pen, and so that my sincerity should not be doubted.

One last word.

Massenet has been much imitated; he did not imitate anyone.

26

PAULINE VIARDOT

(Ecole buissonnière,
Pierre Lafitte, 1913, 217–223)

A lfred de Musset, who adorned Maria Malibran's tomb with immortal flowers, has left us a description of the beginnings of Pauline Garcia's career;[1] we can find traces of it too in the articles of Théophile Gautier. From both sources we can see that these beginnings were not ordinary. For those who know, personalities like this reveal themselves instantly, before they have come to full flower. Pauline was then very young; and soon afterwards she married M. Viardot, then the director of the Théâtre-Italien and one of the finest men of his time. She went abroad to develop her talent and came back to France in 1849, summoned by Meyerbeer to create the role of Fidès in *Le prophète*.

Her voice was enormously powerful, had a prodigious range and was equal to every technical difficulty but, marvellous as it was, it did not please everybody. It was not a velvet or crystalline voice, but rather rough, compared by someone to the taste of a bitter orange, and made for tragedy or myth, superhuman rather than human; light music, Spanish songs and the Chopin mazurkas she transcribed for the voice, were transfigured by it and became the triflings of a giant; to the accents of tragedy, to the severities of oratorio, she gave an incomparable grandeur.

I never had the pleasure of hearing Malibran, but Rossini spoke to me about her. He preferred her sister. Mme Malibran, he told me, had the advantage of beauty; and in addition she died young, leaving the memory of an artist in full possession of her powers; but as a musician she was not the equal of her sister and would not have been able, like her, to survive the decline of her voice.

[1] Marie Malibran (1808–1836) and Pauline Viardot (1821–1910) were the daughters of the famous singer Manuel Garcia.

Mme Viardot was not beautiful: she was worse. The portrait painted of her by Ary Scheffer is the only one that captures the look of this unique woman and gives an idea of her strange, powerful fascination. What made her particularly captivating, even more than her singing talent, was her character—certainly one of the most astonishing I have come across. She was a fluent speaker and writer in Spanish, French, Italian, English and German, kept up with the literature of every country, and was in correspondence with the whole of Europe.

She could not remember learning music; in the Garcia family, music was the air they breathed. She also protested against the legend that made father Garcia out to be a tyrant, bullying his daughters to get them to sing. I do not know how she learnt the secrets of composition; apart from handling the orchestra, she knew them all and the numerous *lieder* she wrote on French, German and Spanish texts testify to an impeccable technique. In contrast to most composers for whom nothing is more urgent than publicity for their products, she concealed hers as though they were a fault; it was extremely hard to persuade her to have them performed; the least of them, though, would have done her honour. She announced as a popular Spanish song one with a savage tone and a relentless rhythm, which Rubinstein was infatuated with; it took me several years to get her to admit she was the composer.

In collaboration with Turgenev, she wrote some sparkling operettas that have remained unpublished and have only ever been performed in private.

A curious story will show the flexibility of her compositional talent.

As a friend of Chopin and Liszt, her tastes naturally oriented her towards the future, while M. Viardot's musical opinions were as old-fashioned as could be; he found Beethoven too advanced.

One day when he had as a guest a friend with similar opinions, Mme Viardot announced her intention of letting them hear a magnificent aria by Mozart that she had discovered; and she sang them a long aria, with recitatives, arioso and a final allegro, which was praised to the skies, and which she had quite simply written for the occasion. I have read this aria; even the sharpest critic might have been taken in by it.

But we shouldn't imagine from this that her compositions were pastiches; on the contrary, they had a highly original flavour. Why is it that those that were published are so little known? One is led to believe that this admirable artist had a horror of publicity. For over half her life she taught pupils, and the world was unaware of it.

They were superb festivals of art, those Thursday evening parties that some survivors still remember, given by the Viardots in the days of the Empire in their house on the rue de Douai, splendidly adapted to its aesthetic destiny. From the reception rooms, where Ary Scheffer's famous portrait was displayed and where secular instrumental and vocal music was performed, you went down a few steps to a gallery of fine paintings, at the end of which was a marvellous organ, a masterpiece by Cavaillé-Coll; this was the temple of sacred music, there resounded arias from the oratorios of Handel and Mendelssohn that the singer gave in London during the season and that she could not programme in Paris concerts, which refused to entertain these vast compositions. On the organ, as on the piano, I had the honour of being her regular accompanist.

But passionate as she was about singing, she was more so about music. She played the piano admirably; in private she wrestled successfully with the most taxing difficulties; at her Thursday gatherings she confined herself to chamber music, with a particular liking for the violin and piano duets of Henri Reber, so delicately written, but unknown to the amateurs of today who, rather than the pure juice of the vine served in crystal glasses, prefer poisonous brews presented in cups of gold. They need profusion, painted ceilings, stifling ostentation. They would not understand the poet who sang: *O rus, quando te aspiciam!*[2] They will never understand the supreme distinction of simplicity. Reber's chaste Muse is not made for them.

Being as erudite a musician as you could find, she subscribed from the first to the complete edition of J. S. Bach. Everyone knows what an astonishing revelation this publication was: each year ten church cantatas emerged from the secular shadows and each year brought new surprises with these works of such variety, unexpectedness and power to move. Until then we thought we knew Bach; we were now learning to know him and to discover in the incomparably virtuosic composer a wide-ranging poet—of whom the *Well-tempered Clavier* had in the meantime given us some idea. But the beauties of this famous work needed light shed on them; in the absence of any indications, views differed as to how they should be interpreted. In the cantatas the meaning of the words shows the way and, by applying formal analogies, we can see clearly what the composer's intentions were in his harpsichord pieces.

One fine day the annual volume contained a cantata in several movements, written for contralto solo accompanied by strings, oboe, and an obbligato organ part—that is to say, one that does not confine itself to filling out the harmonies.[3] The organ was there, the organist too; the instruments were brought together, the baritone Stockhausen was put in charge of the small orchestra, and Madame Viardot sang the cantata. I doubt whether the composer had ever heard it sung like that! I have kept the memory of that day as one of the most precious of my musical life. My

[2] "O countryside, when shall I see you again!" Horace, *Satires* I, 6.

[3] Almost undoubtedly the Cantata No. 170 *Vergnügte Ruh'* . I am grateful to Nicholas Anderson for his expert advice on this point.

mother and M Viardot were the only listeners to this unique performance. We did not dare repeat it before an audience that was unprepared; what would nowadays have certainly been a great success would then have been a good thing wasted. Nothing is more depressing than to see an audience remain cold in the presence of a great work! Better to keep treasures that would not be appreciated for yourself.

One thing will always militate against the popularity of these vocal works of Bach; their resistance to translation. When translated into French, they lose their savour, their charm, and sometimes are on the edge of becoming ridiculous.

One of the most astonishing facets of Madame Viardot's talent was her facility for entering into every style, from the old Italian music in which she had been brought up (and whose beauties she revealed to me whereas, on my own, I had seen only its weaknesses) to Schumann, Gluck, and even Glinka which she sang in Russian. Nothing was foreign to her; she was at home everywhere.

As a close friend of Chopin, she had very precise memories of his playing and used to give invaluable advice as to how his music should be interpreted. From her I learnt that the playing of this great pianist (or rather this great composer) was much simpler than is generally imagined, and as far removed from vulgar mannerism as from cold correctness. From her I learnt the secrets of the true *tempo rubato* without which Chopin's music is disfigured, and which is nothing like the dislocations through which it is all too often caricatured.

I have mentioned her great talent as a pianist; one could judge it at a concert given by Madame Schumann in which, after Madame Viardot had sung Schumann songs accompanied by the famous pianist, the two great artists joined in playing the illustrious composer's Duo for two pianos, a piece bristling with difficulties, *with equal virtuosity.*[4]

When her voice began to fail, she was advised to devote herself to the piano; that would have been a new career and a second source of fame for her. But she did not want to and for many years presented the sad spectacle of a genius struggling against adversity, in the shape of a voice that was broken, disobedient, unequal and unreliable; and a whole generation knew her only from this image that was unworthy of her.

What damaged her voice so young was her overweening love of music; she wanted to sing everything that she loved, and she sang Valentine in *Les Huguenots*, Donna Anna in *Don Giovanni*, and other roles too that she should not have attempted if she wanted to preserve her instrument.

She admitted as much at the end of her life.

[4] *Andante and Variations* Op. 46.

"Don't do what I did," she said one day to a young female singer; "I wanted to sing everything and I ruined my voice!"

Happy those natures of flame that consume themselves, and glory to those swords that use the scabbard!

27

FOUR POEMS TO FRIENDS

1. A Madame Pauline Viardot
(*Rimes familières*, Calmann-Lévy,
1890, 21–22)

Gloire de la Musique et de la Tragédie,
Muse qu'un laurier d'or couronne tant de fois,
Oserai-je parler de vous, lorsque ma voix
Au langage des vers follement s'étudie?

Les poètes guidés par Apollon vainqueur
Ont seuls assez de fleurs pour en faire une gerbe
Digne de ce génie éclatant et superbe
Qui pour l'éternité vous a faite leur soeur.

Du culte du beau chant prêtresse vénérée,
Ne laissez pas crouler son autel précieux,
Vous qui l'avez reçu comme un dépôt des cieux,
Vous qui du souvenir êtes la préférée!

Ah! comment oublier l'implacable Fidès
De l'amour maternel endurant la supplice,
Orphée en pleurs qui pour revoir son Eurydice
Enhardi par Eros pénètre dans l'Hadès!

Grande comme la lyre et vibrante comme elle,
Vous avez eu dans l'Art un éclat nonpareil.
Vision trop rapide, hélas! que nul soleil
Dans l'avenir jamais ne nous rendra plus belle!

Glory of Music and of Tragedy,
Muse whom the gilded laurel oft has crown'd,
How shall I speak of you, when helplessly
My voice on verse's shore is cast aground?

Those poets guided by Apollo's might
Alone have flowers enough for a bouquet
Fit for that genius, so proud and bright,
That hath made you their sister, and for aye.

Revered high priestess in the shrine of song,
Let not its precious altar shattered be,
You who received it from the heavenly throng,
You who live on, supreme, in memory.

Ah! how can we forget iron-will'd Fidès,
Braving maternal love's profoundest woe,
Or tearful Orpheus, whose impassioned gaze
Seeks out his own Eurydice below!

As great and vibrant as the ancient Lyre,
In Art your glory shone as none before—
Alas, too fleeting! Nor shall Phoebus' fire
For us its radiant beauty e'er restore!

2. A M Gabriel Fauré
(*Rimes familières*, Calmann-Lévy,
1890, 27–29)

Ah! tu veux échapper à mes vers, misérable!
    Tu crois les éviter.
Ils sont comme la pluie: il n'est ni Dieu ni Diable
    Qui les puisse arrêter.

Ils iront te trouver, franchissant les provinces
    Et les départements,
Ainsi que l'hirondelle avec ses ailes minces
    Bravant les éléments.

Si tu fermes ta porte, alors par la fenêtre
    Ils te viendront encor,
Etincelants, cruels, comme de la Pharètre
    Sortent des flèches d'or;

Et tu seras criblés de rimes acérées
    Pénétrant jusqu'au coeur;
Et tu pousseras des clameurs désespérées
    Sans calmer leur fureur.

Pour te défendre, Aulète à l'oreille rebelle,
    Tu brandiras en vain
Du dieu Pan qui t'a fait l'existence si belle
    La flûte dans ta main.

Elle rend sous ta lèvre experte et charmeresse
    Un son voluptueux
Qui nous donne parfois l'inquiétante ivresse
    D'un parfum vénéneux;

Des accords savoureux, inouïs, téméraires,
    Semant un vague effroi,
Apportant un écho des surhumaines sphères,
    Inconnu avant toi.

Mais l'essaim de mes vers, tourbillonnant, farouche
    Sur elle s'abattra,
Obstruant les tuyaux; le sens deviendra louche
    Des sons qu'elle émettra;

Puis, jouet inutile entre tes mains d'athlète,
    La flûte se taira.
O vengeance terrible et dont l'ingrat poète
    Le premier gémira!

Car, pour lui, le retour de la rose ingénue
    Après l'hiver méchant,
Après un jour brûlant la fraîcheur revenue
    Ne valent pas ton chant!

Ah! so, you wretch, you want t'escape my verse!
    You think you'll circumvent 'em!
They're like the rain: nor God's nor Devil's curse
    Can possibly prevent 'em.

They'll seek you out whate'er the future brings
    Of travels here and there,
Just like the swallow with its slender wings
    Braving the stormy air.

So shut your door, then through the window see
   Them flocking to your side,
Sparkling and cruel, as, from the quiver free,
   The golden arrows glide.

And you'll be rent with sharp and stinging rhymes
   That strike right to the heart;
You'll shout despairingly a thousand times,
   No calm will you impart.

In vain, rebellious minstrel, you will try
   To use the flute of Pan
As a defence, whose sound has set you high
   Among the sons of Man.

Your skilled enchanter's lips elicit hence
   A long, voluptuous lay
That brings to us at times th'unsettling scents
   Of some poisoned bouquet;

Choice chords, uncharted, bold, in listeners' ears
   Spreading a vague misgiving,
Bringing an echo from immortal spheres
   Unknown till you were living.

But then my swarm of verses, fiercely swirling,
   Will batten fast on to 't,
And block your apertures; a nasty skirling
   Will issue from your flute.

Then, useless plaything in your expert hands,
   The flute will silent lie.
O terrible revenge, at whose demands
   The poet first will sigh!

For him, you see, the rose's sweet returning
   After the winter's wrong,
Or cooling breezes after midday's burning
   Are nothing to your song!

3. Sonnet, Written in Algeria, 1 January, Year Unknown
(Philippe Fauré-Fremiet, *Gabriel Fauré*, Albin Michel, 1957, 51–52)

Monsieur Gabriel Fauré
Le bon an je vous souhaite
De l'ergot jusqu'à la crête,
En Ut, en Sol, même en Ré!
Votre nom soit admiré!
Du succès gagnez le faîte
Et que la gloire vous fête!
Soyez partout adoré!

Sur mon rocher solitaire
Quand je regarde en arrière
Loin, bien loin dans le passé,
J'y trouve plus d'une larme;
Mais un souvenir me charme:
C'est de vous avoir bercé.

Dear Monsieur Gabriel Fauré,
To you all New Year's joy be sped
From tip of toe to top of head,
In G, in D, and even A!
May admiration light your way!
May you to glory's heights be led,
Far may your wondrous triumphs spread—
Let all th'adoring world survey!

Upon my lonely rock, when I
Look back with a nostalgic eye,
Far back down hist'rys long highway,
No little sadness there I find;
But one sweet mem'ry comes to mind:
I rocked the cradle of Fauré.

4. A Madame Augusta Holmès
(*Rimes familières*, Calmann-Lévy, 1890, 43–44)

Il est beau de passer la stature commune;
    Mais c'est un grand danger:
Le vulgaire déteste une gloire importune
    Qu'il ne peut partager.

Tant qu'on a cru pouvoir vous tenir en lisière
    Dans un niveau moyen,
On vous encourageait, souriant en arrière
    Et vous disant: c'est bien!

Mais quand vous avez eu le triomphe insolite,
    L'éclat inusité,
Cet encouragement banal et vain bien vite
    De vous s'est écarté;

Et vous avez senti le frisson de la cime
    Qui, seule dans le ciel,
N'a que l'azur immense autour d'elle, l'abîme
    Et l'hiver éternel.

On craint les forts; celui qui dompte la chimère
    Est toujours détesté.
La haine est le plus grand hommage: soyez fière
    De l'avoir mérité.

It's fine to go beyond the common frame;
    But danger's lurking there:
The crowd detest an unexpected fame
    In which they cannot share.

And while they think they've got you on a lead,
    A harmless popinjay,
Encouragement and smiles are what they feed
    You, saying, "Good! Hooray!"

But when your triumph, so surprising, comes,
    And glory unforeseen,
This empty, drab encouragement becomes
    A distant smithereen;

And then you feel the wind around the peak
    That in the sky, alone,
Stands firm in space, eternally a bleak
    Redoubt of ice and stone.

Men fear the strong; who, bloody but unbow'd,
    Wins through, is always spurned.
Hate is the greatest homage: so be proud,
    My dear, of what you've earned.

INDEX

Ugalde, Delphine, 46*n*2
  La fée Carabosse and, 128–29
  Offenbach and, 155
Ulysse (Gounod), 116
  choruses of, 123–24
  failure of, 124
Une Capitulation (*Eine Kapitulation,*
  Wagner), 101–2

Vaccaï, Nicola, 80*n*4
Vacquerie, Auguste, 131–32
Vale of Tempé, 123
Variétés, 151
Vaucorbeil, Auguste-Emmanuel,
  122–23
Venus de Milo, 15
Verdi, Giuseppe
  comedy and, 48
  preludes and, 64
Vert-Vert (Offenbach), 155
Vervoitte, Charles, 32
Veuillot, Louis, 151
Viardot, Pauline, 68, 120–21,
  167–72
Vicomtesse de Grandval, Marie, 133
Villemessant, Hippolyte de, 150
Virgil, 37
virtue, 34
vocal music
  Gounod and, 137
  instrumental music *v.*, 22
  trends of, 42
Vollard, Ambroise, 107*n*3

Wagnerians
  fanaticism of, 102–3
  illusion of, 108–15
Wagner, Richard, 4–11
  Berlioz *v.*, 62–63

  chords of, 154
  comedy and, 48
  Der Ring des Nibelungen, 6–7,
    101–7
  Die Walküre, 38
  difficulty of, 34
  Flying Dutchman, The, 4*n*1, 8
  France and, 107*n*3
  Hugo and, 79
  hyperbole of, 109–10
  leitmotifs and, 109
  Liszt and, 93, 96–97
  Lohengrin, 4–6
  Parsifal, 5–7
  realism and, 35
  Rienzi, 98
  Tannhäuser, 4, 101
  Tristan und Isolde, 4*n*1, 5–6
  worship of, 111–12
Warot, Victor-Alexandre-Joseph,
  134*n*28
Weber, Carl Maria von
  Der Freischütz, 47
  Liszt and, 93
  Wagner and, 62–63
Weber, Gottfried, 160
Well-Tempered Clavier (Bach), 94
William Shakespeare (Hugo), 9–10
wind instruments
  Meyerbeer and, 64
  Wagner and, 112
women, Wagner and, 7
woodwinds, 30–31
writing
  art of, 12
  musical criticism and, 27–28

Zampa (Hérold), 93
Zampieri, Domenico, 17*n*1